FILMS

Embarrassing Movie Debuts

Jami Bernard

PUBLISHED BY CAROL PUBLISHING GROUP

Dedicated to Scott and Barbara Siegel, who have taught me the true meaning of friendship—well, they're still trying—and who are always available for a chat at two in the morning about unions, feminism, socks, rotator cuffs, two-speed reversible drills, that credit card problem, and first films.

Copyright © 1993 by Jami Bernard
All rights reserved. No part of this book may be reproduced in any
form, except by a newspaper or magazine reviewer who wishes
to quote brief passages in connection with a review.

A Citadel Press Book
Published by Carol Publishing Group

Citadel Press is a registered trademark of Carol
Communications, Inc.

Editorial Offices: 600 Madison Avenue, New York, N.Y. 10022
Sales & Distribution Offices: 120 Enterprise Avenue, Secaucus,
N.J. 07094
In Canada: Canadian Manda Group, P.O. Box 920, Station U,
Toronto, Ontario M8Z 5P9

Queries regarding rights and permissions should be addressed to
Carol Publishing Group, 600 Madison Avenue, New York, N.Y. 10022

Carol Publishing Group books are available at special discounts
for bulk purchases, for sales promotions, fund raising, or
educational purposes. Special editions can be created to specifications.
For details contact: Special Sales Department, Carol Publishing
Group, 120 Enterprise Avenue, Secaucus, N.J. 07094

Manufactured in the United States of America
10 9 8 7 6 5 4 3 2

Library of Congress Cataloging-in-Publication Data

Bernard, Jami.
    First films : illustrious, obscure, and embarrassing movie debuts
by Jami Bernard.
      p.   cm.
    "A Citadel Press book."
    ISBN 0–8065–1402–7
    1. Motion picture actors and actresses—Interviews.   2. Motion
picture producers and directors—Interviews.   3. Motion picture
acting.   4. Motion pictures—Production and direction.   I. Title.
II. Title: Movie debuts.
PN1998.2.B47   1993
791.43′092′2—dc20   92–37571
                                                                      CIP

CONTENTS

ACKNOWLEDGMENTS

I'm as grateful to those who pitched in as to those who took the cue from my dour answering machine message and left me alone. And so, my deepest gratitude to:

Doug Buffo and the boys at World of Video, where they know a thing or two, plus:

RESEARCHERS: My sister, Diane Bernard, and her Lotus spreadsheet; Stacey Ross for her unaccountably cheerful fact-checking; Stephen Schaefer and his junketeering ways; Henry Jaglom for several encounters straight out of one of his movies; Myron Rushetzky, who didn't realize there would be *that* much work in return for this little mention; Mike Schlesinger, Larry Cohn, and Bruce Goldstein for their long memories; Marianne Goldstein for her twin abilities to organize and soothe; Ron and Howard Mandelbaum at Photofest for their patience and knowledge—and, of course, their photos. My friends and agents, Scott and Barbara Siegel, who gave countless hours of their time and resources when they could have been out having dessert. Plus Stephen Louis, Pat Walcheske, M. George Stevenson, Chris Bowen, Roy Frumkes, Mason Wiley, Jim Byerley, Dwight Brown, Monty Arnold, Milton Goldstein, Gail Klinger, and Mark Simpson.

FRIENDS: The following people supported my desire either to be coddled frequently or left alone: Amanda Kissin, JoAnne Wasserman, Batton Lash, Lisa Tindall, Howard Feinstein, Russell Calabrese, Carole Lee, Diane Stefani, Larry Friedman, Rita Zausner, Terry Smolar, Amy Pagnozzi, Mark Hamilton, Ben Petrone, Maria Umali, and Sue Pivnick.

FILM FOLK: Thanks to the celebrities who took the time to reflect on their careers. And for helping me gain access to them, I am indebted to the movie studios, the video companies, and to Nina Stern, Christina Ferguson, Jane Ayer, Louise Stanton, Anne Stavola, Dorrit Ragosine, Terry Greenberg, Jule Kuendorf, Cara White, Jeremy Walker, Julian Schlossberg, Cynthia Swartz, Judy Arthur, Fritz Friedman, Clint Culpepper, Marilu Eagles, Michael Scriamente, and Maria La Magra. Also, the folks at the Margaret Herrick Library in L.A. and at the Museum of Modern Art Film Department.

EDITORS: Thanks to my editor, Gail Kinn, and my peripatetic publisher, Steve Schragis. And to the loyal magazine editors in my life: Dave McDonnell, Tony Timpone, Lou Mulkern, Bruce Apar, Susan Baar, Anne Reischick, and Roy Hemming. And to my very first editors, Vincent P. O'Connor, Barry Michaels, Elizabeth Hardwick, and Jerry Tallmer.

FILM FESTIVALS: Many of the interviews that appear in this book took place at the following festivals: Toronto, Montreal, Cannes, Berlin, Locarno, Edinburgh, Sarasota, Miami, U.S.A. (in Dallas), Fort Lauderdale, Morocco—and, of course, the New York Film Festival. Smoothing my way were Joanne Ney, Steve Grenyo, Noah Cowan, Robert Gray, Michelle Mahieux, Joyce Pierpoline, Henri Behar, Mark Urman, Catherine Verret, Samantha Dean, Norman Wang, and Sophie Gluck.

And a final thank-you to my patient family, to whom words are everything: Sam and Gloria Bernard, Diane and her cats—and my parrot, Sensei, whom I taught to dance the lambada.

INTRODUCTION

"Everything you need to know about a filmmaker can be seen in his first film."
—*Orson Welles*

L ike first love, first films occupy a special place in the hearts of actors and filmmakers. Not necessarily a *pleasant* special place, but then not everyone made a feature film debut as ground-breaking as Orson Welles did when he directed *Citizen Kane*. Kevin Costner, for instance, made his debut among the beach-blanket-bimbo set in *Sizzle Beach, U.S.A.* For every Warren Beatty starting out in *Splendor in the Grass*, there's a Patrick Swayze in *Skatetown U.S.A.*

Some actors' stellar futures can be read like tea leaves in their first films. How others ever made it in Hollywood after their early bombs is as great a mystery as what happened to the missing six hours of Erich von Stroheim's *Greed*. This is why watching a first film can be an intellectual challenge or a goof.

As a film critic, for me the occupational equivalent of winning the lottery is finding an unknown actor and correctly predicting future fame. *First Films* is a book that turns that endeavor upside down, and it's a game any movie-lover can play: watching your favorite actors in their first appearance and comparing them—favorably, unfavorably, indifferently—to their later work. Look at the poise Michelle Pfeiffer has gained since she played an insecure carhop in *Hollywood Knights*. See how miscast is Sean Penn as the conscientious cadet in *Taps*.

Another pleasure of first films is that of discovery. You probably think Jennifer Beals's first film was *Flashdance*, or that Cher's was *Goodtimes*, or that little Drew Barrymore's first day job was babysitting E.T. In this book, "first" means the very first time you can glimpse someone in a theatrical feature film (no TV-movies, shorts, or documentaries). That means that long before *Night Moves*, postadolescent Melanie Griffith was an extra in a scene with her twice-future husband Don Johnson, in *The Harrad Experiment*. And years before *Foxes*, Laura Dern stayed close to her mom's apron strings in *White Lightning*.

Many actors for obvious reasons wish their first movies never took place. This book by no means wishes to embarrass them. It is well known that Paul Newman hated *The Silver Chalice*; it is understood that Annette Bening would probably have preferred to start in something other than *The Great Outdoors*. In neither case does a turkey in their past detract from the excellent work they've done since. An actor with Arnold Schwarzenegger's unprecedented success has little to fear from *Hercules in New York*.

Anyway, no first-timer is expected to have the clout to demand a better role or script. Madonna sued unsuccessfully to keep *A Certain Sacrifice* off video, and two famous actors had X-rated movies in their checkered pasts. Many actors, either because they were powerless to prevent it or because they were young and in great shape, began their careers in the nude.

Interviewing most of the 120 or so actors and directors who appear in this book reconfirmed what I already knew from years of entertainment writing: In Hollywood, it's hard to get at the truth of anything. Many perfectly reasonable celebrities "forget" their first films or tailor their bios according to special definitions—first *starring* role, first *good* role, first *adult* role. Former child star Kurt Russell seemed upset when asked about his early days; he's no longer the person who made those Disney movies. Willem Dafoe was very pleasant about *Heaven's Gate*, even though he'd rather steer viewers toward *The Loveless*, his second movie.

When it comes to the first films of directors, the approach changes. Because good directors always put their personal stamp on a movie, and because their movies taken as a whole reflect a distinct body of work—that's where the auteur theory comes in—a director's debut can provide a wealth of information about an entire career.

Orson Welles would boast that he knew who made a movie merely by watching the first thirty seconds. Even if Welles were exaggerating, it stands to reason that in the early work of filmmakers are planted the seeds of their later careers. As with actors, "first" here is confined to theatrical feature films. An exception: Tim Burton's half-hour *Frankenweenie*, a virtual blueprint for *Beetlejuice*, *Edward Scissorhands*, and *Batman*.

Most of the movies in this book are available on video; the companies listed have either released the movie in the past, so that old cassettes can still be found, or currently own the rights to the title. Companies fold, change hands, lose rights to their libraries, get renamed, and suffer other sea changes. But the general rule of thumb is that titles "on moratorium" come around again, and everything becomes available on video if you wait long enough.

In general, the dates of the movies are their theatrical release dates, except in cases where they were made several years before their release; then the earlier year is noted. Filmographies do not list all TV movies.

Who gets included? While several noteworthy or hellacious debuts were too good to pass up, in general this book contains people at mid-career, whose work is still in flux. I interviewed them on airplanes, at film festivals, in hotel rooms, on press junkets, by telephone, over drinks. I found them variously to be eloquent, arrogant, diffident, nasty, exuberant, insecure, tiresome, frightened. Patrick Swayze taught me the mambo—okay, for two minutes, but he said I had "a knack."

Fame can be quite a crapshoot. It would be very difficult to tell from *Blood Red* that Julia Roberts would become the highest-paid female star in Hollywood, yet you can see in Al Pacino's cameo in *Me, Natalie* the kind of intensity that would make him one of the leading male stars. No matter how well you think you know people's work, you don't *really* know them until you've seen their first films.

BARE BEGINNINGS

Actors Who Got Plenty of Exposure Their First Time Out

A new video box cover design fully capitalizes on Madonna's pre-fame film debut, *A Certain Sacrifice* (1979). In it, Madonna is raped, has group sex, appears in a wet T-shirt, and is smeared with sacrificial blood—a dry run for her future vidclips.

MADONNA

Singer, actress, pop culture phenomenon
First film: *A Certain Sacrifice* (1979), d. Stephen Lewicki
Video Availability: WorldVision
Role: Bruna

"I'm a do-do girl, and I'm looking for my do-do boy."

*E*veryone was impressed with Madonna's supposed film debut as the alter ego of suburban housewife Rosanna Arquette in *Desperately Seeking Susan*. But even before the Susan Seidelman movie, there was a certain, uh, *sacrifice*, on the altar of film in the form of the nearly unwatchable *A Certain Sacrifice*. It is the genuine film debut of Madonna Louise Ciccone, as she is billed.

The Super 8-mm student film, made in 1979 by the evidently untalented Stephen Lewicki, is so bad that the home video version opens with a disclaimer that attempts some serious spin-doctoring. Citing the movie as "a rare piece of music history," it warns that the "raw and intimate experimental style" is fraught with "technical inconsistencies." Meaning that it is difficult to see, hear, or fathom.

The only reason to see it, its claim on "music history" aside, is to get the kind of satisfaction Dorothy got when Toto pulled aside the curtain that revealed the powerful Wizard of Oz for the mere mortal that he was. In this case, the curtain reveals that the self-made Madonna wasn't always in control of her material or of her material girl-ness.

A Certain Sacrifice certainly does presage the Madonna to come. "She was what me and my compadres called a bad girl," says the narrator of Madonna's character, Bruna.

Bruna is not the main character, nor is she the certain sacrifice. But she does manage to expose her breasts often, simulate group sex, get raped in a diner bathroom, indulge in a sexual rite in which her body is rubbed with a dead man's blood, and utter such fodder for her future multi-million-dollar lyrics as: "I suppose you're the mother and you want me to be your child." Conceptually, it could pass for one of Madonna's controversial sex-baiting music videos.

Back in 1979, Madonna was a brunette, didn't shave under her arms, wore an innocent barrette to hold back her hair, and sported a shrill, whiny voice that has only been matched in her subsequent career by the irritating tonalities in *Who's That Girl?* She seems thoroughly game for her scenes, whether it be frolicking under a park sprinkler while brandishing a gun or kissing the men and women in her "family of lovers" as they strip her and grope her.

The plot of this movie may defy film scholars for decades to come, but it seems to revolve around a rape-revenge.

Madonna has never fared very well in her films, except perhaps in the documentary *Truth or Dare*, which followed her on the road during her Blond Ambition tour. The sexual flaunting and religiosexual rites of *A Certain Sacrifice* have more to do with the imagery and tableaux she has incorporated into her successful arena act and controversial book of nude photos (*Sex*) than with her attempts at serious acting.

A Certain Sacrifice is most likely an embarrassment to Madonna today—not just because it was so awful, but because it lacked the self-determination that characterizes everything she has done since.

A Certain Sacrifice, 1979
Desperately Seeking Susan, 1985
Vision Quest, 1985
At Close Range, 1986 (song)
Shanghai Surprise, 1986
Who's That Girl? 1987
Bloodhounds of Broadway, 1989

Dick Tracy, 1990
Truth or Dare, 1991 (also exec. producer)
A League of Their Own, 1992
Shadows and Fog, 1992
Blast 'Em (docu), 1992
Peter's Friends (newsreel footage), 1992
Body of Evidence, 1993

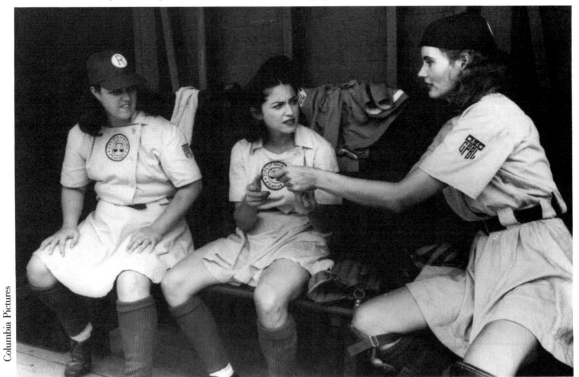

Columbia Pictures

Madonna (center) sasses baseball teammates Geena Davis (right) and Rosie O'Donnell in *A League of Their Own* (1992), part of her ongoing quest for a serious film career. O'Donnell's response when Madonna offers to unbutton her blouse for the spectators: "You think there are men in this country who ain't seen your bosoms?" Well, if they ain't, they can always rent *A Certain Sacrifice*.

SYLVESTER STALLONE

Actor
First Film: *A Party at Kitty and Stud's* (renamed
  The Italian Stallion) (1970)
Video Availability: Adult video stores
Role: Stud

"Mmmmm."

Sylvester Stallone has built a career on his muscles, and he displays every one of them—
if you get my drift—in the 1970 soft-core movie *A Party at Kitty and Stud's*, later retitled
The Italian Stallion with a few extra lines of dialogue added to cash in on his fame.

Sylvester Stallone gives a limp performance in *A Party at Kitty and Stud's. (1974).*

As Stud, Stallone wears a watch and a medallion on a chain, and that's it. His hair is overgrown and his body is only half of what it would be by the time he had bulked up for *Rocky*. Although he does not actually have intercourse in the film, he displays little of the talents necessary for a career in legitimate film, or in adult film, either; let's just say he's no WILLEM DAFOE.

For those who care, he is uncircumcised.

His bios list Woody Allen's *Bananas* as Sly's film debut, which naturally sounds a lot more prestigious. In that 1971 comedy, an unbilled Stallone plays a subway thug. Woody buries his head in a copy of *Commentary* while Stallone and a partner gang up on a little old lady sitting next to him. At the end of the sequence, as Stallone closes in menacingly on Woody, his sneer is visible. This wordless scene is perhaps a harbinger of the sparse scripts in Stallone's future.

A Party at Kitty and Stud's, 1970
Bananas, 1971
The Lords of Flatbush, 1974
The Prisoner of Second Avenue, 1975
Capone, 1975
Death Race 2000, 1975
Farewell, My Lovely, 1975
No Place to Hide, 1975
Cannonball, 1976
Rocky, 1976 (also screenplay)
F.I.S.T., 1978
Paradise Alley, 1978 (also director, screenplay)
Rocky II, 1979 (also director, screenplay, choreography boxing)
Victory, 1981
Nighthawks, 1981

First Blood, 1982 (also screenplay)
Rocky III, 1982 (also director, screenplay and choreography boxing)
Staying Alive, 1983 (director)
Rhinestone, 1984 (also screenplay)
Rambo: First Blood Part II, 1985 (also screenplay)
Rocky IV, 1985 (also director, screenplay)
Cobra, 1986 (also screenplay)
Over the Top, 1987 (also screenplay)
Rambo III, 1988 (also screenplay)
Lock Up, 1989
Tango and Cash, 1989
Rocky V, 1990 (also screenplay)
Oscar, 1991
Stop! or My Mom Will Shoot, 1992
Cliffhanger, 1993

But here he is in a stunning career turnaround in his second movie, *Bananas* (1971), harassing an old lady on the subway while Woody Allen pretends he's invisible.

BO DEREK

Actress
First Film: *Fantasies* (1973), d. John Derek
Video Availability: Fox Video
Role: Anastasia

"Bye, bye, sun, see you tomorrow!"

*B*o Derek reveals every ounce of acting talent she will ever exhibit right there in her first movie, *Fantasies*, a ridiculous soft-core romance set in the Aegean.

The teenage Bo was billed as Kathleen Collins—her given name is Mary Kathleen Collins—after being "discovered" on the beach by John Derek, a man whose marital life has been conducted something like the teen musical group Menudo, whose members have to leave after they reach a certain age. Bo is John's fourth wife; all the others looked just like her at her age.

Bo Derek finds yet another excuse to get naked in *Fantasies* (1973), the fantasies being those of director John Derek, who discovered Bo in the Aegean and married her. Here Bo—billed by her real name, Kathleen Collins—contemplates why the boy who was raised as her brother won't make a pass at her.

Photofest

Bo plays Anastasia, who was raised as a sister to Damir (Peter Hooten), even though they are not technically siblings. That gets filmmaker John Derek off the hook on charges of making a movie about incest.

As Anastasia and Damir grow up, they both begin noticing her developing "bumps." It is hard not to notice her bumps, since Anastasia displays them quite regularly in a variety of sexy poses, including a night swim, wet T-shirts, and a photo shoot that has little to do with the plot, such as it is. She frequently stands up in rowboats to display her form, even though she is always wobbling and about to fall into the water.

The characters speak as woodenly and formally as if they were taught to read from ancient textbooks, and a peculiar musical soundtrack provides such saccharine lyrics as: "White ships with tourists will bring new prosperity for my island."

If you're wondering whose fantasy *Fantasies* is, John Derek is credited as director, screenwriter, and photographer.

The script is designed to bring out Bo's playful teenage nature. "Bye bye, sun, see you tomorrow!" she calls out merrily to the setting orb. "You are crazy," says Damir. "No... I am a woman!"

The movie is taken up with much discussion over whether Anastasia is truly a woman or still a girl, and the movie ends when Damir locates the perfect bathtub for her, thus baptizing their newly sexual relationship.

Bo at seventeen has the same lean body and sharp profile she will have in her later, similarly undemanding films, such as *Bolero* and *Tarzan, the Ape Man*, although from the front her young face looks less defined. (Are we talking nasal reconfigurations?)

In Las Vegas at a video convention to promote *Ghosts Can't Do It*, which went straight to cassette, Bo seemed very sweet but not very deep, and failed to shed light on just about any topic, particularly her career, which has included minor producing credits.

Her best work to date has been in her cornrows in slow-motion as the perfect girl in Blake Edwards's *10*, a movie that wisely gives her little to say or do. "Who wants to see a Bo Derek movie where she doesn't take off her clothes?" John Derek once said about his wife. Maybe she'll get lucky and John will spring her from the marriage when she hits forty.

Fantasies, 1973
Orca, the Killer Whale, 1977
10, 1979
A Change of Seasons, 1980

Tarzan, the Ape Man, 1981
Bolero, 1984 (also producer)
Ghosts Can't Do It, 1990 (also producer)
Hot Chocolate, 1992

AMANDA DONOHOE

Actress
First Film: *Castaway* (1987) d. Nicolas Roeg
Video Availability: Warner Home Video
Role: Lucy

Tea and toast on a tropical island

*A*manda Donohoe, who has been underclothed and oversexed for most of her acting career, appropriately enough began in film completely naked—save for a leather belt and hunting-knife sheath.

In *Castaway*, she plays Lucy, an Eve to Oliver Reed's Adam. They meet through the personals and agree to play husband and wife on a deserted island for a year. The movie is based on a true story.

The castaways soon learn to hate each other as if they had been married a lifetime. Donohoe recoils from Reed, who develops nasty boils on his legs and feet. During most of the movie, directed in a malevolently obsessive style by Nicolas Roeg, Donohoe romps nude in the surf while Reed suffers from allergic reactions and lack of sex.

Copyright © Warner Brothers

Amanda Donohoe makes a revealing debut in *Castaway* as Oliver Reed's equally stubborn partner on a deserted island. Reed hated his costar because she brought her boyfriend along to watch the sex scenes being filmed.

9

Offscreen, life was imitating art. "Amanda, like a lot of beautiful women, is preoccupied with her own beauty," snarled the notoriously outspoken Reed at a fancy restaurant right after filming. "She was preoccupied with her TOAST for BREAKFAST in the morning. Amanda can eat lots and lots of TOAST all the time, with her two makeup ladies and all of them talking about knitting, washing machines, and TOAST. I'd go on the set and hear all this TWITTER. I'd like to slap tea and toast on their FACES."

Reed also complained about Donohoe's boyfriend of the moment, "a good-looking, handsome fellow," who was always hanging around the tropical set. "When we were filming a love scene, her guy was so close to her he was sitting on her face," complained Reed with typical overstatement.

These comments are relayed to an amused Donohoe. "That's very Oliver," she says. "Oliver is really a very sensitive guy, but he is from that generation of guys where there is an enormous pressure to succeed and be masculine. Oliver hides his sensitivity through overtly macho behavior. Off the set, he could be a little wild occasionally. Emotionally, it was quite draining. We'd all heard Oliver stories, but nobody knew quite how Ollie can be. Anyway, I gave him as good as he gave me. At the end I think there was a mutual respect."

The daughter of British antiques dealers, Donohoe went on to make two movies with Ken Russell, *The Lair of the White Worm*, in which she plays a vampy serpent, and *The Rainbow*, an adaptation of a D. H. Lawrence novel and a prequel to Russell's *Women in Love*, the movie in which Oliver Reed rolled around nude with Alan Bates. In *The Rainbow*, Donohoe rolls around nude with actress Sammi Davis.

Donohoe's apparent comfort with her body in *Castaway* also led her to be cast as an object of sexual obsession in then-boyfriend Nick Broomfield's *Dark Obsession*, and as the bisexual lawyer of the TV series "L.A. Law."

Foreign Body, 1986 (Donohoe claims *Castaway* was made first)
Castaway, 1987
The Lair of the White Worm, 1988

The Rainbow, 1989
Dark Obsession, 1989
One Way to Paradise, 1989
Paper Mask, 1990

SPALDING GRAY

Actor, monologuist
First Film: *The Farmer's Daughter* (1973)
Video Availability: VCA
Role: Naked guy

The monologuist's nightmare

Spalding Gray likes to talk about himself. As a monologuist, that's his job. He shares his experiences as a bit player in *The Killing Fields* in his filmed monologue *Swimming to Cambodia*. He verbally battles all the permutations of writer's block in *Monster in a Box*. His life is an open book.

Except when it comes to his film debut in *The Farmer's Daughter*. No, not the 1947 *Farmer's Daughter* in which Loretta Young ran for Congress. The *other Farmer's Daughter*, available only in specialized video stores on the seedy side of town. It stars Spalding Gray and porn queen Gloria Leonard in a rustic setting.

Things can get very boring down on the farm, so Gray ties Leonard by her wrists to the

Spalding Gray poses with the unfinished manuscript he calls the monster in a box. He has managed to keep something else under wraps for many years: his unconvincing debut in the porn movie *The Farmer's Daughter*.

bedpost. He then goes one distinct step further than SYLVESTER STALLONE did in *his* first movie.

In another scene, two underlings bring Gloria to her knees in front of Gray, perhaps the better to appreciate one of his monologues. Like Stallone, Gray is no WILLEM DAFOE, although the two work together at the Wooster Group experimental theater in New York.

In *Impossible Vacation*, the highly autobiographical novel that had been Gray's "monster in a box," he humorously describes getting "two crisp $50 bills" for acting in a porn film. The scene involves him and another man, plus a woman who had to "fluff" the men up before the scene could get under way. "By the time [the crew] got set up again, Gary and I had begun to wither, and all they got were two rather wilted dicks that were mostly held up by our own hands. They looked more like display specimens in some medical journal than like erotic male members."

His assessment of the porn experience: "Had the film been about a man crying at the slightest cue instead of getting erect, I would have become an overnight star."

In any case, Gray has paid his dues for his lurid past. The lack of dialogue and narrative in *The Farmer's Daughter* must have been hard on the future monologuist.

The Farmer's Daughter, 1973
Variety, 1983
Almost You, 1984
The Communists are Comfortable (And Three Other Stories), 1984
The Killing Fields, 1984
True Stories, 1986

Swimming to Cambodia, 1987
Beaches, 1988
Clara's Heart, 1988
Heavy Petting, 1988
Stars and Bars, 1988
Monster in a Box, 1992

NED BEATTY

Actor
First Film: *Deliverance* (1972), d. John Boorman
Video availability: Warner Home Video
Role: Bobby

"We beat it, didn't we?"

*N*ed Beatty isn't too thrilled that people still come up to him on the street and ask him to squeal like a pig. He wasn't even so crazy about *Deliverance* while he was filming it, and tried to quit. "I don't know where I was going, because we were forty miles from anywhere, but Burt [Reynolds] ran after me and talked me out of it," says Beatty.

Deliverance is a famous man-against-nature movie in which fours pals test their manhood against a white-water-rafting trip that goes awry. "Sometimes you have to lose yourself before you find anything," says Reynolds, the leader of the four rafters, in one of his finest performances.

Burt Reynolds (rear) by contrast is the lucky one in the white-water-rafting and male-bonding film *Deliverance* (1972); all he gets is a bullet in the leg. But Ned Beatty, in his film debut, is raped by mountain men who make him squeal like a pig.

One of the foes of the quartet is the river itself; the rafting scenes are quite exciting. Another foe is a group of backwoods mountain men who as a result of generations of inbreeding have developed some serious social problems, not to mention tooth decay. *Deliverance* is remembered primarily for two things: the "Dueling Banjos" song, and Ned Beatty being raped by the mountain men.

"Drop your pants," they command Beatty, while Jon Voight is tied helplessly to a tree nearby and forced to witness his pal's degradation. "Go piggy, gimme a ride!" they taunt him. "Squeal! Louder!"

"We beat it, didn't we?" begs Beatty at the end of the grueling trip. "You don't beat the river," replies Reynolds through gritted teeth, a bullet lodged in his leg.

"It was a very macho set, in the positive sense of 'macho,'" reflected Beatty over drinks at the Toronto Festival of Festivals, where he was promoting *Hear My Song*. "We worked well together; we were very confrontational. The movie itself was about being macho. Like the characters, if there were problems on the set, we chewed each other out."

Director John Boorman cast the thirty-six-year-old actor after seeing him on Broadway in *The Great White Hope*, and since then, Beatty has made approximately fifty movies.

"I've never made a film that good since then," sighs Beatty nostalgically, even though distributor Miramax touted him for an Oscar for playing an elusive Irish tenor in *Hear My Song*. (He did get a nomination for *Network* in 1976.) "Since *Deliverance*, it's been all downhill."

Deliverance, 1972
The Life and Times of Judge Roy Bean, 1972
The Last American Hero, 1973
The Thief Who Came to Dinner, 1973
White Lightning, 1973
W. W. and the Dixie Dancekings, 1974
Nashville, 1975
All the President's Men, 1976
The Big Bus, 1976
Mikey and Nicky, 1976
Network, 1976
Silver Streak, 1976
Exorcist II: The Heretic, 1977
Gray Lady Down, 1977
Alambristal, 1978
Superman, 1978
1941, 1979
American Success Company, 1979
Promises in the Dark, 1979
Wise Blood, 1979
Hopscotch, 1980
Superman II, 1980
The Incredible Shrinking Woman, 1981
The Toy, 1982
The Ballad of Gregorio Cortez, 1983
Stroker Ace, 1983

Touched, 1983
Restless Natives, 1985
Back to School, 1986
The Big Easy, 1986
The Fourth Protocol, 1987
Rolling Vengeance, 1987
The Trouble With Spies, 1987
After the Rain, 1988
Midnight Crossing, 1988
Physical Evidence, 1988
Purple People Eater, 1988
Shadows in the Storm, 1988
Switching Channels, 1988
The Unholy, 1988
Ministry of Vengeance, 1989
Time Trackers, 1989
Twist of Fate, 1989
Big Bad John, 1990
Captain America, 1990
Chattahoochee, 1990
A Cry in the Wild, 1990
Repossessed, 1990
Fat Monroe (short), 1990
Hear My Song, 1991
Going Under, 1991
Angel Square, 1991

Blind Vision, 1992
Prelude to a Kiss, 1992
Illusions, 1992
120-volt Miracles, 1993
Ed and his Dead Mother, 1993

WILLIAM HURT

Actor
First Film: *Altered States* (1980), d. Ken Russell
Video Availability: Warner Home Video
Role: Dr. Eddie Jessup

"Real, mensurate, quantifiable, tangible, incarnate..."

*W*illiam Hurt's pale intensity was perfect for Ken Russell's cinema of religiosexual excess, although Hurt got to *Altered States* before Russell did. The director stepped in to replace Arthur Penn on the troubled shoot of the trip-filled movie that is better enjoyed in an altered state of one's own. The shoot continued to be troubled, and screenwriter Paddy Chayevsky eventually denounced Russell and assumed a pseudonym.

Hurt begins and ends the movie in the nude, in keeping with the theme of recapturing humanity's essential Adam and Eve-ness. He plays Dr. Eddie Jessup, Harvard psychology

William Hurt can't even enjoy a one-night stand with one of his college students in *Altered States* (1980) without noticing strange changes in his forearm, courtesy of some genetic regression caused by long soaks in the isolation tank.

Jerry Ohlinger

wunderkind, who is fascinated by the religious allegory found in the rantings of schizo-phrenics. Eddie may be just this side of crazy himself, immersing himself for hours at a time in isolation tanks, ingesting harmful doses of Mexican hallucinogenic drugs, and seeking to regress not only his mind, but his physical self, to a primordial state.

He manages to regress far back enough that when he breaks out of the isolation tank, he runs off to the zoo to snack on "a small sheep."

Eddie's obsession with "memory as energy" wreaks havoc with his home life. (See DREW BARRYMORE.) Wife Blair Brown describes their lovemaking: "I feel like I'm being harpooned by some raging monk in the act of receiving God," and accuses him of being "a Faust freak."

Based on Chayevsky's novel, *Altered States* depends on wild, psychedelic visuals to simulate the doctor's experiences and on rushed delivery of complicated, pseudo-scientific dialogue—such as when Eddie pontificates on his goals: "I think the true self is a real, mensurate, quantifiable, tangible, and incarnate fruit... *and I'm gonna find the fucker!*"

Although like ROBERT DUVALL, Hurt worried that his thinning hair might keep him from the big time, his willingness to play impassioned men stuck in their own psychic isolation tanks enabled him to play the impotent Vietnam vet in *The Big Chill*, the imprisoned gay window dresser in *Kiss of the Spider Woman* (for which he won an Oscar), the dupe obsessed with Kathleen Turner in *Body Heat*, and even the style-over-substance newscaster whose shallowness is the cross he has to bear in *Broadcast News*.

Comfortable with his body and enamored of physical roles, Hurt often bares more than his tortured soul in his movies. In fact, if you freeze-frame the scene in *Broadcast News* where he is making shadow pictures with his body, you can see all of him.

Altered States, 1980
Eyewitness, 1980
Body Heat, 1981
The Big Chill, 1983
Gorky Park, 1983
Kiss of the Spider Woman, 1985
Children of a Lesser God, 1986
Broadcast News, 1987

The Accidental Tourist, 1988
A Time of Destiny, 1988
Alice, 1990
I Love You to Death, 1990
Until the End of the World, 1991
The Doctor, 1991
The Plague, 1992

JOBETH WILLIAMS

Actress
First Film: *Kramer vs. Kramer* (1979), d. Robert
   Benton
Video Availability: Columbia/TriStar
Role: Phyllis Bernard

"Do you like fried chicken?" "Very much."

"*K*ramer, I just met your son," says a discombobulated JoBeth Williams after that memorable scene in *Kramer vs. Kramer* in which, clad only in black-rimmed spectacles, she runs into Dustin Hoffman's six-year-old son on the way to the bathroom.
   Kramer vs. Kramer was the well-acted weepy that championed father's rights, somewhat at

JoBeth Williams provides Dustin Hoffman with his first meaningful relationship after his wife leaves him to raise their little boy alone in *Kramer vs. Kramer* (1979). This dinner date scene was cut from the movie; in the next scene, Williams famously encounters the kid in Hoffman's hallway while wearing nothing but black-rimmed eyeglasses.

the expense of Meryl Streep, who played the mother who walks out on her husband and child to "find herself." Once found, she returns for a battle royal over custody of floppy-haired Justin Henry. By this time, father and son have got their act together, including their ritualistic bonding over morning French toast.

Williams plays Kramer's business associate Phyllis Bernard, the first woman Papa Kramer has the courage to date after becoming a single dad. Phyllis's awkward nude encounter with the child ("Do you like fried chicken?" he asks. "Very much," she answers, positioning her hands strategically) is better remembered than the courtroom scene that pits Kramer versus Kramer.

Early typecasting? Five years later, the likable former soap actress would run naked down a high school corridor to convince Nick Nolte she cares, in *Teachers*.

Kramer vs. Kramer, 1979
The Dogs of War, 1980
Stir Crazy, 1980
Endangered Species, 1982
Poltergeist, 1982
The Big Chill, 1983
American Dreamer, 1984
Teachers, 1984

Desert Bloom, 1986
Poltergeist II: The Other Side, 1986
Memories of Me, 1988
Welcome Home, 1989
Switch, 1991
Dutch, 1991
Stop! or My Mom Will Shoot, 1992
Me, Myself and I, 1992

KATHLEEN TURNER

Actress
First Film: *Body Heat* (1981), d. Lawrence Kasdan
Video Availability: Warner Home Video
Role: Matty Walker

"You're not too smart, are you?"

"*Y*ou're not too smart, are you?" asks sultry Matty Walker (Kathleen Turner) of handsome dim-bulb Ned Racine (William Hurt) in *Body Heat*. "I like that in a man." Turner turns up the heat in this sexy noirish thriller as she baits lawyer Ned to help kill her rich husband and collect the insurance. It's not precisely *Double Indemnity*, although it tries to be, but the debut of both Turner and director Lawrence Kasdan is as steamy as its title—particularly when Ned, who cannot stand the double torment of an unremitting heat wave and Matty's sexuality, breaks a window in her mansion to get to her more quickly.

Husky-voiced Kathleen Turner turns up the thermostat in *Body Heat* (1981), enticing gullible William Hurt to do her bidding in this remake (more or less) of *Double Indemnity* (1944).

Turner enjoyed overnight success with *Body Heat* and went on to establish herself mostly in romantic comedies such as *Peggy Sue Got Married* and *The War of the Roses*, the latter with dashing frequent partner Michael Douglas. She and Douglas developed a kind of old-fashioned Nick 'n' Nora rapport when she played romance novelist Joan Wilder, whose real-life adventures fuel her writing, in *Romancing the Stone* and *The Jewel of the Nile*.

The sultry voice Turner unleashed in *Body Heat* didn't go unnoticed; she is the official—although originally unbilled—voice of the pneumatic, scene-stealing cartoon character Jessica Rabbit in the Roger Rabbit movie and cartoons.

Body Heat, 1981
The Man With Two Brains, 1983
A Breed Apart, 1984
Crimes of Passion, 1984
Romancing the Stone, 1984
The Jewel of the Nile, 1985
Prizzi's Honor, 1985
Peggy Sue Got Married, 1986
Dear America, 1987
The Accidental Tourist, 1988

Switching Channels, 1988
Who Framed Roger Rabbit? 1988 (voice)
Tummy Trouble, 1989 (voice)
The War of the Roses, 1989
Rollercoaster Rabbit, 1990 (voice)
V. I. Warshawski, 1991
A Day at a Time (docu), 1991
House of Cards, 1993
Undercover Blues, 1993
Naked in New York, 1993

FAST STARTS

Can Their Careers Keep the Pace?

MICHAEL KEATON

Actor, former stand-up comic
First Film: *Night Shift* (1982), d. Ron Howard
Available: Warner Home Video
Role: Bill "Blaze" Blazejowski

"I think it's important that I see all of your breasts."

Michael Keaton considers himself lucky. If his TV career hadn't flopped, he may never have gone into movies, and then he wouldn't have become Batman, millionaire by day, vigilante in a cape and tights by night—and paid handsomely for the trouble.

"I think my career would have done fine, probably in television. But that was at a time when almost no one was crossing over" from TV to films, says Keaton in the clipped, wary style that makes him a tough interview. He occasionally punctuates a remark by curling his top lip back from his front teeth like a demented bunny.

Michael Keaton (right) is the ambitious idea man on the graveyard shift at the morgue in the black comedy *Night Shift* (1982). He convinces Henry Winkler to go in with him on a plan to unionize prostitutes.

"If you think back, right then that sort of thing just didn't happen. I'll tell you who managed to move out of TV into movies at that time, John Travolta, but that was it. Fortunately, my TV series ["All's Fair"] had not gone on, because it would have been tough to move to film. So I really wanted that movie."

That movie was the comedy *Night Shift*, a sleeper hit from which little had been expected. After all, the director, Ron Howard, was still fixed in people's minds as the harmless TV kid Opie from "The Andy Griffith Show." Howard cast his "Happy Days" pal Henry Winkler (the Fonz) in the lead, and Keaton was virtually unknown except along the stand-up comedy circuit, where he was doing jokes about being brought up in Pittsburgh (where he changed his name from Michael Douglas). The plot—about two night-shift morgue attendants who moonlight as pimps—sounded tasteless.

In "Night Shift," Keaton plays Bill "Blaze" Blazejowski, a restless morgue attendant on the lookout for the better chance. Since the night shift is slow on stiffs, the freewheeling Billy rents out the hearse with himself as chauffeur for proms and frat parties. This is all to the consternation of his more cautious coworker, Charles Lumley (Winkler), a former Wall Street broker who is developing a gentlemanly crush on his prostitute neighbor (Shelley Long).

Keaton is first seen in silhouette through a translucent door, gyrating and singing "Jumpin' Jack Flash." Essentially an idea man—he claims he dreamed up the concept of the moist towelette, and he has another scheme to pack mayonnaise right in the can with the tuna fish—Billy tape-records his every thought. (And this was years before TV's "Twin Peaks" made self-dictation cool.)

Billy convinces Charles that they become pimps, or "love brokers," who offer the girls a health plan plus shares in a fast-food franchise. Billy's sales pitch to the local hookers amounts to a stand-up routine, in which he breaks down the word "prostitute" into its component parts, finishing triumphantly with the embedded word "tit," and ending his spiel with a flourish: "At this moment I think it's important that I see all of your breasts."

"That role was enormous fun to play, and an enormously fun experience," says Keaton. "I just had a great time, and I thought it was a good, rich character. It paved the way for a whole career."

Night Shift might have died by dawn without Keaton, who was singled out by critics for what later became his trademark—canny comic timing on the edge of a psychotic breakdown.

His second film played that to the hilt. In *Mr. Mom*, Keaton plays the house husband who gradually goes to seed while his wife becomes successful. In a dark universe, *One Good Cop* could be considered the sequel; Keaton plays a good detective gone bad for the love of three little orphans left in his care.

Being on the edge is a personal trait Keaton was encouraging even during his stand-up days. "Sometimes just a *look* can send you into therapy for months," was one of his routines. Another involved an existential reading of the Bazooka Joe bubblegum comic.

Keaton didn't fare too well in more traditional romantic leads in *Touch and Go* and *The Squeeze*. But as long as there was something crazy, pent-up, and destructive about his character, he did well—like the yuppie trying to kick the habit in *Clean and Sober*, or the mental patient lost on the streets of New York in the quixotic *Dream Team*. In *Pacific Heights* he is a tenant so hateful he breeds giant roaches just to drive his landlords out.

Tim Burton harnessed all that dangerous energy when he directed Keaton in *Beetlejuice* as an exorcist-for-hire, a leering, hyperkinetic hipster in a fright wig who cleans out haunted houses and cops feels from both the quick and the dead. Burton then took a chance on Keaton in the title role of *Batman*, despite an uproar from comics fans who feared he would play it more like the Joker.

Of course, *Batman* and *Batman Returns* gave Keaton his most famous role to date, a character perfectly in keeping with the tightly wound persona he has developed in movie after movie. Far from the campy nature of the original TV series, Batman as played by Keaton is just—as he might put it—a look away from a few months of therapy. Keaton is gleeful, although in interviews he is so guarded he almost never laughs. "The way I see it, I've got two jobs. I'm an actor, and I'm Batman. It's a pretty good gig."

Night Shift, 1982
Mr. Mom, 1983
Johnny Dangerously, 1984
Gung Ho, 1986
Touch and Go, 1986
The Squeeze, 1987
Beetlejuice, 1988

Clean and Sober, 1988
Batman, 1989
The Dream Team, 1989
Pacific Heights, 1990
One Good Cop, 1991
Batman Returns, 1992
Much Ado About Nothing, 1993

Keaton's wild improvisation and fright wig made him a memorable exorcist-for-hire in Tim Burton's *Beetlejuice* (1988), here with black-humored Winona Ryder. Later Burton would loyally cast him as *Batman*.

WARREN BEATTY

Actor, director, producer, writer
First Film: *Splendor in the Grass* (1961), d. Elia Kazan
Video Availability: Warner Home Video
Role: Bud Stamper

"Please, Deenie!"

*F*irst love drives Natalie Wood crazy in Warren Beatty's first movie, *Splendor in the Grass*, about two teenagers whose relationship is destroyed by conflicting parental, social, and moral forces. Offscreen, the two stars consummated what they could not in William Inge's screenplay, and the sexy movie set the tone for Beatty's lifelong career image as a high-class seducer.

Although stories about Beatty's love life are legion, he describes a "graph of inaccuracy"

Natalie Wood assures newcomer Warren Beatty she'd do anything for him, "anything at all," in *Splendor in the Grass* (1961). When society prevents her from following through on her promise, she goes nuts. Offscreen, there were no such restrictions between the two stars.

one can chart where the more information he gave the press about himself, the more stories it made up about him—which is why he was a media recluse for so many years.

History would have been mighty different if Beatty had made his debut in *Parrish*. He and Jane Fonda were to make their debuts together in this melodrama about love and tobacco farming, under the direction of Josh Logan. According to *Movieline* magazine, after reading the script all three of the principals jumped ship, leaving Troy Donahue to star in the ill-fated film. Fonda made her debut instead in Logan's *Tall Story*, and Beatty found splendor with Natalie Wood.

Elia Kazan, Beatty's first director, praised him as "an actor without any technique" in the sense that the Stella Adler–trained lad lent himself naturally to the role of Bud, whose imperious father won't let him marry high school sweetheart Deenie (Wood). Deenie suffers a breakdown and spends the rest of the movie trying to recover her sense of self.

Beatty quickly emerged as more than just an actor. "You get a lot more interested in film when you direct a couple of times," says Beatty, who has also produced and written for the screen. He is indeed charming in person and chooses his words with such care that a single sentence can take a long time to wind itself to a close.

Although he had directed himself on several occasions, most notably in *Reds* and *Dick Tracy*, the cerebral actor describes it as a "schizophrenic existence, in which you have to be quite in control to direct, and then out of control in order to act. In directing a movie what you really are is an audience. I never know how to separate these things."

Splendor in the Grass, 1961
The Roman Spring of Mrs. Stone, 1961
All Fall Down, 1962
Lilith, 1964
Mickey One, 1965
Kaleidoscope, 1966
Promise Her Anything, 1966
Bonnie and Clyde, 1967 (also producer)
The Only Game in Town, 1970
$, 1971

McCabe & Mrs. Miller, 1971
The Parallax View, 1974
The Fortune, 1975
Shampoo, 1975 (also producer, screenplay)
Heaven Can Wait, 1978 (also director, producer, screenwriter)
Reds, 1981 (also director, producer, screenwriter)
Ishtar, 1987 (also producer, songs)
The Pick-Up Artist, 1987 (exec. producer)
Dick Tracy, 1990 (also director, producer)
Bugsy, 1991
Truth or Dare, 1991

Jane Fonda almost made her film debut opposite Warren Beatty, but instead he went off to make *Splendor in the Grass* and she got stuck grabbing the affections of hoop star Anthony Perkins in *Tall Story* (1960).

ALAN ARKIN

Actor, director
First Film: *The Russians Are Coming, The Russians Are Coming* (1966), d. Norman Jewison
Available: MGM/UA Home Video
Role: Rozanof

"Everyone to get from street!"

"*P*lease to remain absolutely good-behaved," commands Alan Arkin in the fractured English he speaks throughout *The Russians Are Coming! The Russians Are Coming!* the 1966 comedy hit that launched his mostly comic but never meteoric film career.

Arkin says he has never thought of himself as funny. He is serious and somewhat edgy, and can be a little irritable on personal subjects such as his belief in reincarnation and past-life recall. His "earliest memory," in this life anyway, was of wanting to be an actor. When he found it hard to break in, he learned to play guitar and traveled around the world with the folk group the Tarriers, whose one claim to fame was "The Banana Boat Song." Arkin says he was forced to learn to be funny by appearing with Chicago's famed Second City improvisation theater group in the early sixties.

"I was terrible for six months, then I found a couple of characters I guess I did well"— including, importantly, a decent Khrushchev. "I just haven't got the courage anymore for improv. It's too demanding. You felt like you were in front of a firing squad every night, fifty times a night, for years."

Improv goes in for accents and foreign-language gibberish, two qualities that would come

Alan Arkin arrives unexpectedly at a small boating resort after his Russian submarine goes aground in the comedy *The Russians are Coming! The Russians Are Coming!* (1966). His training in improv helped him "speak" Russian for the part.

27

in handy for Arkin's role in *The Russians Are Coming!* as the leader of a group of Soviet submariners who accidentally run aground at a New England vacation island.

Arkin, as Rozanof, leads his band of comrades ashore to knock at the door of the procrastinating New York musical-comedy writer (Carl Reiner, with whom Arkin had worked on Broadway in *Enter Laughing*). Swarthy, uniformed, and armed, Arkin tries to pass his men off as traveling Norwegians on a goodwill NATO tour. Like a game of "telephone," the Russians' search for a boat to tug their submarine out to sea is successively misinterpreted until the locals think there is a Soviet invasion in progress.

Director Norman Jewison first offered Arkin the Reiner role, but Arkin held out for Rozanof, who has such show-stopping scenes as coaching his men to blend in with the locals by saying in a thick accent, "Emergency! Everyone to get from street!" Peter Ustinov was already signed for Rozanof. "And then, thank God, Peter Ustinov made too much money in the United States that year, and he couldn't work in another American film. So I did a screen test for it. I said I'd do a screen test provided I didn't have to read lines. I wanted to improvise. Norman and I did the screen test together, and it was a lot of fun, and I got the part."

Arkin has had a varied career, including directing (*Little Murders*) and stage work. He won an Oscar nomination for his dramatic role as the deaf-mute in *The Heart Is a Lonely Hunter* (1968) and made an impossible role possible as Yossarian, the tormented bombardier in a crazy war, in *Catch-22* (1970).

Still, he is largely identified with his comic roles, including several other Rozanof-worthy characters—dry, exasperated types who bumble into things beyond their reach, as when he teamed with Peter Falk in *The In-Laws* (1979) as a dentist drawn into a web of Latin espionage. Lately, he has largely been playing irascible patriarchs, like the cranky father of three warring sons in *Coupe de Ville* (1990), the *über*-suburban father in *Edward Scissorhands* (1990), and the prickly inventor in *The Rocketeer* (1991).

The Last Mohican (short), 1966
The Russians Are Coming, The Russians Are Coming, 1966
Wait Until Dark, 1967
Woman Times Seven, 1967
The Heart Is a Lonely Hunter, 1968
Inspector Clouseau, 1968
T.G.I.F. (short), 1968 (also director)
The Monitors, 1969
Popi, 1969
Catch-22, 1970
Little Murders, 1971 (also director)
Last of the Red Hot Lovers, 1972
Freebie and the Bean, 1974
Rafferty and the Gold Dust Twins, 1974
Hearts of the West, 1975
The Seven Per-Cent Solution, 1976
Fire Sale, 1977 (also director)
Improper Channels, 1979

The In-Laws, 1979 (also executive producer)
The Magican of Lublin, 1979
Simon, 1980
Chu Chu and the Philly Flash, 1981
Full Moon High, 1981
Deadhead Miles, 1982
The Last Unicorn, 1982 (voice)
The Return of Captain Invincible, 1982
Bad Medicine, 1985
Big Trouble, 1985
Joshua Then and Now, 1985
Coupe de Ville, 1990
Edward Scissorhands, 1990
Havana, 1990
The Rocketeer, 1991
Glengarry Glen Ross, 1992
So I Married an Axe Murderer, 1993
Tamakawa, 1993

VAL KILMER

Actor
First Film: *Top Secret!* (1984), d. Jim Abrahams, Jerry
  Zucker, David Zucker
Video Availability: Paramount Home Video
Role: Nick Rivers

"Swing that rug!"

*V*al Kilmer plays an Elvis Presley–type singer who gets sucked into some espionage high
  jinks during a tour of East Germany in *Top Secret!*, one of the series of *Airplane!*-like
movies that poke fun at film genres.

"How do we know he's not Mel Torme?" asks a suspicious spy, whereupon Kilmer, as Nick
Rivers, launches into a rocking "Straighten Out the Rug," replete with preposterous sight
gags.

Val Kilmer finds romance with Lucy Gutteridge during an unlikely parachute jump in *Top Secret!*
(1984), in which he sings like Elvis. One day he will sing even more like Jim Morrison, in Oliver
Stone's *The Doors*.

No, not Mel Torme, but Kilmer makes a pretty good Presley. And if Presley, then why not...Jim Morrison? Seven years after *Top Secret* Kilmer was the spit 'n' image of the rock legend in Oliver Stone's *The Doors*, even singing his own lyrics like Morrison, thus providing a versatility many feared couldn't be behind such pretty looks, part Irish and part Cherokee.

Actually, Kilmer is extremely intelligent and well spoken, with a dry sense of humor. "Sure, I've had visions," he said after making *Thunderheart*, in which he played a part—Native American FBI agent who becomes sensitive to his heritage while investigating a murder. "I know visions can happen. After all, I live out in crystal-land. Wait...I'm getting a vibe from that shard!"

Playing either Elvis or Morrison fits Kilmer's fascination with men embodying "mythic qualities...I've always been intrigued by American folklore and folk heroes." He has tried to avoid typecasting, although not just because of career considerations: "I get bored easily, and if I do one comedy, I tend to get offered only comedies for a while."

Kilmer's attraction to acting has to do with the powerful experience of moviemaking. "They really can rope off Sunset Boulevard in the middle of the night," he marvels. "You can feel a character in a literal way, a three-dimensional way. While making a movie, you can live in different times. It's a fascinating way to learn about life."

Top Secret, 1984
Real Genius, 1985
Top Gun, 1986
Willow, 1988
Kill Me Again, 1989
The Doors, 1991
Thunderheart, 1992
True Romance, 1993
The Real McCoy, 1993

BARBRA STREISAND

Singer, actress, director, producer
First Film: *Funny Girl* (1968), d. William Wyler
Video Availability: Columbia/TriStar Home Video
Role: Fanny Brice

"I'm the greatest star."

"It came too easy. I haven't suffered enough."

Barbra Streisand talking about her sudden fame after winning an Oscar for *Funny Girl*?

Close, but not quite. Actually, it's a line uttered by Streisand as she played singer-comedian Fanny Brice in that movie, which was nearly as autobiographical for Barbra as it was for Fanny. Except that to hear Streisand tell it, she suffered plenty.

Like Brice, Streisand had to overcome the limitations of her New York ethnic background, nontraditional looks, and lack of family support to break into show business. "I knew I had to get out of where I was," says Streisand. "There had to be more to life than what I was experiencing. And I guess I thought about being famous when I was a kid, and wanting to be the best at everything, at anything I would do."

Copyright © Columbia Pictures

Barbra Streisand prepares to shock Flo Ziegfeld as an ultrapregnant bride in the opening number of her new career as a Ziegfeld girl. *Funny Girl* (1968), about the legendary entertainer Fanny Brice, was a glorious beginning to Streisand's varied career.

Mere success was not enough, either for Barbra or her alterego, Fanny, who sings "I'm the Greatest Star" ("I am by far, but nobody knows it") as she tries to get a job on the chorus line; Fanny eventually became a star of the Ziegfeld Follies. *Funny Girl* made Streisand a star overnight, and yet she still battles Hollywood for recognition (or an Oscar nomination, anyway) for being a female director (*Yentl*, *The Prince of Tides*).

Streisand has fought a nearly lifelong battle with her ambivalence about fame. "I was looking at an early clip of myself the first time I was on television, and you can see the excitement of the cameras and the lights. God, it was so exciting to be on TV for the first time," she says. "And then I looked at videos from the opening night of *Funny Girl*, where you have all these people talking, and then they're interviewing me. And my voice is so drained, and kind of disappointed. Stardom didn't sit well with me. It drove me into analysis, it gave me psychosomatic illnesses. I all of a sudden thought, what do people expect of me? You know, how great do I have to be? And to live up to people's expectations. It was tough, it was really tough."

A sign of how fame has colored the public's perception of her is that in person, she is far tinier than you'd expect of someone with such a voice, such a reputation, such nails, "such a gift," as she sings in *Funny Girl*. She says she is very hurt by the way the media has portrayed her as manipulative and egotistic. "I remember seeing Anne Francis, who was in *Funny Girl*, get on TV and say, 'Well, I had a bigger part, but Barbra Streisand cut me out.' I went, what is she talking about? I didn't have any control over that film. Willie Wyler cut that film. Why do people talk about me this way?"

Funny Girl, 1968
Hello, Dolly!, 1969
On a Clear Day You Can See Forever, 1970
The Owl and the Pussycat, 1970
Up the Sandbox, 1972
What's Up Doc? 1972
The Way We Were, 1973
For Pete's Sake, 1974
Funny Lady, 1975
A Star is Born, 1976 (also executive producer)
The Main Event, 1979 (also producer)
All Night Long, 1981
Yentl, 1983 (also director, producer and screenplay)
Directed by William Wyler (docu), 1986
Nuts, 1987 (also producer)
Listen Up, 1990
The Prince of Tides, 1991
The Warner Bros. Story (docu), 1991 (cohost)

TED DANSON

Actor
First Film: *The Onion Field* (1979), d. Harold Becker
Video Availability: New Line Home Video
Role: Ian Campbell

"Hey, big man, how big are you?" "Not that big."

Ted Danson as Ian Campbell, a gentle, serious-minded cop who plays the bagpipes and who will go to great lengths not to wake his wife when he comes home late, bites the dust early on in *The Onion Field*, a cop thriller based on the Joseph Wambaugh novel.

Campbell's death sparks the central tragedy of *The Onion Field*—his partner's (John Savage) gradual breakdown from the guilt he feels over leaving Campbell and running for his life.

The Onion Field is remarkable for the edgy performance of James Woods as the small-

Bagpipe-playing cop Ted Danson is cool under pressure while scary James Woods holds him hostage in *The Onion Field* (1979), based on a true story. Except for *Three Men and a Baby* (1987) and its sequel, Danson's movie career hasn't been that hot.

time hood who forces Campbell to drive to a deserted onion field in Bakersfield, California, where he will shoot him abruptly. "Hey, big man, how big are you?" he asks Danson, who keeps his cool even though he has an intimation of his death and touches his partner's hand just before he's shot. "Not that big," he responds peaceably.

Tall, strong-jawed Danson, whose trademark thatch of hair is these days courtesy of a hairpiece, was a teacher at the Actors Institute in Los Angeles when he made *The Onion Field*. While he has enjoyed a variety of dramatic roles, including that of the son of dying Jack Lemmon in *Dad*, his immense popularity stems from his many years as a likable lothario behind the bar on the TV show "Cheers," and from being the least responsible of the three occasional dads of *Three Men and a Baby* and its sequel.

Thanks to those roles, he is perceived as an actor of lightweight comedies. "But you know, you do rim shots for nine months out of the year, but there's a sadness in me that I'd like to explore as an actor," says Danson. "As an actor, I'd like to push the dark side."

In *The Onion Field*, he was only a catalyst for the dark side of others. But he was comfortable with the cops-and-robbers aspect of the work, because when he was a kid, his favorite game was the Old West equivalent, cowboys and Indians.

"That's how I grew up, I *lived* a Western," says Danson, full of nervous energy during an interview in which he tosses small pieces of paper at targets, takes off his shoes, and taps his foot incessantly. "All my friends were literally Hopi and Navajo Indians, or ranchers, and we had horses to ride, and we had bows and arrows with little rubber balls on the end, and shields, and we played cowboys and Indians for real."

With few exceptions, Danson's screen image is of a good guy—although sometimes stupid or narcissistic—but Danson tires easily of his saintly reputation. "You know, you're only as nice as you are a shit, as nice as you are bad," he says. "It's not like there's only this one side of the coin. I know some truly remarkable, giving people, who know how petty and angry and *killer* they are inside, but they choose not to act on those things. At least as an actor, you have the option of showing the other side in a controlled setting."

The Onion Field, 1979
Spider-Man the Dragon's Challenge, 1980
Body Heat, 1981
Creepshow, 1982
Little Treasure, 1985
A Fine Mess, 1986
Just Between Friends, 1986
Three Men and a Baby, 1987
Cousins, 1989
Dad, 1989
Three Men and a Little Lady, 1990
Made in America, 1993

CARRIE FISHER

Actress, novelist, script doctor
First Film: *Shampoo* (1975), d. Hal Ashby
Available: Columbia/TriStar Home Video
Role: Lorna

"You wanna fuck?"

"She hates her mother," is how Warren Beatty's character assesses Lorna, the teenager in tennis whites who has frankly seduced him that afternoon. Lorna has guessed that her mother is one of many lovers of Beatty's, who plays a peripatetic hairdresser who is "doing too many heads," so she screws him as a kind of passive-aggressive revenge tactic.

It is a funny and startling—certainly memorable—debut for Carrie Fisher, the daughter of Eddie Fisher and Debbie Reynolds who two years later would coil her hair into two faintly ridiculous earmuffs as Princess Leia, occasional love interest in the *Star Wars* saga.

Carrie Fisher comes in from the tennis court and wants to play ball with Warren Beatty, her mother's lover, in *Shampoo* (1975).

35

Looking as teeny-bopperish as possible for *Shampoo* in knee socks and a kerchief, Fisher offers Beatty a baked apple, a series of pointed questions ("Are you gay? Are you queer?"), points a knife at him, angrily announces, "I'm nothing like my mother!" and then matter-of-factly says the line that made 1975 audiences roar and Warren Beatty swallow hard—"You wanna fuck?"

Ironically enough, Fisher's erratic acting career came full circle back to her own mother when she wrote the largely autobiographical novel *Postcards From the Edge*, which was turned into a Mike Nichols film starring Meryl Streep, about an actress trying to beat her twin addictions to substances and to her egotistical actress-mother.

Aside from the Princess Leia roles, which she abhorred, Fisher's most popular moments have continued to be *Shampoo*-like—short and snappy. Although Lorna was aggressively obnoxious, her later character parts offer refinements on Fisher's own brand of urbane sarcasm: the friend who minutely catalogs available men in *When Harry Met Sally...*, the jaded comedy agent in *This Is My Life*, the libidinous casting agent who makes a hunky actor disrobe to audition for a walk-on as a waiter in *Soapdish*, Dianne Wiest's smugly competitive catering partner in *Hannah and Her Sisters*.

Shampoo, 1975
Star Wars, 1977
Mr. Mike's Mondo Video, 1979
The Blues Brothers, 1980
The Empire Strikes Back, 1980
Under the Rainbow, 1981
Return of the Jedi, 1983

Garbo Talks, 1984
The Man with One Red Shoe, 1985
Hannah and Her Sisters, 1986
Hollywood Vice Squad, 1986
Amazon Women on the Moon, 1987
The Time Guardian, 1987
Appointment With Death, 1988
The 'burbs, 1989
Loverboy, 1989
She's Back, 1989
When Harry Met Sally..., 1989
Postcards From the Edge, 1990 (screenplay from novel)
Awakenings, 1990 (co-wrote, uncredited)
Sibling Rivalry, 1990
Drop Dead Fred, 1991
Soapdish, 1991
This Is My Life, 1992
Sister Act, 1992 (co-wrote, uncredited)
So I Married an Axe Murderer, 1993 (cowrote, uncredited)

Fisher's most identifiable film role has been as Princess Leia of the *Star Wars* trilogy, a girl with what appears to be twin cinnamon buns in her hair.

EDDIE MURPHY

Actor, comic
First Film: *48 HRS.* (1982), d. Walter Hill
Video Availability: Paramount Home Video
Role: Reggie Hammond

"Experience some of my bullshit, cowboy."

"*I* liked *48 HRS.* a lot," says Eddie Murphy of his first movie. "The thing is, a young guy bursting into a room and being obnoxious and getting his way and talking bullshit to the authorities, that's cocky, but as you get older, it's kind of obnoxious, you can get sick of seeing this guy pull this shit. As I get older, I want to do comedy that's more cerebral."

Murphy made a stellar debut in *48 HRS.* as Reggie Hammond, a convict who is sprung from prison for forty-eight hours to help detective Jack Cates (Nick Nolte) track down a vicious cop-killer. Reggie is dapper, cool, and as quick with a one-liner as Jack is with the trigger. Typical to the genre, the two develop a begrudging respect for each other.

Because it was directed by Walter Hill, *48 HRS.* is very violent, and the language is snappy, crude, misogynistic, and homophobic—all the elements of Murphy's early stand-up routines. The character of Jack is a drunk and a racist, and Reggie spends most of his time looking for "pussy" and "trim."

The scene that drove audiences wild, and which precipitated the spectacularly successful *Beverly Hills Cop* series, was when Reggie humbles an entire barful of redneck swine using only his hypnotic fast-talk to play off white fears of black men. "Come in and experience some of *my* bullshit, cowboy," he boasts to Jack as he enters the bar, strong-arms a few patrons, and delivers a string of threats. "I'm your worst fuckin' nightmare, man—a nigger with a badge," even though the badge isn't his.

That's exactly the kind of thing Murphy now says he is trying to move away from. The eager kid that he was has been replaced by a smooth, serious young man with better skin than most cosmetics models, who wears a sweatshirt and a $30,000 Rolex at the same time. He's a man whose soft voice and economical movements bespeak someone who is so rich and successful he doesn't have to do anything he doesn't want, not even raise his voice to be heard.

"I can't even watch some of the early movies. I went through the same things that any young male growing up in America does, and those are the stages of my growth you can see on-screen—*fuck that, fuck the homos, that bitch can kiss my ass.* You have to remember that I got famous at nineteen, and I haven't been that same cat in ten years. I was really tripping

Eddie Murphy intimidates a barful of crackers in *48 HRS.* (1982), with Nick Nolte, and a career of wisecracking style was born.

48-HRS-5056-18

back then. My head was right where it was supposed to be at that age when you have a broken heart and you got on a purple leather suit and you're standing on a stage and saying, *Fuck the bitch!* I was a kid, and things like sensitivity happen later as you get older."

Murphy had time to develop a relationship with the camera during his stint on "Saturday Night Live," starting when he was nineteen. His ease on-screen, coupled with several trademark qualities—that slow-burning laugh, for instance, which unfortunately is dubbed in overseas markets—made him an instant star.

You can see how much clout he gained by watching *Another 48 HRS.*, the sequel made eight years later and carefully tailored to showcase Murphy. Nolte's salty character is reduced to a sad sack.

This pandering to Murphy because of his star status has cost him dearly in several pictures, particularly his own directorial debut, *Harlem Nights*, a nasty movie that Murphy also wrote, starred in, and executive-produced. "I think it's sad what happened to him," says John Landis, who directed Murphy in his second film, *Trading Places*, and later in *Coming to America*, where they had a public falling-out. "It's sad what happens to some nice kids who become stars, when no one around them will tell them the truth or stand up to them," says Landis.

That doesn't mean Murphy was thoroughly blinded, even before his highly touted New Maturity. "I hated *The Golden Child* a lot. I had this feeling I wanted to whip somebody's ass, but I didn't know who to beat up," he jokes. "I wasn't crazy about *Beverly Hills Cop II*, but it was okay. I hated *Best Defense*. I wasn't happy with *Raw*, I can't even watch it now."

Murphy claims the days of his misogyny and homophobia are over. "Some people get older and just stay where they are, remain insensitive," says Murphy. "Twenty years from now, if you still see me doing the same things, you can tell me I'm a straight-out misogynist fuckin' pig."

48 HRS., 1982
Trading Places, 1983
Best Defense, 1984
Beverly Hills Cop, 1984
The Golden Child, 1986
Beverly Hills Cop II, 1987
Eddie Murphy Raw, 1987
Hollywood Shuffle, 1987
Coming to America, 1988
Harlem Nights, 1989 (also directed)
Another 48 HRS., 1990
Boomerang, 1992
The Distinguished Gentleman, 1992
Beverly Hills Cop 3, 1993

WHOOPI GOLDBERG

Actress, comic, talk show host
First Film: *The Color Purple* (1985), d. Steven
    Spielberg
Video Availability: Warner Home Video
Role: Miss Celie

"I call him Mistuh."

*W*hoopi Goldberg made a sensitive dramatic debut in *The Color Purple*, playing the heroine of Alice Walker's novel—a timid black woman who has spent her life being mistreated by white southern society and black men, and who finally learns strength through sisterhood (and, though it is glossed over in the Steven Spielberg movie, through lesbianism). At no time in the movie does Goldberg's background in stand-up comedy peek through.

Stand-up comic Whoopi Goldberg makes a strong dramatic debut in *The Color Purple* (1985), where she's shown here having a lesbian flirtation with Margaret Avery. Goldberg—given name Caryn Johnson—would never play "meek" again. Her career was briefly set adrift among ill-conceived comedies, but got back on track with and Oscar for *Ghost* (1990).

In *The Color Purple*, Goldberg is dignified and restrained, attributes she would use later in the dramas *The Long Walk Home* and *Clara's Heart*.

But for five years after that most promising film debut, Whoopi appeared in dog after dog. Her career was about as dead as Patrick Swayze's character was in *Ghost*, the movie that finally resurrected Goldberg's career (and Demi Moore's, too), and won her an Oscar.

It seemed Hollywood just didn't know what to do with the irreverent Goldberg, who was smart and funny—but also black, female, and dreadlocked. Here are some of her subsequent film credits, each one more awful than the last: a computer programmer drawn into some espionage shenanigans in *Jumpin' Jack Flash* (see PENNY MARSHALL); an undercover cop in *Fatal Beauty*; an itinerant dying of a brain tumor in *Homer & Eddie*; a troubled out-of-work actress in *The Telephone*; a cat burglar who knows too much in *Burglar*.

Although Goldberg sued to prevent *The Telephone* from being shown, she vehemently defends her career path, post-*Purple*. "*Jumpin' Jack Flash* does not cure cancer, but it's entertaining," she argued at Cannes, where she was promoting her scene-stealing small role in *The Player*. "*Fatal Beauty* has a strong woman character. Was I supposed to continue to play the downtrodden black woman for most of my career? I was *already* a downtrodden black woman. When Meryl Streep does six or seven types of roles, she's the premier actress. When I do it, I'm having a 'rough career.'"

Then the defender of *Fatal Beauty* complained about how movies like *Wayne's World* are ruining the cinema.

Amazingly, considering the short memory of most Hollywood types, Goldberg lingered in the consciousness as a major talent who just hadn't found the right vehicle. She made bomb after bomb, relieved only by *Clara's Heart*, in which she played a sympathetic Jamaican maid.

At long last, *Ghost*. As a wisecracking medium through whom the dead Patrick Swayze can communicate with the grieving Demi Moore, Goldberg finally showed what she can whip up with a small, street-smart part. She parlayed that into a couple of similar near-cameos, as a soap writer in *Soapdish* and as an unflappable cop in *The Player*, and emerged as the star of a hit in *Sister Act*, as a singer posing as a nun. Maybe her early movies were just trying too hard.

The Color Purple, 1985
Jumpin' Jack Flash, 1986
Burglar, 1987
Fatal Beauty, 1987
The Telephone, 1988
Clara's Heart, 1988
Beverly Hills Brats, 1989
Homer & Eddie 1989
Ghost, 1990

The Long Walk Home, 1990
Soapdish, 1991
Wisecracks (docu), 1991
The Player, 1992
Sarafina!, 1992
Sister Act, 1992
Made in America, 1993
National Lampoon's Loaded Weapon 1, 1993
Naked in New York, 1993

SHIRLEY MACLAINE

Actress
First Film: *The Trouble With Harry* (1955), d. Alfred
   Hitchcock
Video Availability: MCA Home Video
Role: Jennifer Rogers

"Lightly, Sam, I have a very short fuse."

S hirley MacLaine's career has been through a number of unexpected changes since her stellar debut in Alfred Hitchcock's *The Trouble With Harry*, still the preeminent corpse comedy among its many imitators. "I'm in it for the long haul," says MacLaine about her career goals. "I'm not a sprinter, I'm a long-distance runner."

MacLaine, who was trained to be a ballerina, played Jennifer Rogers, married to the omnipresent corpse named Harry and so well rid of him she hardly bats an eye when she finds out he's dead. She even fixes some lemonade for the lad who finds the body.

Shirley MacLaine (with Edmund Gwenn) shows her winsome ways in Alfred Hitchcock's black comedy *The Trouble with Harry* (1955). Harry is MacLaine's husband, found dead in the woods, and Shirley couldn't be more cheerful.

Once Harry is discovered in the woods, the residents of a small New England town have a dickens of a time trying to get rid of the corpse. The script's black humor is full of double entendres, such as when John Forsythe kisses MacLaine, and she says, "Lightly, Sam, I have a very short fuse."

MacLaine is perky and personable in her first role, blithely tossing off such lines about second-husband Harry as, "We didn't have a wedding night because his horoscope said, 'Don't start new projects.'" Of course, this was years before horoscopes, channeling, and past lives would rank higher on MacLaine's résumé than *The Apartment* or *Terms of Endearment*.

MacLaine doesn't mind jokes about her spiritual beliefs "as long as they are funny" and explains her interest in the metaphysical as "a longing for a sense of inner peace in a competitive world."

Career competition, on the other hand, has never scared her off, and she has been able to make wide-ranging choices in her roles, including a fairly recent string of cantankerous old ladies in *Steel Magnolias, Madame Sousatzka* and *Postcards From the Edge.*

"I've never experienced super-super-stardom like Travolta or Streisand," she admits. "But I do have all this more lateral experience which has enabled me to be less egocentric. I'm a natural to plunge into character work."

The Trouble With Harry, 1955
Artists and Models, 1955
Around the World in 80 Days, 1956
Hot Spell, 1958
The Matchmaker, 1958
The Sheepman, 1958
Some Came Running, 1958
Ask Any Girl, 1959
Career, 1959
The Apartment, 1960
Can-Can, 1960
Ocean's Eleven, 1960
All in a Night's Work, 1961
The Children's Hour, 1961
Two Loves, 1961
My Geisha, 1962
Two for the Seesaw, 1962
Irma La Douce, 1963
John Goldfarb, Please Come Home, 1964
What a Way to Go!, 1964
The Yellow Rolls-Royce, 1964
Gambit, 1966

Woman Times Seven, 1967
The Bliss of Mrs. Blossom, 1968
Sweet Charity, 1969
Two Mules for Sister Sara, 1970
Desperate Characters, 1971
The Possession of Joel Delaney, 1972
The Year of the Woman, 1973
The Other Half of the Sky: A China Memoir, 1974
Sois belle et tais-toi, 1977
The Turning Point, 1977
Being There, 1979
A Change of Seasons, 1980
Loving Couples, 1980
Cannonball Run II, 1983
Terms of Endearment, 1983
Madame Sousatzka, 1988
Steel Magnolias, 1989
Postcards From the Edge, 1990
Waiting for the Light, 1990
Defending Your Life, 1991
Used People, 1992

LILY TOMLIN

Actress, comedian
First Film: *Nashville* (1975), d. Robert Altman
Video Availability: Paramount Home Video
Role: Linnea Reese

"I love you"—in sign language

"*I* don't mind making films," shrugs comedian and one-woman-show-stopper Lily Tomlin, whose first film is probably still her best one, Robert Altman's *Nashville*.

In it, the director who raised overlapping dialogue and entwined stories to an art cast Tomlin as Linnea Reese, gospel singer and loving mother of two deaf children. She is lured only once to another man's bed, when philanderer Keith Carradine sings "I'm Easy" across a

Nashville (1975) gospel singer Lily Tomlin (with Robert DoQui), about to commit her first act of adultery, is thoroughly won over as she sits in a bar listening to Keith Carradine sing "I'm Easy" just for her. All heads turn.

crowded barroom—full of many other ex-lovers—to her alone.

"I don't get offered that many parts, and they don't attract me," says Tomlin, who spent many years with writer Jane Wagner developing her smash show *The Search for Signs of Intelligent Life in the Universe*, which was eventually made into a film. She had big successes in *9 to 5*, about working women who rebel against the patriarchy, and *All of Me*, in which she and Steve Martin share one body (his). But she prefers the personal connection she gets with a live audience, "and when I was famous enough to draw an audience, I wanted a certain control over what I was doing."

While still developing her TV "Laugh-In" characters of Ernestine the telephone operator and Edith Ann, the little child in the big rocking chair, Tomlin optioned a story she wanted to make into a movie. Robert Altman was set to direct it. "At that time, very few people crossed over from TV to film, but I never dreamed I couldn't get my film made," she says.

She couldn't. "Altman punched someone in the mouth at a party, fell in the swimming pool, and it never got made," deadpans Tomlin.

Altman didn't forsake her. He gave Tomlin the part in *Nashville* that was originally slated for Louise Fletcher, and the movie is now considered one of the all-time greats.

She got a chance to work with another former comedian when she played the madam of a brothel in Woody Allen's *Shadows and Fog*. Allen's directorial style? "'Be mirthful,' he said, and that was all he said."

It's a good thing she prefers theater, because Tomlin doesn't find herself up for the juicy film roles. She has made her peace with that, but there are some regrets. "Sure," she says, sighing, "I may have a fantasy that I'll get a part like Anjelica Huston's in *The Grifters*."

Nashville, 1975
The Late Show, 1977
Moment by Moment, 1978
9 to 5, 1980
The Incredible Shrinking Woman, 1981
All of Me, 1984
Lily Tomlin, 1986
Big Business, 1988
The Search for Signs of Intelligent Life in the Universe,
    1991
Shadows and Fog, 1992
The Player, 1992
Short Cuts, 1993

PETER RIEGERT

Actor
First Film: *National Lampoon's Animal House* (1978),
   d. John Landis
Video Availability: MCA Home Video
Role: Boon

Hanging around with a bunch of animals

*H*is girlfriend thought he was "an immature jerk" who spent his time "hanging around with a bunch of animals getting drunk every weekend." That was high praise for Peter Riegert's character, Donald "Boon" Schoenstein, in *National Lampoon's Animal House*, the movie that single-handedly brought back food fights, toga parties, burping, and passing out drunk.

Peter Riegert debuts (to the left of John Belushi) as the most emotionally stable of the frathouse boys in *Animal House* (1978). To the right of Belushi is "Thomas" Hulce, who made his debut the previous year in *⁹/₃₀/55* with Dennis Quaid.

2109-17

The movie also marked the debuts of Kevin Bacon and Karen Allen and the second film for both Tom Hulce and John Belushi, who in his first scene can be seen peeing in the driveway.

Animal House is set in 1962 at Faber College, whose motto is "Knowledge Is Good." It details the struggle of rowdy Delta House to stay in the beer-guzzling business despite its poor grades, loser members, and antiauthority pranks. "I played the sensitive one," says Riegert, "in charge of entertainment for the fraternity."

Later he'd play the sensitive pickle merchant who convinces Amy Irving there are good men out there after all, in *Crossing Delancey*.

Riegert started in showbiz doing a TV commercial, his only one ever, "a chicken commercial, in which I wore a hat and a moustache. Auditioning for commercials is even more ridiculous than trying to get a regular acting job. I mean, they really make you feel like less than human."

He lucked into *Animal House*, which spoiled him. "It made me think acting was so easy—oh, you show up, make a movie, and a lot of people go to see it. What's the big deal? Now I know how hard it is. Now I'm amazed when there's an audience, especially in a culture our size, that makes a connection to a movie."

Thirteen years later, Riegert again worked with director John Landis in the comedy *Oscar*, and although Landis is known for his brutal bluntness, Riegert appreciates his style. "That technique can be kind, actually, if it's done in the right way. There's no value to be told things are going well if they're not. The thing that I feel the strongest about John, and this goes for both times I worked with him, is that his belief in what I can do is so strong that I felt absolutely confident that I can make as big a fool of myself as is necessary."

National Lampoon's Animal House, 1978
Americathon, 1979
Head Over Heels, 1979
National Lampoon Goes to the Movies, 1982
The City Girl, 1983
Le Grand Carnival, 1983
Local Hero, 1983
Un homme amoureux, 1987
The Stranger, 1987
Crossing Delancey, 1988
That's Adequate, 1989
Beyond the Ocean, 1990
A Shock to the System, 1990
The Object of Beauty, 1991
Oscar, 1991
The Runestone, 1991
Utz, 1992
Passed Away, 1992

BOMBS

Early Fiascos That Haunt the Famous

JESSICA LANGE

Actress
First Film: *King Kong* (1976), d. John Guillerman
Video Availability: Paramount Home Video
Role: Dwan (That's right, *Dwan*)

"I owe my life to a movie—Deep Throat."

Jessica Lange gave up a promising career as a waitress at the Lion's Head bar in Greenwich Village to scream and squirm her way through the 1976 Dino De Laurentiis remake of *King Kong*. In it, she survives a shipwreck with her lipstick intact, only to become the plaything of a horny ape.

Her name is Dwan—"Like Dawn, except I switched two letters to make it more interesting," she simpers. When finally donated by island natives as a sacrificial bride to

If Jessica Lange had told King Kong, "Be gentle with me, it's my first time," she would have been telling the truth. Lange's inauspicious debut in the 1976 remake of *King Kong* included scenes such as this, in which the ape is about to remove her blouse to consummate his primate lust.

King Kong, he of the flared nostrils and ill-fitting monkey suit, Dwan tries to guess his astrological sign, and calls him a "nice, sweet, sweet monkey." After bopping him on the nose, she apologizes. "Sometimes I get too physical—it's a sign of insecurity."

The ape, too, gets physical. He tickles her with his hairy index finger, managing to remove the top of her sacrificial dress in the process. (But the jewelry stays put; the end credits thank Bulgari for the sparklers.)

Jeff Bridges, with enough facial hair to have essayed the simian role himself, saves Dwan, and soon this love triangle—hairy guy, hairy ape, semiclad girl—is aboard a steamer bound for New York (where Joe Piscopo debuts as a carnival broker).

An aspiring actress like Lange, Dwan gets her shot at fame by enlisting in a King Kong roadshow, reenacting her tribal marriage to him in front of paying customers. Her career alternative would be "tap-dancing at Rotary clubs," according to Charles Grodin, who provides the film's only distinguishing moments of comic relief.

Lange must have felt the same conflict about accepting her part in *King Kong*. Astonishingly, her career quickly recovered and she became a serious and respected actress, with several Academy Award nominations and one win for *Tootsie*. She reprised her waitressing days by playing a barmaid in *Night and the City*, in a bar actually based on the Lion's Head. Knowing what a terrific actress she has turned out to be, her feat of playing bubble-headed Dwan can be construed as a marvel of achievement.

By the way, Dwan guesses that Kong is an Aries. Lange herself was born on the cusp between Aries and Taurus.

King Kong, 1976
All That Jazz, 1979
How to Beat the High Cost of Living, 1980
The Postman Always Rings Twice, 1981
Frances, 1982
Tootsie, 1982
Country, 1984
Sweet Dreams, 1985
Crimes of the Heart, 1986
Everybody's All-American, 1988
Far North, 1988
Music Box, 1989
Men Don't Leave, 1990
Blue Sky, 1991 (unreleased)
Cape Fear, 1991
Night and the City, 1992

KEVIN COSTNER

Actor, director
First Film: *Sizzle Beach, U.S.A.* (1974), d. Richard
   Brander
Video Availability: Vestron
Role: John Logan

"L.A. women seem to be very impressed with money…"

*W*hen Madonna put her finger in her throat and made like she was going to throw up after
   Kevin Costner's backstage visit to her, as observed in *Truth or Dare*, perhaps she was
thinking back to Costner's film debut in a little jiggle-fest called *Sizzle Beach, U.S.A.*

If not for Costner's subsequent fame, *Sizzle Beach, U.S.A.* might have washed out with the
tide. Instead, the 1974 movie was enshrined on video in 1986. It serves to remind Costner of
his humble beginnings whenever his head swells too much from all those Oscars he won for
Dances With Wolves.

Kevin Costner proves irresistable to Sean Young in *No Way Out* (1987). He was irresistible to
women even as far back as his debut in *Sizzle Beach USA* (1974), where he was a ranch owner; by
the time of *No Way Out*, he would conduct his romances in the backseat of a limo rather than on
horseback.

Dances With Wolves broke new ground by including dialogue in the Lakota language, with English subtitles. *Sizzle Beach* could have used a few subtitles too—the sound is so bad (although not nearly as bad as the acting) that portions are hard to make out, and naturally you won't want to miss a single frame of this saga about three bimbos in search of a bikini top.

The three women share a house in Malibu as they pursue their interests, which mostly involve revealing their breasts to the camera as often as possible. One of them is a health fanatic, so she rides her stationary bike topless. Another wants to be a singer, but first she must take a naked shower. The third is named Dit, perhaps short for Ditz, a wannabe actress who cannot act her way out of a paper bag but who is very good at unzipping her top, the Method way.

It is this last lassie who catches the eye of our lanky young hero, John Logan, as played by Costner. He is in very few scenes, but I can tell you that at least one of them puts him in close contact with bare breasts.

John is a wealthy owner of horse ranches, and therefore wears a cowboy hat in all his scenes. This is what's known in the business as "characterization."

At first, he doesn't want Dit *("Dit, that's a name I'm not gonna forget!")* to know he's rich, because "L.A. women seem to be very impressed with money, and I want to keep a low profile." Soon the cat is out of the bag, and Dit is out of her duds. Dit isn't impressed by money, but after this discovery about John's finances she goes right to bed with him, or rather, right to a shag rug in front of a roaring fire. John kisses her and she bares her breasts.

If only director Richard Branden had done to Costner what Lawrence Kasdan would later do to him in *The Big Chill*—cut his role entirely out of the film during the editing process. (Costner played a corpse in that movie.) On the positive side, Costner is absolutely the most

Costner's easy, loping grin makes him the best cowboy on the horizon of *Sizzle Beach U.S.A.*; in the very next scene he is by the fireside with a topless girl.

talented of any of the performers in *Sizzle Beach, U.S.A.*, and despite a certain awkwardness, he delivers his lines smoothly and interestingly.

Costner's impassiveness has matured into an ironic stance. With the exception perhaps of his energetic performance in *Silverado*, Costner is usually slow and measured in his roles, a device that has earned him a reputation for gravity and stature. That is how he is able to hold the moral center of *The Untouchables, Dances With Wolves, Robin Hood: Prince of Thieves, JFK*, and the bodyguard reluctant to get involved with his client in the movie of the same name.

Sizzle Beach, U.S.A., 1974
Shadows Run Black, 1981
Night Shift, 1982
Stacy's Knights, 1982
The Gunrunner, 1983
Table for Five, 1983
Testament, 1983
American Flyers, 1985
Fandango, 1985
Silverado, 1985
No Way Out, 1987
The Untouchables, 1987
Bull Durham, 1988
Chasing Dreams, 1989
Field of Dreams, 1989
China Moon (coproducer), 1990 (unreleased)
Dances With Wolves, 1990 (also director, producer)
Revenge, 1990 (also executive producer)
Robin Hood: Prince of Thieves, 1991
JFK, 1991
Truth or Dare, 1991
The Bodyguard, 1992

MICHELLE PFEIFFER

Actress
First Film: *Hollywood Knights* (1980), d. Floyd
  Mutrux
Video Availability: N/A
Role: Susie Q

"I have an audition in the morning."

"*Hollywood Knights*, a low-rent ripoff of *American Graffiti*, featured three film debuts. Robert Wuhl in the lead plays the girl-crazy head of a 1965 teen gang called the Hollywood Knights, who hang out at the drive-in when they're not mooning people from their car windows. First-timer Tony Danza has a considerable part. But Michelle Pfeiffer, sporting her old nose and too much eyeliner, has the smallest role as Suzie Q, a carhop at Tubby's drive-in, where her job requires her to wear tall white go-go boots.

Suzie's an aspiring actress who dreams of hitting it big, but not at the expense of her relationship with Danza. "Oh, I forgot," says Danza, his voice oozing with sarcasm, "you're gonna be a famous *actress*."

One of Michelle Pfeiffer's most self-assured lines in *Batman Returns* (1992) is a simple "Meow," playing a mousy secretary turned Catwoman.

Danza could eat his words today, because within a few movies, along about *Grease 2*, Pfeiffer did indeed become a famous actress, now one of the top in Hollywood—but no thanks to *Hollywood Knights*. Although she does have the beginnings of that slightly mournful beauty and willowy stance that marks *The Russia House, Dangerous Liaisons,* and *Tequila Sunrise*, there's none of the self-confidence that she'd need for the day she'd slither across a piano in *The Fabulous Baker Boys* or crack a mean whip as Catwoman in *Batman Returns*.

In person, Pfeiffer is almost painfully thin and can be very shy. "I can act, but I can't talk," she says to explain her awkwardness when working without a script.

Her voice back in 1980 clearly needed work, but you can't expect much from a film whose highlight is Wuhl punctuating "Volare" at the high school dance with amplified farts.

Hollywood Knights, 1980
Falling in Love Again, 1980
Charlie Chan and the Curse of the Dragon Queen, 1981
Grease 2, 1982
Scarface, 1983
Into the Night, 1985
Ladyhawke, 1985
Sweet Liberty, 1986
Amazon Women on the Moon, 1987
The Witches of Eastwick, 1987

Dangerous Liaisons, 1988
Married to the Mob, 1988
Tequila Sunrise, 1988
The Fabulous Baker Boys, 1989
The Russia House, 1990
Frankie and Johnny, 1991
Batman Returns, 1992
The Age of Innocence, 1993
Love Field, 1992

In her first movie, *Hollywood Knights* (1980), Pfeiffer is a beautiful but mousy carhop; even Tony Danza as her boyfriend gets better billing.

NICK NOLTE

Actor
First Film: *Return to Macon County* (1975), d. Richard
   Compton
Video Availability: Vestron
Role: Bo Hollinger

"...And don't you forget it!"

*I*t wasn't much of a stretch in *Return to Macon County* for Nick Nolte to run afoul of the law
as a smart-mouthed lad on his way to California with pal Don Johnson to race their
souped-up stock car. In his early twenties, Nolte had been convicted of selling fake draft
cards. Later he would endure three divorces and a palimony suit, not to mention his
successful battles with drugs and alcohol. It seems Nolte, at least in terms of actorly
research, has had ample opportunity to see the inside of a courtroom and the bottom of a
barrel.

   Return to Macon County is Nolte's first theatrical film after a few TV-movies, a brief

Gentlemanly drag racer Nick
Nolte defends aspiring actress
Robin Mattson in the woods
in *Return to Macon County*
(1975), where the good ol'
boys of the region make his
brief stopover a hell on earth.

57

modeling career, and a youth spent playing football. He plays Bo Hollinger, who with Harley McKay (Johnson) makes the mistake of driving their car, replete with flames painted around the wheels, across the Macon County line. Cross that line, and you've got trouble, bub, in the form of rednecks looking for a fight and a local cop who'll never forgive Bo for punching him in the nose.

Between car chases and drag races, Bo falls for a quirky aspiring actress who wants to exchange waitressing for the life of a Hollywood starlet. Love gets Bo very confused; it's the start of Nolte's career playing conflicted, pent-up men. "I know what I'm gonna do, I'm gonna *do* what I wanna do, and don't you forget it!" he admonishes Junell, the Hollywood hopeful.

The handsome, beefy actor with the lived-in face—although when asked about an almost-certain facelift he jokes that he got a "testicle tuck" instead—attacks each role with such single-minded gusto that Nolte can raise even bad movies a notch.

"All films are a lot of work," he says, absentmindedly rubbing cigarette ash into the white table linen in front of him as he talks. "When the material is fascinating it doesn't take a toll, it's more of an exploration."

The material of *Macon County* was far from fascinating, but Nolte quickly resolved to seek out better scripts. "When I started acting, right away it was apparent to me that if I wanted to be involved in the literature of playwrights, it was the material that was important. I looked at a play and said, geez, this is about human life, the human condition. Not only can I read it, I can participate in it. So immediately from Day One, I was feeling satisfied artistically from the inside."

Nolte always lets his intuition be his guide. "I never embraced the concept of doing something in order to do something else. I've always done the films I wanted to do; they were my choices. Unlike the common perception, the material doesn't come to you from studios, it comes to you from other people, and usually by happenstance, circumstance, and luck, the artists that want to tell the story that certain people are interested in, they usually hook up in some odd way. A director wants an actor in his film who is not necessarily 'box office,' but who is into the material of the story he is telling. I wouldn't do this line of work if I couldn't do what I wanted to do."

Even when he gets the right movie, "I don't want to be bigger than the story, either. I have no interest in that."

After a callow youth on film, Nolte matured to play complicated, somewhat weary men. These pained characters—like the painter who needs constant female inspiration in Martin Scorsese's "Life Lessons" segment of *New York Stories* or the convict-turned-actor in *Weeds*—are right up Nolte's alley, since "I don't search for happiness; I don't find it an embraceable concept. I wouldn't play that game. I guarantee you you'll be miserable if you go for happiness. 'Cause you can't sustain it. It's much easier to accept the moment as it comes."

But he agrees that he is driven to fill the void between assignments. "There's something inside of me that's propelled to tell stories, I don't know where that comes from. Usually I finish a film and sit around and start churning, what's the next story?"

The next story after *Macon County* was 1977's *The Deep*, which most people *think* was Nolte's first movie. He has had a few other clinkers, like *Everybody Wins*, a psychological mess in which Nolte falls for Debra Winger, who has multiple personalities, each more rotten than the last—written by, of all people, Arthur Miller.

Otherwise, Nolte has shown in both comedy and drama, from *North Dallas Forty* on up to *The Prince of Tides* and *Cape Fear*, that he is one of America's sturdiest leading men, if still slightly unsung.

Return to Macon County, 1975
The Deep, 1977
Who'll Stop the Rain, 1978
Heart Beat, 1979
North Dallas Forty, 1979
48 HRS., 1982
Cannery Row, 1982
Under Fire, 1983
Teachers, 1984
Grace Quigley, 1985
Down and Out in Beverly Hills, 1986
Extreme Prejudice, 1987

Weeds, 1987
Farewell to the King, 1989
New York Stories, 1989
Three Fugitives, 1989
Another 48 HRS., 1990
Everybody Wins, 1990
Q&A, 1990
The Prince of Tides, 1991
Cape Fear, 1991
The Player, 1992
Lorenzo's Oil, 1992
I'll Do Anything, 1993

Nolte cuddles his shrink and lover, played by Barbra Streisand, in *The Prince of Tides*, a movie for which Nolte had to explore his emotions both on- and off-screen.

STEVE GUTTENBERG

Actor
First Film: *The Chicken Chronicles* (1977), d. Francis
   Simon
Video Availability: New Line Home Video
Role: David Kessler

Phoning it in

*D*avid Kessler sells fried chicken take-out at Chicken on the Run and hopes to get his
girlfriend to bed before high school graduation in a few weeks. That gives you more than
you need to know about the *The Chicken Chronicles*, a knock-off of *American Graffiti* and
Steve Guttenberg's inauspicious film debut.

    Guttenberg's easy *Chicken Chronicles* charm has got him a lot further than his actual
talent, in such films as *Cocoon, Three Men and a Baby, Diner,* and so many brain-numbing

Fast-food waiter Steve Guttenberg and girlfriend Meredith Baer ponder their impending high school
graduation in *The Chicken Chronicles* (1977). Guttenberg has sex and fried chicken on the brain.
One wonders what he had on the brain in the *Police Academy* series.

Police Academy movies that he is still identified with the series even though he only made it through the fourth installment.

At least he's honest. "My biggest problem as an actor is the tendency to take the easy road, the road we always tend to fall back on," he says, although he is not nearly so charming in person as in the movies. He breezes in fifteen minutes late for a twenty-five minute interview like a big-time movie star.

"There's a tendency to phone it in, and that's something I'm very aware of, because it's something I tend to want to do," says the actor who phoned it in for *Short Circuit, Can't Stop the Music,* and *High Spirits.* "I always take the easy road out. But I know that the harder road is the one that's much more responsible and much more worthwhile. The important thing is, you're in the entertainment business, so you have to entertain."

Guttenberg had intended to be a dentist, but acting turned his head.

"What's important to realize is that when you're an actor, you're ensconced with self-interest. And when you're playing in a film that's an ensemble, like *Three Men and a Baby,* self-interest gets in the way," he says, calling early success "a strange bubble to be under."

One thing Guttenberg has learned over time, that he didn't know when first making *The Chicken Chronicles,* is how to deal with the false friendships that result from the pressure-cooker atmosphere of movie sets. "I used to get upset about this," he says. "You spend three or four months together, intensely. By the end of the first week, you're telling each other your deepest, darkest secrets about everything. I mean, about things that you would never tell your best friends. But you have to learn that when you stop work, you move on, and you may not see each other for two years again."

Or, in the case of the *Police Academy* movies, more often than that.

The Chicken Chronicles, 1977
The Boys From Brazil, 1978
Players, 1979
Can't Stop the Music, 1980
Diner, 1982
The Man Who Wasn't There, 1983
Police Academy, 1984
Bad Medicine, 1985
Cocoon, 1985
Police Academy 2: Their First Assignment, 1985
Police Academy 3: Back in Training, 1986
Short Circuit, 1986
Amazon Women on the Moon, 1987
The Bedroom Window, 1987
Police Academy 4: Citizens on Patrol, 1987
Surrender, 1987
Three Men and a Baby, 1987
Cocoon: The Return, 1988
High Spirits, 1988
Don't Tell Her It's Me, 1990
Three Men and a Little Lady, 1990

PATRICK SWAYZE

Actor, dancer, singer, songwriter, skater, carpenter
First Film: *Skatetown, U.S.A.* (1979), d. William A.
   Levey
Video Availability: N/A
Role: Ace

Former "dance dude" in the fast lane

S *katetown, U.S.A.* offers lighthearted slices of life at the roller disco for people who aren't very demanding about entertainment. Aside from sharing with *Roller Boogie* the dubious honor of being virtually the only movies about the roller disco fad of the late seventies, its claims to fame are that it is one of the few films Playmate Dorothy Stratten made before she was murdered and that it is Patrick Swayze's film debut.

Still lean from his youth studying ballet at the Harkness and Joffrey schools and dancing

Patrick Swayze knows how to show a girl a good time at the roller rink in *Skatetown USA* (1979). Here he partners April Allen, who had done skating shows with Swayze in their younger Houston days.

with the Feld company (his mother, Patsy, is a choreographer of some note), Swayze shows undeniable talent—if not particularly as an actor, then as a skater. Early in his professional life he was a performer in an ice show, and within a couple of movies he would be Rob Lowe's hockey pal in *Youngblood* (see KEANU REEVES).

His career did a *grand jeté* when he played another athletic role, that of the Catskills dance instructor in *Dirty Dancing*. His fearlessness about punishing his body, despite an old football injury that has required several operations, led him to go parachute jumping in *Point Break*. He is so inured to pain that he once sliced off the tip of a finger with an electric planer and didn't notice until several hours later.

Swayze and his wife, Lisa Niemi, live on a ranch, and it may set even more girlish hearts aflutter if they knew that in his spare time, their idol likes to *rope steer*.

"I never wanted to be known as the Dance Dude," he says of his film debut, listening in the background to both a radio nearby and a television playing in another room. "In the beginning of my career, I kept it quiet in order to fight the stigma of the dancer turned actor."

The aftermath of *Dirty Dancing* kept Swayze ambivalent for years to come. "All I know is that I didn't have women screaming for me when I was growing up," he says. "It's a trade-off, being a star. Your privacy is gone. But then there's your career, so you deal with it. You deal with the fact that the way you zip up your zipper in the bathroom could wind up in the newspapers."

Skatetown, U.S.A., 1979
The Outsiders, 1983
Uncommon Valor, 1983
Grandview, U.S.A., 1984
Red Dawn, 1984
Youngblood, 1986
Dirty Dancing, 1987

Steel Dawn, 1987
Tiger Warsaw, 1988
Next of Kin, 1989
Road House, 1989
Ghost, 1990
Point Break, 1991
City of Joy, 1992

Swayze's lean dancer's body won him several athletic roles, including his most famous as a Catskills dance instructor in *Dirty Dancing* (1987).

STEVE MARTIN

Actor, comic, screenwriter
First Film: *Sgt. Pepper's Lonely Hearts Club Band*
   (1978), d. Michael Schultz
Video Availability: MCA Home Video
Role: Dr. Maxwell Edison

"Bang, bang, Maxwell's silver hammer..."

*H*is fans tend to think *The Jerk* was Steve Martin's first film, and Martin doesn't go much out of his way to correct them. Maybe he has survivor's guilt. The embarrassing *Sgt. Pepper's Lonely Hearts Club Band* just about killed the careers of his costars, particularly Peter Frampton and the Bee Gees.

Sgt. Pepper is a movie in which Beatles songs are loosely strung together with a thin narrative and in which Peter Frampton sings to a character named Strawberry Fields as she's lying in a glass-topped coffin.

Photofest

Is it the Jerk? No, it's Steve Martin singing "Maxwell's Silver Hammer," one of the high points of *Sgt. Pepper's Lonely Hearts Club Band* (1978), the dud that sank the careers of virtually everyone else in it.

If it was fade-out time for Frampton and the Bee Gees, it was just the beginning for Martin, whose frenzied rendition of "Maxwell's Silver Hammer" is about the only bright spot in the movie. His raucous early comedies, like *All of Me*, in which he played a man and woman sharing one body, paved the way for more gentle, adult comedies like his Cyrano de Bergerac update *Roxanne*, or the more personal *L.A. Story*, which does for Martin's hometown what Woody Allen movies do for his.

"I'm more mature now, I've had more experience, and I hope that I would hesitate to settle and say this is my style," says Martin, who is pleasant in person, but guarded and formal, and nearly never makes a joke while being interviewed—perhaps for fear it won't translate well. "I think I've changed in every movie, grown in every movie."

Martin was a successful comedy writer and stand-up comic, selling out arenas and wearing an arrow through his head. He was a hit on "Saturday Night Live" and with Johnny Carson. But when he switched to movies, he "didn't know how to get to the calm center."

When he made *The Lonely Guy*, he confided his fears to costar Charles Grodin. "I don't know how to be funny in a movie," he told Grodin. "When I was onstage, I knew how to be funny, and I don't know how to be funny in a movie."

Martin, more handsome and refined in person than on-screen, says he's licked that problem in the intervening years. "When I was doing stand-up, I was completely, 100 percent confident, and now I feel that way again about film. It's about the size, the intimacy; it's the indefinable nut or nub of something that you can hang on to. Before I felt like I was all over the place, and now I feel like I know what I'm doing."

Sgt. Pepper's Lonely Hearts Club Band, 1978
The Jerk, 1979 (also screenplay)
The Kids Are Alright, 1979
The Muppet Movie, 1979
Pennies From Heaven, 1981
Dead Men Don't Wear Plaid, 1982 (also screenplay)
The Man With Two Brains, 1983 (also screenplay)
All of Me, 1984
The Lonely Guy, 1984
Movers & Shakers, 1985
Little Shop of Horrors, 1986
Three Amigos! 1986 (also screenplay, executive producer)
Planes, Trains, and Automobiles, 1987
Roxanne, 1987 (also screenplay, executive producer)
Dirty Rotten Scoundrels, 1988
Parenthood, 1989
My Blue Heaven, 1990
L.A. Story, 1991 (also screenplay, executive producer)
Father of the Bride, 1991
Grand Canyon, 1991
Housesitter, 1992
Leap of Faith, 1992
Daddy's Little Dividend, 1993

PAUL NEWMAN

Actor, director
First Film: *The Silver Chalice* (1954), d. Victor Saville
Video Availability: Warner Home Video
Role: Basil

No fun at the toga party

*I*n the history of lousy film debuts, *The Silver Chalice* gets top marks. Paul Newman was so embarrassed by his first role—wearing a toga as the artisan Basil in Ancient Greece—that he later took out a full-page ad in the trades apologizing and urging people not to see the movie.

Basil is designing a silver chalice for Christ to drink from at the Last Supper, but Jack Palance is screwing up the works. (It's Lorne Greene's first movie too.)

And to think Newman almost made his debut in *East of Eden*. He tested with James Dean, another gorgeous actor who was often up for the same roles as Newman. The screen test has

Copyright © Warner Brothers

Not *Animal House*, but *The Silver Chalice* (1955)—in which Paul Newman unhappily begins his brilliant career in a toga. He took out trade ads advising people not to see him play a Greek artist designing a cup for the Last Supper.

survived and shows the two handsome rivals bantering flirtatiously. "Kiss me," says Dean. "Not here," says Newman.

Dean went *East* and Newman went Greece. But the latter's career rebounded two years later with his next role, as boxer Rocky Graziano in *Somebody Up There Likes Me*, a part that had been meant for Dean before he died in that car crash heard round the world.

The Silver Chalice, 1954
Somebody Up There Likes Me, 1956
The Rack, 1956
The Helen Morgan Story, 1957
Until They Sail, 1957
Cat on a Hot Tin Roof, 1958
The Left-Handed Gun, 1958
The Long, Hot Summer, 1958
Rally Round the Flag, Boys! 1958
The Young Philadelphians, 1959
Exodus, 1960
From the Terrace, 1960
The Hustler, 1961
Paris Blues, 1961
Adventures of a Young Man, 1962
Hud, 1963
A New Kind of Love, 1963
The Prize, 1963
The Outrage, 1964
What a Way to Go! 1964
Lady L, 1965
Harper, 1966
Torn Curtain, 1966
Cool Hand Luke, 1967
Hombre, 1967
Rachel, Rachel, 1968 (director, producer)
The Secret War of Harry Frigg, 1968
Butch Cassidy and the Sundance Kid, 1969
Winning, 1969
King: A Filmed Record...Montgomery to Memphis (docu), 1970

WUSA, 1970 (also producer)
Sometimes a Great Notion, 1971 (also director)
They Might Be Giants, 1971 (producer)
The Effect of Gamma Rays on Man-in-the-Moon Marigolds, 1972 (director, producer)
The Life and Times of Judge Roy Bean, 1972
Pocket Money, 1972
The Mackintosh Man, 1973
The Sting, 1973
The Towering Inferno, 1974
The Drowning Pool, 1975
Buffalo Bill and the Indians, or Sitting Bull's History Lesson, 1976
Slap Shot, 1977
Quintet, 1979
When Time Ran Out, 1980
Absence of Malice, 1981
Fort Apache, the Bronx, 1981
The Verdict, 1982
Harry & Son, 1984 (also director, producer, screenplay)
The Color of Money, 1986
The Glass Menagerie, 1987 (director)
Hello Actors Studio, 1987
John Huston (docu), 1988
Blaze, 1989
Fat Man and Little Boy, 1989
Mr. & Mrs. Bridge, 1990
What's Wrong With This Picture? (cameo), 1990
The Hudsucker Proxy, 1993

TOM SELLECK

Actor
First Film: *Myra Breckinridge* (1970), d. Michael
  Sarne
Video Availability: Fox Video
Role: Stud

Talent agent seeks "position"

*L*isted only as a "stud" in the credits, Tom Selleck appears in *Myra Breckinridge* for less
than half a minute as a potential boy-toy for Mae West, then well into her eighties. She
was taken by Selleck's performance in a Pepsi commercial, and as Cher might say, had him
washed and brought to her tent. Selleck plays a talent agent, minus moustache, for whom
West hopes to find a "position."

Mae West is naturally interested in finding a "position" for an awkwardly grinning—and smooth-
cheeked—Tom Selleck in the campy *Myra Breckenridge* (1970). Tom only got about 17 seconds of
screen time; the other actors weren't so lucky.

In real life, Selleck rejects the studly image that has trailed him ever since. "There's a romantic side to men that we don't necessarily get credit for," he says earnestly, adding that heartbreak is "harder on men."

"There's a great emotional health I see in women that I envy. Men often expect somebody to read our feelings—wouldn't it be romantic if she knew what I was feeling—because as a man, I don't want to talk about it."

But sex object has been his fate, thanks to his Marlboro Man looks. He even looked good as a dead body in *Coma*, where he signed into the hospital for a football knee injury and wound up suspended eerily from wires in an experimental warehouse for comatose patients.

Ever since *Myra Breckinridge*, Selleck has stayed true to form, following up that awful movie with many other awful movies—such as *Daughters of Satan, Her Alibi,* and *Mr. Baseball*—right up to today. In fact, although he became a big TV star with the long-running "Magnum, P.I.," his only film successes have been with the two *Three Men and a Baby* movies, in which he played the most sensitive male of the trio, and the most marriageable.

Myra Breckinridge, 1970
The Seven Minutes, 1971
Daughters of Satan, 1972
Coma, 1978
High Road to China, 1983
Lassiter, 1984
Runaway, 1984
Three Men and a Baby, 1987
Her Alibi, 1989
An Innocent Man, 1989
Quigley Down Under, 1990
Three Men and a Little Lady, 1990
Christopher Columbus: The Discovery, 1992
Mr. Baseball, 1992
Folks! 1992

ALEC BALDWIN

Actor
First Film: *Forever, Lulu* (1987), d. Amos Kolleck
Video Availability: Columbia TriStar
Role: Buck

"Parting is such sweet sorrow..."

"You've gotta watch yourself, there are a lotta creeps around here," Alec Baldwin warns Hanna Schygulla in the bomb *Forever, Lulu*, a movie that plays with all the awkward pacing of a foreign film dubbed into English.

In his first role, Baldwin turns out to be not a creep but a cop who saves Schygulla's life and is rewarded with a roll in the hay—actually, a roll among the seafood in a Fulton Fish Market warehouse. And to think Schygulla was contemplating suicide earlier that week because—on top of losing her job and being chased by the mob for two suitcases full of money and drugs she inadvertently stole—it appeared that there were no available men in New York.

Alec Baldwin gets protective around Hanna Schygulla in the dreary comedy *Forever, Lulu* (1987) He plays a cop who goes to night school and reads Shakespeare.

Debbie Harry is billed prominently and does little in this extremely unfunny comedy, probably to put viewers in mind of the doppelgänger effect created by Madonna and Rosanna Arquette in *Desperately Seeking Susan.*

Baldwin doesn't enter the picture until near the end, first wearing white high-top sneakers and a black leather jacket, and later looking ill at ease in a policeman's uniform. He affects a Brooklyn accent to quote Shakespeare, but it's no *Kiss Me Kate.*

Even in such a silly role, Baldwin manages to generate the kind of raw heat that would quickly mark him as a sex symbol and also make him so excellently nasty in *Miami Blues*, a movie in which he casually breaks a man's finger, and in *Glengarry Glen Ross*, in which when asked his name he spits: "Fuck you, that's my name." He also displays a hint of the comic flair that made him a natural in *Prelude to a Kiss* and a standout supporting actor as Melanie Griffith's lingerie-obsessed Staten Island boyfriend in *Working Girl* and Michelle Pfeiffer's middle-class mafioso husband in *Married to the Mob.*

The subject of his looks makes him uneasy, however, and in fact he had "an insuperable aversion to dailies," the playbacks of each day's scenes, until *The Hunt for Red October,* when costar Sean Connery "taught me how to watch them, just to see if what you're doing works."

Baldwin says his early film career was marked by being "very excited, bouncing around the set." Unsolicited career advice from his coworkers ran to the order of: "Save energy."

Forever, Lulu, 1987
Beetlejuice, 1988
Married to the Mob, 1988
She's Having a Baby, 1988
Talk Radio, 1988
Working Girl, 1988
Great Balls of Fire, 1989
Alice, 1990
The Hunt for Red October, 1990
Miami Blues, 1990
The Marrying Man, 1991
Prelude to a Kiss, 1992
Glengarry Glen Ross, 1992

RICK MORANIS

Actor, comedian
First Film: *Strange Brew* (1983), d. Rick Moranis and
  Dave Thomas
Video Availability: MGM/UA Home Video
Role: Bob McKenzie

"All you hosers in Russia and Hawaii, greetings!"

*W*ith the success of the beer-swilling McKenzie brothers skits on the Canadian TV show
"SCTV," Rick Moranis and Dave Thomas branched out to make *Strange Brew*, an
insipid comedy relying heavily on jokes about beer, bodily functions, and low IQs.

On "SCTV," the McKenzie brothers would analyze movies, usually concluding, "Things
blowed up good, *real* good," and calling each other a hoser, which is Canadian for jerk.

Opening up the simple skit for the big screen meant pasting a plot over the sketchy

Rick Moranis and Dave Thomas bring their moronic McKenzie brothers routine from "SCTV" to
film in *Strange Brew* (1983). What worked in blackout sketches has a long way to go in a film,
every frame of which seems to have another beer joke.

characters of the two brothers, something like what was done years later (and more successfully) with *Wayne's World*.

The self-reflexive plot of *Strange Brew* finds the two stars of the ersatz "Great White North" TV series starring in their own movie, one about a brewery where an ingredient is rendering people stupid and making them want to play hockey. The ingredient has no discernible effect on the McKenzie brothers, as they already are quite stupid.

The brothers are hired to provide "quality control" on the assembly line; mostly they just drink the beer in massive quantities. Moranis gets locked in a vat and has to drink his way out, then relieves himself at some length, putting out a nearby fire in the process.

Although Thomas hasn't fared nearly so well, Moranis—who emphasizes his nerdy looks and skinny frame—has made a decent if undiversified living as a Ghostbuster and as the mad scientist of the *Honey, I...* movies. (First he shrinks the kids, then he blows up the baby.)

"Am I a nerd in real life? Yes, I am. More so in real life than on the screen," says a rather stern Moranis, who doesn't lend himself to a happy-talk kind of interview. "If I take my glasses off, I can't see anything. It's just the way I look. I'm a short guy and I wear glasses, so these roles are unavoidable for me. Anyway, I don't only do nerds. I do sleazes, weasels, geeks, goofs."

Moranis, originally a comedy writer, is one of the more successful alumni of "SCTV," along with John Candy. "It was a unique situation," he says of the incredibly popular "SCTV." "I know why it was good and why we can't do it anymore. When you're young and hungry and green and you're in Edmonton and you're on at twelve-thirty at night, and your producer is letting you go way over budget, and you have seven people who all have the common goal of breaking out and becoming rich and famous, you're gonna get good stuff. As soon as the network realizes, hey, this is good, let's put this on in prime time, it's over. Because you now have people flying up to Edmonton telling you, *no no no no*, this should be a close-up, don't do that. And all of a sudden they're measuring that which shouldn't be measured.

"And when you take those same seven people, and you give them agents and lawyers and business managers and accountants and you throw them in Hollywood, and their salaries are competing, and the studios want them to do this and this and this—you've perverted it, you've corrupted it, and it's over."

Strange Brew, 1983 (also director, screenplay)	*Spaceballs*, 1987
Ghostbusters, 1984	*Ghostbusters II*, 1989
Streets of Fire, 1984	*Honey, I Shrunk the Kids*, 1989
The Wild Life, 1984	*Parenthood*, 1989
Brewster's Millions, 1985	*My Blue Heaven*, 1990
Club Paradise, 1986	*L.A. Story*, 1991
Head Office, 1986	*Honey, I Blew Up the Kid*, 1992
Little Shop of Horrors, 1986	*Splitting Heirs*, 1993

PIA ZADORA

Actress, singer
First Film: *Santa Claus Conquers the Martians* (1964),
  d. Nicholas Webster
Video Availability: New Line Home Video
Role: Girmar the Martian

"The doll has a teddy bear's head…!"

*I*n *The Lonely Lady* (1983), Pia Zadora plays a screenwriter who has to crawl over a lot of bodies to make it in Hollywood. As she's standing there triumphantly holding her Oscar and having a flashback to how she got there, perhaps she is also remembering her movie debut at age eight or so (depending on which published birthday you're going by) in *Santa Claus Conquers the Martians.*

Little Pia, painted all in green, plays one of two Martian children whose "only interest is in watching meaningless Earth programs on the video." It turns out her malaise is because there is no Santa Claus on Mars, so her dad and some other Martians beam down to Earth and steal St. Nick right out of his North Pole factory. "All this trouble over a fat little man in a red suit," grouses one Martian.

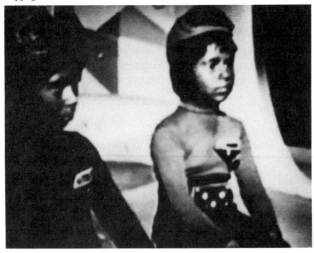

Twelve-year-old Pia Zadora (right) in green makeup watches too many Earthling sitcoms on television for a proper Martian girl, in *Santa Claus Conquers the Martians* (1964).

Santa arrives on Mars and immediately elicits peals of laughter from Pia with such jokes as: What is soft and round and green and toasted in the fireplace? A Martian-mallow.

Zadora took up acting early in life at the encouragement of the nuns at Our Lady Queen of Martyrs School in Forest Hills, Queens, because she was such a shy, introverted child. As Girmar the Martian, Pia gives a restrained and rather uninteresting performance, livening up only when things at the Martian toy factory go awry. "The doll has a teddy bear's head, and the teddy bear has a doll's head!" she squeals helpfully.

It would be difficult while watching *Santa Claus Conquers the Martians* to flash-forward seventeen years to when the grown Zadora, now a sex kitten aspiring to a real film career, would costar with the great Orson Welles in *Butterfly*, a movie her rich husband, Meshulam Riklis, basically bought for her.

After a few much-joked-about flops—the members of the Golden Raspberries, who give out awards to the worst movies every year, made a field trip to see *The Lonely Lady* on its opening day—Zadora has had much better success with a singing career.

Santa Claus Conquers the Martians, 1964
Butterfly, 1981
Fake Out, 1982
The Lonely Lady, 1983
Voyage of the Rock Aliens, 1985
Hairspray, 1988

ADOLESCENT APPROACHES

Hollywood Hatchlings

CHRISTIAN SLATER

Actor
First Film: *The Legend of Billie Jean* (1985), d.
  Matthew Robbins
Availability: Fox Video (Key)
Role: Binx

"Eat plants and leaves and stuff! And go huntin'!"

*W*hat does Christian Slater think made him stand out in the movie he says is his first, *The Name of the Rose*?

"My penis," he replies in that Jack Nicholson drawl he has appropriated for the current generation.

Actually, you never see his manhood—boyhood, really—in *The Name of the Rose*. And, come to think of it, that wasn't his first film. But let's go with it for a moment.

Helen Slater (backseat, and apparently no relation) is floored by Christian Slater's way with a gun in his early teenage debut in *The Legend of Billie Jean* (1985). The next time he used a gun he created a bigger stir, in the high school cafeteria in *Heathers* (1989).

Slater as a tonsured monk helps Sean Connery make like Sherlock Holmes to solve some monastic murders in *The Name of the Rose* (1986), a movie wrongly considered to be the teen idol's debut.

Although never actually on-screen, Slater's appendage does get a workout in *The Name of the Rose*, in which he plays novice Adso of Melk. He's in the care of Sean Connery, who is the Sherlock Holmes of the monk set back in thirteenth-century Italy. "The devil is hurling beautiful boys out of windows," is how William Hickey—stroking Slater's tremblingly beautiful face—describes the monastery's dilemma.

Early in the film, Slater pees into an earthen bowl for lack of locating the local loo. And although his penis cannot be glimpsed even with the most excellent of freeze-frames, he does display the rest of his fifteen-year-old body in a tussling sex initiation with a seductive peasant girl. "The actress in the scene [Valerina Vargas] guided me through," says Slater gratefully. "The love scenes were shot on a stone cold floor with dead fish lying around, not the most sexual thing at all. I don't like to be filmed while I'm making love. I won't do a love scene if it's grotesque and lewd and there's no point to it."

Spoken like a true sex symbol, although it wasn't until his high school rebel in *Heathers* three years later that Slater became such an icon. The black comedy *Heathers* cemented Slater's reputation for not playing by the rules—he takes care of his social problems by killing off the high school's snobby elite. In 1990's *Pump Up the Volume*, another teen counterculture movie, Slater is the voice of a new generation as an anonymous radio pirate deejay who tells it like it really is and who also pretends to masturbate on the air.

In fact, his role as a shy, sensitive, inexperienced monk (with a tonsured hairdo) is an

79

anomaly in his movie career, whereas his role as a renegade kid brother in 1985's *The Legend of Billie Jean* is more like it. In this, his *real* first movie, he rides a motorbike, brandishes a gun (a toy one), and wisecracks while he and his sister go on the lam.

Binx Davy and his sister, the soon-to-be-legendary Billie Jean (Helen Slater; no relation), become heroes to kids across the nation who respond to Billie Jean's rallying cry of "fair is fair" and her own self-comparisons to Joan of Arc, or at least to Jean Seberg. They come to represent antiauthoritarian courage, and look forward to a life in Vermont, where, as Binx puts it, they will "live in the woods! Eat plants and leaves and stuff! And go huntin'!"

In his first film, Christian still looked like a child. The famous cheekbones were not so well defined, and his bleached-blond hair flopped all over the forehead that within a couple of years would always be on display. The sardonic back talk is there, although he doesn't yet have that cool control that makes him seem so much older than his years.

And those tender years haven't kept Slater out of the gossip columns. "I've had a tendency in my blurry past to get a little crazy," he admits, chain-smoking Marlboros in a way that would drive an adolescent girl wild. He's close enough to his blurry past that he is still in touch with the doctor who delivered him back in 1969, but maybe not close enough to remember *The Legend of Billie Jean*. But then, who does?

The Legend of Billie Jean, 1985
The Name of the Rose, 1986
Twisted, 1985
Gleaming the Cube, 1988
Personal Choice, 1988
Tucker: The Man and His Dream, 1988

Heathers, 1989
The Wizard, 1989
Pump Up the Volume, 1990
Tales From the Darkside, the Movie, 1990
Young Guns II, 1990
Robin Hood: Prince of Thieves, 1991
Mobsters, 1991
Star Trek VI: The Undiscovered Country, 1991
Kuffs, 1992
Ferngully, The Last Rain Forest (voice), 1992
Where the Day Takes You, 1992
Baboon Heart (Adam's Heart), 1993
True Romance, 1993
The Last Party, 1993

No longer the juvenile sidekick or the timid monk, the cool, laconic Slater is now considered a young Jack Nicholson; he *talks* like him, anyway.

MOLLY RINGWALD

Actress
First Film: *Tempest* (1982), d. Paul Mazursky
Video Availability: Columbia TriStar Home Video
Role: Miranda

"I'm not exactly beautiful; besides, I'm a virgin."

"*I* dreamt I was smoking pot at a Go-Gos concert," says Molly Ringwald. Sighing, as she spins her wheels on a Greek island with her renegade dad, his lover, and a goatherd in *Tempest*, Paul Mazursky's desultory update of the Shakespearean shipwreck story.

"What's with her?" asks John Cassavetes, playing Ringwald's father, who has fled to this island from his bad marriage.

"It's called puberty," says Susan Sarandon, his Aegean lover, while wife (and real-life wife) Gena Rowlands is back home cheating on him.

Before the Brat Pack, Molly Ringwald was a member of the Bard Pack, in Paul Mazursky's update of the Shakespearean shipwreck play. Ringwald plays Miranda in *Tempest* (1982), daughter of sparring Gena Rowlands and John Cassavetes.

Raul Julia is the concupiscent goatherd who watches Ringwald bathe naked in the sea, then lures her to his cave to view his Sony Trinitron. "I want to balander you with my bonny johnny," he wheedles. But Ringwald, as Miranda, is hoping for a more suitable candidate to divest her of her virginity. "I want to put heels on and go to a concert. I want a frozen daiquiri," she whines, running from the cave of Kalibanos.

Apt sentiments for an actress who would spend her youth branded as a member of Hollywood's "brat pack" of young actors who cared more for frozen daiquiris than for the art of acting. Ringwald got off to a good start with *Tempest*, which earned her a Golden Globe nomination. She then made her reputation in the John Hughes oeuvre of suburban teen-angst comedies like *Sixteen Candles*, *The Breakfast Club*, and *Pretty in Pink*.

"I haven't had the Great Role yet, although I've been in some great movies," says Ringwald, whose career slipped off track after *Pretty in Pink*. "I don't believe in regrets. Most people my age haven't decided what to do with their lives, and I feel I've only just started. I'm sure I'll have plenty of movies that will be big box office."

The red-haired Ringwald, who describes herself as "passionate and angry," began in show business at age four, singing with the jazz band of her father, Bob Ringwald. She made *Tempest* at age fourteen, and in it she harmonizes on "Why Do Fools Fall in Love" with Sarandon while splashing in the water; she hopes to make a real musical some day.

Tempest also "introduces" Sam Robards, the son of Lauren Bacall and Jason Robards, who plays Freddy, Miranda's romantic interest. "I watched dailies on *Tempest*, but there was a kissing scene with Sam, and I ran out of the room before the kiss. It made me cringe," admits Ringwald. Although she blames the press for some of her image problems, she concedes that "perhaps I haven't been as wise as I thought I was" concerning career choices. "At fourteen I thought I knew it all. I thought I was brilliant."

Tempest, 1982
P.K. and the Kid, 1982
Spacehunter: Adventures in the Forbidden Zone, 1983
Sixteen Candles, 1985
The Breakfast Club, 1985
Pretty in Pink, 1986
King Lear, 1987

The Pick-Up Artist, 1987
For Keeps, 1988
Fresh Horses, 1988
Strike It Rich, 1989
Betsy's Wedding 1990
Face the Music, 1993

Ringwald, all grown up, in *Betsy's Wedding*—sans the red locks that made her famous.

RIVER PHOENIX

Actor
First Film: *Explorers* (1985), d. Joe Dante
Video Availability: Paramount Home Video
Role: Wolfgang Muller

"Dad's gonna kill me!"

*R*iver Phoenix plays what he calls a "computer whiz nerd" in Joe Dante's *Explorers*, a boy in a scientist's jacket who monkeys with his basement computer and finds a way to manipulate energy fields so he and his two school pals can go tooling around town in a rebuilt carnival tilt-a-whirl. One clever scene has them hovering in their own UFO in front of a drive-in screen where a sci-fi B-movie is playing.

"I went out on a standard cattle call for four auditions," says Phoenix in a very serious, intent way, which must have been why Dante made him the scientist of the group. "At the time I had a cast on from a motorcycle accident, and I had plumped out pretty good. I told Dante I can do this part, I know I can. He cared for me and wanted me to be in the project somehow."

In *The Explorers* (1985), scientifically minded River Phoenix and pals convert an old rusty Tilt-a-Whirl into a spaceship so they can hover over the local drive-in, then visit with extraterrestrials.

83

As Wolfgang Muller, Phoenix is an adjunct to star Ethan Hawke, a science fiction nut who dreams he's traveling in a computerized dimension. Dante attempted to take the movie in two directions—as a reminder not to lose the childhood ability to dream and as a loving send-up of pop culture, which he would later do with more finesse in *Gremlins 2*.

The fourteen-year-old Phoenix displays in *Explorers* the remarkable maturity that made him such a standout in *Stand By Me* and *Running on Empty* (for which he was nominated for a supporting-actor Oscar). In fact, the few movies in which he played a "typical" teen, such as *A Night in the Life of Jimmy Reardon*, bombed.

"I think *The Mosquito Coast* was the most daring thing I've done, because it was advanced for my age," said Phoenix over dinner during the 1991 Toronto Festival of Festivals. In *The Mosquito Coast*, he is the son of an inventor (Harrison Ford) whose obsessions are destroying the family.

The Mosquito Coast is not nearly as daring as the role of a narcoleptic hustler searching for home in *My Own Private Idaho*, the film for which Phoenix had traveled to the festival.

Privately, Phoenix can be as studious as Wolfgang Muller; at a press conference the next day, however, he seemed hostile and incoherent. "It's difficult, the actual process of communicating," he explains haltingly. Friends chalk it up to shyness.

And so, River Phoenix describing how he works up a character: "I read some, and look some, and observe some, and spend time thinking, and thinking some more. Any comments I would have are built into the work."

Explorers, 1985
The Mosquito Coast, 1986
Stand By Me, 1986
Little Nikita, 1988
A Night in the Life of Jimmy Reardon, 1988
Running on Empty, 1988
Indiana Jones and the Last Crusade, 1989
I Love You to Death, 1990
Dogfight, 1991
My Own Private Idaho, 1991
Sneakers, 1992
Silent Tongue, 1993

MATT DILLON

Actor
First Film: *Over the Edge* (1979), d. Jonathan Kaplan
Video Availability: Orion
Role: Richie White

"I only have one law..."

Matt Dillon was fourteen years old when he was plucked from Mamaroneck High School outside of New York City. He had been found skulking around the halls while cutting classes, and so they sent him off—not to detention, but to be a scowling, misunderstood teen in *Over the Edge*. The underappreciated little movie is about teens rebelling against conformity in a cookie-cutter housing tract.

"I only have one law—a kid who tells on another kid...*is a dead kid*," vows Dillon, playing Richie White, the kind of rebel Dillon built his early career on in such films as *The Outsiders* and *Rumble Fish*. His handsome, muscular looks, James Dean irreverence, and ease with the camera took him through the eighties and in 1989 he made a spectacular leap into adult roles as an addict trying to kick in *Drugstore Cowboy*.

Over the Edge also "introduces" Vincent Spano as an outlaw teen who rides a motorbike and shoots pellet guns at cops, but Spano actually made his debut earlier the same year in the forgettable *The Double McGuffin*.

Over the Edge, 1979
Little Darlings, 1980
My Bodyguard, 1980
Liar's Moon, 1981
Tex, 1982
The Outsiders, 1983
Rumble Fish, 1983
The Flamingo Kid, 1984
Rebel, 1985
Target, 1985
Native Son, 1986
The Big Town, 1987
Dear America, 1987
Kansas, 1988
Bloodhounds of Broadway, 1989
Drugstore Cowboy, 1989
A Kiss Before Dying, 1991
Singles, 1992
Blast 'Em (docu), 1992
Face the Music, 1993

Courtesy New York Shakespeare Festival

Nonactor Matt Dillon makes a strong first impression in *Over the Edge* (1979) playing a misunderstood teen who rebels against the sterility of a housing project where the kids have nowhere to go.

ALLY SHEEDY

Actress
First Film: *Bad Boys* (1983), d. Rick Rosenthal
Video Availability: HBO Home Video
Role: J.C.

"I don't want you to die—I love you."

"They tell you a lot of fairy tales about what it's like," says Ally Sheedy about the travails of working in film. In her very first one, her boyfriend comes to terms with his sense of outrage only after Sheedy is raped by his nemesis.

In *Bad Boys*, Sheedy plays J.C., the loyal girlfriend of misunderstood juvenile delinquent Sean Penn, who has been sent to the Rainford Juvenile Correctional Facility. J.C.'s father gives her a big talk about how Penn will never amount to anything, but she won't hear of it.

The rapist, played by Esai Morales, stalks J.C. down what is apparently the darkest, most deserted alley in Chicago and rapes her to get back at Penn, with whom he has a grudge match.

Penn breaks out of the pen and runs home to comfort J.C. Her big dramatic moment comes when she turns her face to the camera and reveals a badly bruised eye; it is now that Penn learns to cry and to care. Morales is put in the same cell block, and there is the expected confrontation, with an unexpected ending; *Bad Boys* is actually a pretty good movie.

The cat-faced Sheedy, at twelve the author of a best-selling children's book, would soon become famous as one of the Brat Pack cast of *The Breakfast Club*, playing the weird girl who never combs her hair and eats strange lunch from a paper bag. Later, she would drop partially from sight, beset by eating disorders and the problems sudden fame often bring on the young.

"I've always wanted to act, and I didn't want to fall into any ruts," she says. "I wanted it to be wonderful and have happiness and be very peaceful and not have to turn into a maniac."

To that end, along about the time Sheedy made *Maid to Order*, about a rich girl turned overnight into a poor maid for a Beverly Hills family, Sheedy took up meditation, the point of which was to get her busy, no-good beta brain waves to subside to happy-making alpha waves. After that, her career went into somnolent delta waves, which she is attempting to fix.

Bad Boys, 1983
WarGames, 1983
Oxford Blues, 1984
The Breakfast Club, 1985
St. Elmo's Fire, 1985
Twice in a Lifetime, 1985
Blue City, 1986
Short Circuit, 1986
Maid to Order, 1987
Heart of Dixie, 1989
Fear, 1990 (not released theatrically)
Betsy's Wedding, 1990
Only the Lonely, 1991
The Pickle, 1993
Kiss and Tell, 1993

Hollywood Book & Poster

Ally Sheedy's main acting task in her first film, *Bad Boys* (1983), is to convince teen convict Sean Penn that she loves him. Only after she is raped does he begin to deal with his feelings.

ROB LOWE

Actor
First Film: *The Outsiders* (1983), d. Francis Coppola
Video Availability: Warner Home Video
Role: Sodapop Curtis

"Lookit your tuff hair!"

As Arsenio Hall put it at the time, Rob Lowe had finally made a movie people wanted to see. That was when he was caught with his pants down in a home video that showed him having sex—for what seems like an eternity—with an underage girl he had picked up at a political rally. Judging by the video, Lowe certainly could have made more of an impression than either SLY STALLONE or SPALDING GRAY in *their* specialized first films.

But that video came well into his career, several years after Lowe's debut in Francis Coppola's notable teen movie, *The Outsiders*, which featured just about every up-and-comer of the new generation eventually known as the Brat Pack. Lowe is fifth-billed as Sodapop Curtis in a cast that includes Patrick Swayze, Matt Dillon, Emilio Estevez, Tom Cruise,

Rob Lowe (second from left) makes his debut as Sodapop in *The Outsiders* (1983). Director Francis Ford Coppola certainly had an eye for future talent—from left, Emilio Estevez, Lowe, C. Thomas Howell, Matt Dillon, Ralph Macchio, Patrick Swayze, and Tom Cruise.

Ralph Macchio—and C. Thomas Howell, through whose eyes the story of misunderstood adolescence unfolds. Lowe plays one of Howell's beloved older brothers, the good-looking one, although the rest of the case gives him a run for the money. He leisurely steps out naked from the shower, but the view is blocked by Swayze and Cruise horsing around in the foreground. He grieves over Howell's newly shorn and bleached locks—"Lookit your tuff hair!"—because their long hair identifies them as "greasers" from the wrong side of town. In his debut, Lowe is a bit stiff, but surely pretty.

Lowe has tried to counteract the effect of his pretty looks in several ways. One is by wearing intellectual-looking glasses, although he doesn't need them. Another is by taking a few roles against type; in 1987's *Square Dance* he played a retarded violinist, which surely kept the crowds away. He was rather better as a psychotic con artist in 1990's *Bad Influence*—a movie just getting rolling during Lowe's sex, lies, and videotape scandal—in which James Spader's sex scenes are secretly videotaped. The filmmakers deny either switching the actors' parts to avoid extra controversy or adding the videotape touch to cash in on it. Hmmm.

The Outsiders, 1983
Class, 1983
The Hotel New Hampshire, 1984
Oxford Blues, 1984
St. Elmo's Fire, 1985
About Last Night..., 1986
Youngblood, 1986
Square Dance, 1987
Illegally Yours, 1988
Masquerade, 1988
Bad Influence, 1990
Stroke of Midnight, 1991
The Dark Backward., 1991
Wayne's World, 1992
The Finest Hour, 1992

ANDREW McCARTHY

Actor
First Film: *Class* (1983), d. Lewis John Carlino
Video Availability: Vestron
Role: Jonathan

Forever a virgin

*W*hen Andrew McCarthy finally broke out of teen roles to play a journalist on the run in the thriller *Year of the Gun*, he was grateful. "It's a different kind of part—I'm not dragging around a dead body or kissing a mannequin or anything."

The dead body was in *Weekend at Bernie's*, the dummy in *Mannequin*, but McCarthy doesn't mind that he got his start in what he calls "silly movies" that date all the way back to his first one, *Class*. In that, he plays obnoxious Rob Lowe's virginal college roommate, who winds up having an affair with the roomie's sophisticated mother (Jacqueline Bisset).

Andrew McCarthy suffers the ignominy of being locked out of his dorm during a hazing, wearing women's underwear, in *Class* (1983). Rob Lowe in his second film plays his prankish roommate.

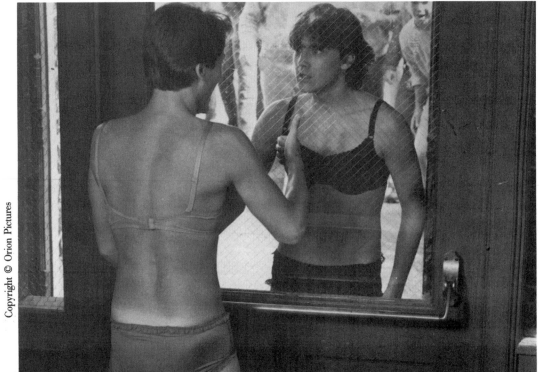

Thanks to his youth and inoffensive manner, McCarthy went on to other silly teen-type roles in *Heaven Help Us, Pretty in Pink*, and *St. Elmo's Fire*. "I was young—what was I going to play but a nineteen-year-old guy?" protested McCarthy at the Toronto Festival of Festivals, where he seemed uncomfortable touting his new manhood in *Year of the Gun* (which he followed up with a return to his old self in *Weekend at Bernie's II*).

"I was plucked out of acting school to do *Class*. It felt like treading water, trying not to drown. I didn't even know what 'marks' were." (For the uninitiated, the floor of a movie set is "marked" so that actors know where to stand in a scene.) "The director was patient, and especially Jackie [Bisset] was patient—she could have run roughshod over me."

McCarthy had several sex scenes with the older Bisset. "It was terrifying. I was so naive then. I was lucky in that if I knew a little more, it would have been worse. Anyway, you make your first movie, and it's not like you're finished—there's a lot to learn, even which camera angle is better for you. You're a virgin every time."

Class, 1983
Heaven Help Us, 1985
St. Elmo's Fire, 1985
Pretty in Pink, 1986
Less Than Zero, 1987
Mannequin, 1987
Waiting for the Moon, 1987
Fresh Horses, 1988
Kansas, 1988
Weekend at Bernie's, 1989
Docteur M., 1990
Jours tranquilles a Clichy, 1990
Year of the Gun, 1991
Only You, 1992
Weekend at Bernie's II, 1993

PATRICK DEMPSEY

Actor
First Film: *Heaven Help Us* (1985), d. Michael Dinner
Video Availability: HBO Home Video
Role: Corbet

"Hey, Danni, you gettin' any?"

O nly in his mid-twenties, and already Patrick Dempsey is bitterly philosophical about fame and the actor's dilemma.

"People love a beginner, but when you're too successful, people don't want you to be too good," he complains, chain-smoking and stamping his foot under the table.

Somehow, Dempsey feels the press or public has turned on him since his career has faltered. He started strong in *Heaven Help Us*, Michael Dinner's big-screen directorial debut, an effective comedy about a Brooklyn Catholic school. Dempsey plays an obnoxious student named Corbet who teases Danni, a counter waitress played by Mary Stuart Masterson. It was the beginning of a career as a wisecracker.

Patrick Dempsey (right) has a grinning beginning in the Catholic school comedy *Heaven Help Us* (1983), with Mary Stuart Masterson and Stephen Geoffreys. Though his career has been lagging, he made an early name for himself playing the love object of older women.

Dempsey reacts defensively, almost suspiciously, to a question about *Heaven Help Us*. When he does open up after some coaxing, he sounds as if he's just left an est seminar.

"An actor is a product of circumstances and the energy, an energy force that comes through you. Early in your career, you're open to that energy. There's a whole religious aspect to it, spiritual. Stardom doesn't feel hollow if you know what it is."

Dempsey was speaking at the trendy Laura Belle restaurant in Manhattan after playing young Meyer Lansky in the teen dud *Mobsters*, at a time in his life "when I'm just coming up after being down for a while. For a while, I got caught up in the lights, the glamour side of it. I was getting sucked in, the hype, the ego. The temptation of being around so many beautiful women, it's like, which one should I choose? It's a constant battle. But what really turns me on is the work."

Dempsey got married at age twenty-one to Rocky Parker, sixteen years his senior, and most of his successes were movies in which he attracts older women (*In the Mood*, *Loverboy*). He may not be a hit with people his own age, though; rumor had it that his costars froze him out on the set of *Mobsters*.

"I know where I've got to go after now," he says, not sharing his destination. "I don't care what people think. I have to be passionate, committed to an outer manifestation of something inside." Excuse me?

Heaven Help Us, 1985
Meatballs III, 1986
Can't Buy Me Love, 1987
In the Mood, 1987
Il Giovane toscanini, 1988
In a Shallow Grave, 1988
Some Girls, 1988
Happy Together, 1989
Loverboy, 1989
Coupe de Ville, 1990
Run, 1991
Mobsters, 1991
R.S.V.P., 1992
Face the Music, 1993

HORRORS

Careers That Give You the Creeps

JAMIE LEE CURTIS

Actress
First Film: *Halloween* (1978), d. John Carpenter
Video Availability: Media Home Entertainment
Role: Laurie Strode

"Guys think I'm too smart."

*E*ver since he dressed in a clown suit to kill his older sister for necking with her boyfriend, Michael's juices have been flowing every Halloween like clockwork. It's fifteen years later, and judging by the point-of-view camera and the heavy breathing, we know Michael is stalking brainy Jamie Lee Curtis, a studious high schooler and a champion babysitter.

The reason we know from the start that Curtis is going to live to carve yet another jack-o'-lantern is because she doesn't date; as everyone knows, premarital sex is the most reliable indicator of impending death in slasher movies. "Guys think I'm too smart," mourns the dateless babysitter who will spend a harrowing night being stalked in the first of the *Halloween* series.

In the slice-&-dice genre, only the one virginal girl in the bunch gets to outwit the serial

A screamer no more, Jamie Lee Curtis is tough as nails as a cop with a thing for her gun, and a boyfriend with a thing for her gun too, in *Blue Steel* (1990).

killer. In *Halloween*, John Carpenter's creepy thriller, all of Laurie's sexually active friends get punished for their lascivious ways while Laurie fixes popcorn and reads bedtime stories to her young charge. The intelligence that kept the men at bay allows Laurie to use her head when all about her are losing theirs, quite literally.

Curtis continued to scream her way through such movies as *The Fog, Terror Train*, and *Prom Night*. But that guys thought Laurie was too smart is an apt description of Jamie Lee Curtis's career; with her strong jawline and stronger bloodline—she is the daughter of Tony Curtis and Janet Leigh—Curtis graduated from scream queen to more intelligent roles, with a brief stopover for that indelible nude scene in *Trading Places*.

She's strong, and yet she still seems to attract psycho killers. As a mannish cop in *Blue Steel*, she winds up with a boyfriend who likes her for her trigger finger.

Halloween, 1978
The Fog, 1980
Prom Night, 1980
Terror Train, 1980
Halloween II, 1981
Road Games, 1981
Love Letters, 1983
Trading Places, 1983
The Adventures of Buckaroo Banzai, 1984
Grandview, U.S.A., 1984
Perfect, 1985
Amazing Grace and Chuck, 1987
Un homme amoureux, 1987
Dominick and Eugene, 1988
A Fish Called Wanda, 1988
Blue Steel, 1989
Queens Logic, 1991
My Girl, 1991
Forever Young, 1992

With parents like Tony Curtis and Janet Leigh, Jamie Lee Curtis had good genes. But it was her good lungs that got her started in Hollywood. *Halloween* (1978) was the first of many screamers before she went legit.

97

HOLLY HUNTER

Actress
First Film: *The Burning* (1981), d. Tony Maylam
Availability: HBO Home Video
Role: Sophie

"What happens if we don't find 'em?"

*F*eisty Holly Hunter made a truly inauspicious film debut with a single line of dialogue to her credit as one of the girl campers in *The Burning*, a nondescript slasher film about a burn victim who stalks teens during their nature-trail outing.

(Future Michelle Pfeiffer boyfriend Fisher Stevens also makes his debut here at age sixteen as a camper who gets his finger chopped off and is later found decapitated.)

Cropsy (Lou David) wasn't a good camp caretaker, so the boys set him afire some years ago as a prank. Now crispy Cropsy is back for revenge, armed with gardening shears and third-degree makeup by fx wizard Tom Savini. He lets loose the Camp Stonewater canoes, and when some of the kids go off to look for them, Hunter gets her big line: "What happens if we don't find 'em?"

A reasonable question, indeed. Maybe we can read into this Hunter's future playing reasonable if excitable characters. In the off-kilter *Raising Arizona*, she is Nicolas Cage's barren wife, who reasons that they should kidnap a baby from a neighbor's batch of quints, since there are so many of them to begin with. In *Broadcast News*, she is a highly principled TV news producer who pencils time into her busy schedule to have a cry.

Author's collection

In *The Burning* (1981), Holly Hunter (left) shivers around the campside to scary stories before all her fellow campers get hacked to death by Cropsy, a former camp caretaker who got charred in a prank.

Hunter went on to play cutely neurotic dynamos, but the camera can barely find her as Sophie amid the other ponytailed campers in *The Burning*. Watch for her sitting petrified around the campfire as the boys tell stories of maniac burn victims.

The Burning, 1981
Swing Shift, 1984
Raising Arizona, 1987
End of the Line, 1987
Broadcast News, 1987
Always, 1989
Animal Behavior, 1989
Miss Firecracker, 1989
Once Around, 1991
Piano Lessons, 1993

BROOKE SHIELDS

Actress, model
First Film: *Alice, Sweet Alice* (a.k.a. *Communion, Holy
    Terror*) (1977), d. Alfred Sole
Video Availability: Various
Role: Karen Spages

Always a pretty baby

*I*t was only after she was a *Pretty Baby* that the filmmakers released *Alice, Sweet Alice*, Brooke Shields's film debut. In it, she's killed off in the first twenty minutes.

   The $400,000 *Alice, Sweet Alice*, with as many titles as murder suspects (*Communion, Holy Terror*), is about a Paterson, New Jersey, Catholic schoolgirl named Alice (Paula Sheppard) who is suspected of several murders, including that of baby sister Karen (Shields, then nine). Karen gets it the day of her first communion, so we don't have to hear her shrill voice for the rest of the movie.

Pretty baby Brooke Shields isn't long for this world in the horror flick *Alice, Sweet Alice* (1977). Her older sister is suspected of knocking her off on the day of her first communion.

Jerry Ohlinger

The former Ivory Snow baby, discovered in infancy by photographer Francesco Scavullo, is best known for being the child prostitute of *Pretty Baby*—just as well, since most of her films have been pretty awful, even if she looked lovely in them. "Range" is not an acting quality often associated with her.

Bright and athletic, Shields has always been under the thumb of stage-mother/manager Teri Shields. Now that she's trying to change her image, Brooke has replaced her mom with a Hollywood agency, but there are other roadblocks. "People have trouble seeing me as an adult," she complains. "They remember me as a teenager, and they have trouble making the transition. I mean, I'm a grown woman!"

Alice, Sweet Alice, 1977
King of the Gypsies, 1978
Pretty Baby, 1978
Just You and Me, Kid, 1979
Tilt, 1979
Wanda Nevada, 1979
The Blue Lagoon, 1980
Endless Love, 1981
The Muppets Take Manhattan, 1984
Sahara, 1984
Brenda Starr, 1989 (released '92)
Speed Zone, 1989
Backstreet Dreams, 1990
Legends in Light (docu), 1993

Shields portrays reporter/clotheshorse Brenda Starr in the ill-fated movie of the same name, with Timothy Dalton. The movie, based on the comic strip, was tied up in litigation for years, and got dismal reviews when it finally appeared in 1992.

JOHN TRAVOLTA

Actor
First Film: *The Devil's Rain* (1975), d. Robert Fuest
Video Availability: Various
Role: Danny

Before melting hearts, he just plain melted

*F*or those with failing eyesight who may easily have missed John Travolta's brief bit in *The Devil's Rain*, the distributors redid the title credits of the awful movie after he became famous, moving Travolta's name to the top of the cast list. This would effectively prevent magazine profiles from touting *Carrie* as the good-natured actor's first film, and further underscores how when it comes to celluloid, you can run but you can't hide.

In *The Devil's Rain*, a zombies-and-revenge flick, Ernest Borgnine gets everyone's goat by turning into a goat-headed demon and melting down most of the cast. Travolta, a zombie, has one line and then puddles up like the rest of them. If you weren't specifically looking for him, you wouldn't find him.

Memories of John Travolta's debut as a zombie in *The Devil's Rain* (1975) give him a headache today. Here he is in a scene from his more successful *Look Who's Talking?* (1989), in which he plays a sensitive cabbie in love with Kirstie Alley's out-of-wedlock baby.

Travolta's fame still rests primarily on his disco moves in *Saturday Night Fever* (1977), where he pulled himself up by his bootstraps by wearing a white suit, latching on to a classy dame, and gyrating to the Bee Gees as no one has done before or since. (See STEVE MARTIN entry for the fate of the Bee Gees.) Sylvester Stallone directed the sequel, *Staying Alive* (1983), proving that you can take the disco-dancer out of Brooklyn, but you can't hustle the box office.

Travolta had a surprise hit on his hands when he played another blue-collar type, this time a taxi driver who makes the perfect babysitter, in *Look Who's Talking* and its sequel. Despite those anomalies, his career has been in the kind of limbo you'd expect from a *Devil's Rain* zombie.

The Devil's Rain, 1975
Carrie, 1976
Saturday Night Fever, 1977
Grease, 1978
Moment by Moment, 1978
Urban Cowboy, 1980
Blow Out, 1981
Staying Alive, 1983
Two of a Kind, 1983

Perfect, 1985
Eyes of an Angel, 1988 (unreleased)
The Experts, 1989
Look Who's Talking, 1989
Look Who's Talking Too, 1990
Shout, 1991
Chains of Gold, 1992
Boris and Natasha, 1992

Courtesy Jerry Ohlinger

John Travolta as we best remember him, stayin' alive and talkin' Brooklyn in *Saturday Night Fever*.

DARYL HANNAH

Actress
First Film: *The Fury* (1978), d. Brian De Palma
Video Availability: Fox Video
Role: Pam

"You can have my seat."

She was lovely as the mermaid in *Splash*, the replicant in *Blade Runner*, and the astronomer beloved by a modern-day Cyrano in Steve Martin's *Roxanne*. But for anyone who thought Daryl Hannah made an acting "stretch" by playing the awkward, bespectacled hairdresser Annelle in *Steel Magnolias*, just catch her debut in *The Fury*.

As Pam, a bit role in which she practically fades into the furniture, Hannah is shy, graceless, overeager to please. "If you're so nervous, why don't you try masturbating," one girl snaps at her.

She plays one of the classmates of Amy Irving, who is miserable because of her unwanted extrasensory powers. Her telepathy is the kind that usually reads minds, moves small objects across desks, or distinguishes circles from triangles on hidden test cards, but for the movie's sake her gift goes several steps further. In the hands of director Brian De Palma, who evidently had not got the subject out of his system with the similar *Carrie* two years before, these ESP powers reveal themselves whenever Irving, as "Gideon," touches someone; her firm handshakes draw both memory and blood. (Watch for Jim Belushi in his debut as well.)

"I usually in the first week of shooting get very nervous and insecure," she says in a soft, hesitant voice, her hands clenched in her lap. Hannah really *is* painfully shy in person and really *can* look geeky when she wears her reading glasses. In fact, "I wore them when I went to read for *Steel Magnolias* and then I wore them in the movie; I thought that was appropriate for the character and it made it easier for me to read anyway."

The Fury gave Hannah plenty of experience to draw from when she went for a similar look in *Steel Magnolias*. "I had specific ideas for the way my character would dress, even down to finding ill-fitting underwear so her pantyline would show through. Certain types of polyester were preferable."

The special effects—a boy on the ceiling, spontaneous bloodletting, etc.—were handled by special effects master Rick Baker. But Hannah needed no help coming up with the geeky, pigtailed look of Pam all on her own. In fact, her subsequent image as a screen beauty still surprises her.

Daryl Hannah (right) recovers from her bad table manners in *The Fury* after a classmate tells her to "go masturbate" in order to calm down.

Although she plays a beauty in most of her roles, the long-limbed, flowing-haired Hannah says she most empathizes with characters who are "displaced, who are lost souls. I keep finding it alarming that in interviews they ask if my beauty is the focus for me."

But it certainly is the focus for many. The image of her that comes most often to mind is the publicity shot for *Splash*, where Hannah is lying prone with her head propped on her arms and her blond tresses artfully covering the human parts of her mermaidhood. The rumor was that Woody Allen asked her to play a bit part in *Crimes and Misdemeanors* just so he could film a kissing scene with her, and then shot take after take that ended up on the cutting-room floor. "They were looking for a Daryl Hannah type, and I said, *I'm* a Daryl Hannah type! My agent said I would hate it. I went in to see Woody, and he was embarrassed to ask. I said, Ask! Ask! I only had one line, but we reshot it a couple of times, then changed the location. He said he loved me, and he tends to work with people again, so I can only hope."

Her shyness is a lifelong affliction, which is why she turned to acting in the first place. "When you make a movie, you have a character and lines, and you can express yourself in a

105

hidden way. It's different just talking to someone, because you're, like, *naked* there. I don't know what to say. I'm shy. I'm somewhat of a recluse, not a party girl. I hate to watch myself played back on the screen. I think to myself, *I feel like a jerk!*"

The Fury, 1978
The Final Terror, 1981
Hard Country, 1981
Blade Runner, 1982
Summer Lovers, 1982
The Pope of Greenwich Village, 1984
Reckless, 1984
Splash, 1984
The Clan of the Cave Bear, 1986

Legal Eagles, 1986
Roxanne, 1987
Wall Street, 1987
High Spirits, 1988
Crimes and Misdemeanors, 1989
Steel Magnolias, 1989
Crazy People, 1990
At Play in the Fields of the Lord, 1991
Memoirs of an Invisible Man, 1992

Daryl Hannah as a sexy replicant in Ridley Scott's futuristic *Blade Runner* (1982), a far more satisfying performance than as a geeky schoolmate in *The Fury* (1978), her film debut.

FALSE STARTS

HARRISON FORD

Actor
First Film: *Dead Heat on a Merry-Go-Round* (1966), d.
 Bernard Girard
Available: Columbia/TriStar Home Video
Role: Bellhop

"Paging Mr. Ellis…"

"*P*aging Mr. Ellis," calls the bellhop as he lopes hopefully through the crowded hotel lobby. Could that be…is *that* the Harrison Ford who so manfully dominates the screen as one of today's most rugged leading men?

The Harrison Ford of *Dead Heat on a Merry-Go-Round* is all but unrecognizable, except for those eyebrows, which were not to be taken seriously until at least seven years later, when Ford played the handsome, cowboy-hatted drag-strip cruiser in *American Graffiti* (1973).

Dead Heat on a Merry-Go-Round stars James Coburn, the kind of craggy, romantic leading man Ford would be one day. In this complicated comedy, Coburn is a charming con man who seduces women to get what he needs to sustain himself while he plans a huge,

Photofest

Harrison Ford in his bellhop gear outside Camilla Sparv's trailer on the set of *Dead Heat on a Merry-Go-Round* (1966), an awkward start for a future Star Warrior.

ridiculously detailed airport heist. Ford has one mercifully brief scene with the star; after Coburn gets the information he needs from Ford the bellhop, he withholds the young man's tip. You would too once you see how awkward Ford is. He is not even listed in the credits.

"I didn't have a career at all, or I wouldn't have had that part," says Ford today, sarcastically, hating the memory of *Dead Heat* almost as much as he hates being interviewed. "I was under contract at Columbia at that time, a seven-year contract which paid $150 a week that first year. I had a very clear sense of how much respect was implicit in that kind of arrangement. I had nowhere to go but up from there."

Ford was a full-grown twenty-four when he won this bit part. Moving uneasily within the confines of his tall, rangy build, he proved a particularly awkward presence on celluloid in his early career, like a man getting accustomed to new limbs that have been grafted onto his body. It is hard to see in his debut the commanding, heroic stance and bitter, self-effacing wit that would make him a fixture of some of the highest-grossing films of the seventies and eighties, including the *Star Wars* and *Indiana Jones* trilogies.

Because of economic necessity, Ford learned by doing. "It took real-life situations, working for money, for me to begin to form a concrete way of working. Until I began to develop a method of work for myself, I had no confidence in my process, and so I had no confidence in the results. Once I felt comfortable with that process and saw it work for me, then I felt much more secure about what I was doing."

American Graffiti was the first role of any substance where Ford felt comfortable. "It was the first time I had a part big enough for me to do the work the way I do it. I had other acting jobs before that, where I would ask the director a question and he would say, 'Don't bother me, *please*, I'm trying to make a movie here. Go away, kid.'"

Ford is one of the few big action-adventure heroes who has been able to diversify his career. He has since made his peace with low-tech action (*Witness*), comedy (*Working Girl*), and drama (*Presumed Innocent*). "I would never play Han Solo again," he says of the scruffy intergalactic pilot of *Star Wars*. "That's a pretty thin character for me. But I would play Indiana Jones again, because I had so much fun doing it."

He also hates his part in *Blade Runner*, in which he played "a detective who did no detecting. There was nothing for me to do except to stand around in some vain attempt to give focus to Ridley Scott's sets." Actually, the problem with *Blade Runner* is that the audience identifies with the androids, who are fighting to survive, while Ford's detective is out to destroy them.

Mature, disciplined, and self-assured, the present-day Ford is ultraserious when discussing his work, despite a few dry asides. (When told that director Mike Nichols described him as a Ferrari, Ford quips, "That means I'm expensive and difficult to maintain.") He admits he feels "dread" before interviews, and when discussing his upcoming projects he seems to have the weight of the world on him. "I have not so much a sense of anticipation" about new roles, "as a sense of impending great responsibility."

He betrays none of the awkwardness of that earnest bellhop of long ago, but he still experiences moments of doubt. "There are days when I can't act my way out of a paper bag. It happens to everybody. On days like that, I do as little as possible; I don't mean as little *work* as possible, just that I become a *minimalist*. Those days kill me."

Dead Heat on a Merry-Go-Round, 1966
The Long Ride Home, 1967
Journey to Shiloh, 1968
Getting Straight, 1970
American Graffiti, 1973
The Conversation, 1974
Heroes, 1977
Star Wars, 1977
Force 10 From Navarone, 1978
Apocalypse Now, 1979
The Frisco Kid, 1979
Hanover Street, 1979
The Empire Strikes Back, 1980

Raiders of the Lost Ark, 1981
Blade Runner, 1982
Return of the Jedi, 1983
Indiana Jones and the Temple of Doom, 1984
Witness, 1985
The Mosquito Coast, 1986
Frantic, 1988
Working Girl, 1988
Indiana Jones and the Last Crusade, 1989
Presumed Innocent, 1990
Regarding Henry, 1991
Patriot Games, 1992
The Fugitive, 1993

Gone is the awkwardness of youth. Ford's weather-beaten insolence is perfected by the time of the *Indiana Jones* series.

ELLEN BARKIN

Actress
First Film: *Diner* (1982), d. Barry Levinson
Availability: MGM/UA Home Video
Role: Beth

"I don't know who I am... am I pretty?"

"*I* can't hold a five-minute conversation with Beth," complains Shrevie (Daniel Stern) in *Diner* about the hapless high school sweetheart he married who doesn't understand his obsession with cataloging his record collection.

There are directors today who probably wish Ellen Barkin were more the Beth type; Barkin is known in the business for being a real scrapper when it comes to pleading the case for her characters. She figures she lost "about 70 percent of the fights with the powers that be" on the set of *Sea of Love*, where she played the prime suspect in a lonely-hearts murder case.

Photofest

The submissive-wife role never darkened Ellen Barkin's doorstep again, even though it was done for gentle comedy in *Diner* (1982). Here she dances with Daniel Stern, the high school sweetheart she marries only to find that their marriage is seemingly on the rocks when she makes the fatal error of misfiling his albums.

111

And yet Barkin, whose wit, off-kilter beauty, Nautilus body, and sensuality have earned her a screen reputation as an intellectual femme fatale, began her film career as Beth in Barry Levinson's *Diner*, about a group of Baltimore high school buddies whose camaraderie is threatened by the intrusion of adult responsibility.

Beth's big scene is when Shrevie finds she hasn't been filing his records properly, both alphabetically and by musical genre and year. Her big sin is that she filed James Brown under "J" and under "rock" instead of "R & B." Beth's teary, befuddled response is similar to later roles in which Barkin can get laughs from her characters' anxiety, most famously when she played an uptight district attorney in *The Big Easy* who gets a change of luck literally at the hands of Dennis Quaid's slightly corrupt but very handsome New Orleans cop.

But what would Beth have made of the character Barkin played in a cameo in *Down by Law*, in which she throws all her no-good boyfriend's earthly possessions out the window during one prolonged temper tantrum?

Nothing in the Beth character hints at the reputation Barkin would soon develop for sex scenes. As an obsessive tightrope walker in *Siesta*, she sucked Gabriel Byrne's thumb—which must have worked because they have been married ever since. In *Sea of Love* she throws Al Pacino against a wall and frisks him after stalking him like a tigress.

"Sometimes sex scenes are good because they're sex scenes, because they're sexy, and good directors direct them and they know how to direct them. But that's rare," says Barkin, who even when seemingly in repose on a sofa has the tense alertness of a feline on a catnap. "I think probably what makes a good sex scene is that maybe you find something out about the character in the course of the scene, instead of just seeing them have some sex act transpire before your eyes."

Barkin says her method of working has always been to reject more scripts than she accepts and to work only every now and then because of an abiding laziness. "I have no hobbies. I like to do nothing," she insists, although she likes to cook and takes acting classes occasionally between gigs.

"I think what makes a great movie actor is just someone up there telling you the truth about whatever they're feeling at that moment. They're telling you a secret about themselves. With Marlon Brando, you were always looking at something that you didn't think you should be privy to. You didn't think you should be allowed to know someone so intimately."

In *Diner*, Beth attempts to ease her marital woes by turning to someone she once dated in high school, a low-class hairdresser with high aspirations, played by Mickey Rourke. (They teamed again in 1989 for the punishing *Johnny Handsome*, in which Barkin plays what she smirkingly calls "a very bad girl.") Barkin ferociously defends Rourke, whom she calls "a great actor" snubbed by Hollywood "because the fashion seems to have moved away from the De Niros and Pacinos, who are scary actors, you never know what they're gonna do."

Barkin claims her late start in acting (she was twenty-eight when she made *Diner*) was due to uncertainty, but she's very certain about the sanctity of acting. "No one would think of going up to a firm, attractive young girl with small breasts and saying, here's a pair of toe-shoes, you look right, maybe you could be a ballet dancer and dance *Swan Lake*. But with acting, people seem to think that anybody could do that, if you look appropriate for the role. I don't believe that. I think that it's like any other instrument, you've got to keep it well oiled."

Diner, 1982
Tender Mercies, 1982
Daniel, 1983
Eddie and the Cruisers, 1983
Enormous Changes at the Last Minute, 1983
The Adventures of Buckaroo Banzai, 1984
Harry and Son, 1984
Terminal Choice, 1985
The Big Easy, 1986
Desert Bloom, 1986

Down by Law, 1986
Made in Heaven, 1987
Siesta, 1987
Johnny Handsome, 1989
Sea of Love, 1989
Switch, 1991
Man Trouble, 1992
This Boy's Life, 1992
Mac, 1992
Into the West, 1992

Barkin exudes sexual confidence in *Sea of Love* (1989), in which Al Pacino must decide if she is a woman who kills her blind dates after taking them to bed.

SEAN PENN

Actor, director
First Film: *Taps* (1981), d. Harold Baker
Video Availability: Fox Video
Role: Alex Dwyer

"Let's say we won the war and let's go home!"

Sean Penn made a false start in *Taps* when he was miscast as the goody-good roommate of TIMOTHY HUTTON at Bunker Hill military academy. Hutton is the one with the leadership credentials, TOM CRUISE is the bad-boy rebel, and Penn—who would later be as famous for taunting the paparazzi or divorcing Madonna as for his film roles—plays the guy who tutors them all in math and science.

"Declare a victory," Penn nervously pleads when his schoolmates hold out against those trying to shut down the academy. "Let's say we won the war and let's go home!"

With its talented, energetic young cast, *Taps* is a decent offering in the defend-our-school school of film. Cruise and Penn both show a remarkable amount of smoldering; watch them

Sean Penn (left) is the solid, studious kid in a mysterious bit of early miscasting in *Taps* (1981). He helps roommate Timothy Hutton with his homework and fears that taking over their military academy will get them into trouble.

on the parade grounds as they pass by for inspection. (Penn rides a horse, a little stiffly.)

"When this is over, you and me are gonna go round and round," threatens Cruise to Penn, who is a little on the yellow side compared to his rough-and-tumble classmates, and who rats on colleague Cruise when he breaks the rules.

Meanwhile, Hutton, the sensitive youth of *Ordinary People*, is the iron-willed leader of the pack in another bit of casting that shows a particular lack of vision, considering that both Penn and Cruise are waiting in the wings.

Penn, the pugnacious son of director Leo Penn, rectified the casting error with his second film, as the memorable surfer Spicoli in *Fast Times at Ridgemont High*, then in the aptly named *Bad Boys* as a juvenile delinquent with an inner decency. He played toughs with a conscience and without, respectively, in *State of Grace* and *Casualties of War*, then made his directorial debut with *The Indian Runner*, about a good brother and a bad brother struggling to handle their family responsibilities. "There's nothing a director ever did to me that I hated that I didn't do to my own actors," he remarked at the Toronto Festival of Festivals, smoking cigarettes and answering questions politely yet warily.

He claims it's the end of acting for him, "unless there's a large amount of money involved, or if I need my pool heated. Otherwise I'll keep directing. I haven't enjoyed acting for a long time."

Thinking back to his first film is painful for Penn, who says his "brain cells aren't retaining what the experience was like. Acting is so focused on such a specific, contained area, that it's really all about maintaining a certain relaxation. So I don't think I was as aware on the first day of my first film as an actor as I was on my first day on my first film as a director."

He admits that as a child, he would hang around his father's sets, and when he was directing *The Indian Runner*, his father returned the favor. "Oh, you already did that other shot?" his father would ask, a gentle reminder that the younger Penn had forgotten to film something he would need later for "coverage."

Acting's loss is directing's gain, since Penn shows a lot of promise on the uneven evidence of *The Indian Runner*. "It may not be a great movie," he admits candidly. "But I like it."

Taps, 1981
Fast Times at Ridgemont High, 1982
Bad Boys, 1983
Crackers, 1984
Racing With the Moon, 1984
The Falcon and the Snowman, 1985
At Close Range, 1986
Shanghai Surprise, 1986
Dear America, 1987
Colors, 1988
Judgment in Berlin, 1988
Casualties of War, 1989
We're No Angels, 1989
State of Grace, 1990
The Indian Runner, 1991 (director)
Blast 'Em (docu), 1992

ANNETTE BENING

Actress
First Film: *The Great Outdoors* (1987), d. Howard
    Deutch
Available: MCA Home Video
Role: Kate

"Honey, you're a stud…!"

*W*arren Beatty would have needed a fairly keen eye to pick out Annette Bening as the future mother of his child if he had seen her in *The Great Outdoors*, the comic piffle that was Bening's introduction to the silver screen. Luckily, Beatty met her instead four years later on the set of *Bugsy*, where he played the famed mobster who dreamed up Las Vegas and she played his lover Virginia Hill, a feisty, sexy moll who gave as good as she got.

In *The Great Outdoors*, Bening makes the best of a bad situation as Kate—adoring, giggly wife to Dan Aykroyd—a role that required her to call out such sweet encouragements as, "Honey, you're a stud; you look great on that horse!"

Strong-willed Annette Bening survived her nondescript debut in the disastrous comedy *The Great Outdoors* (1987), playing Dan Aykroyd's wife on a vacation in the woods.

"It was very standard," comments Bening kindly; it is her code of honor never to speak ill of anyone or anything, not even a turkey.

The Great Outdoors was written (and executive-produced) by John Hughes, that prolific chronicler of teen angst (*The Breakfast Club*) and dull middle-agers out of their element (*Trains, Planes, Automobiles*, the *National Lampoon's Vacation* series). In fact, *The Great Outdoors* is much like the *Vacation* movies; in this case, fellow Canadians Dan Aykroyd and John Candy play rival in-laws who share a log cabin vacation with their wives and children. Most of the humor resides in pitting the built-for-comfort Candy against nature: water-skiing, horseback riding, fishing. This is the kind of movie where the raccoons who ransack the garbage each night have subtitled "conversation" and where Candy wins a steak-eating contest and then throws up.

Bening became adept at sexy roles with a comic edge, but sometimes recharges her batteries by infusing supportive-wife roles with a rare warmth—in *Regarding Henry*, she cuckolds and then redeems wounded lawyer Harrison Ford, and in *Guilty by Suspicion* she is separated from and then shores up blacklisted Hollywood director Robert De Niro.

In *The Great Outdoors*, however, Kate's main chore is to laugh heartily at her pompous husband's jokes. "It's so lonely being wealthy," she sighs to her sister when the menfolk are gone fishin', adding about her sorry sex life, "Sometimes I think the only way I'll get any pleasure is by leaning against the washer during the spin cycle."

"I haven't seen it in so long," says Bening, which is her way of distancing herself from *The Great Outdoors*. "I think it's okay. I had a great experience doing it; it was a lot of fun. It was my first movie, and I learned a lot doing it. It was a big, expensive Hollywood comedy."

Those are pretty much the standard lines for actors who don't want to burn their bridges. Bening adds, "When you've never done a movie before, and you've come from theater, and you're used to getting paid what you're paid in the theater, and you're used to that kind of experience, it's tremendously exciting."

Born in Topeka, Kansas, and raised from the age of seven in San Diego, California, Bening supported herself as a cook aboard a charter scuba-diving boat before studying acting at San Francisco State University. She did some regional theater before divorcing her husband Steven J. White, a theater director, and moving to New York. She was in the play *Coastal Disturbances* when her agent hooked her up with the casting director for *The Great Outdoors*. Her audition tape was sent to L.A.

"That's what they do a lot in New York for actors, since so much of the film industry is in Los Angeles," says Bening. "They come looking for actors here, but they don't always fly you out. They make a videotape of you, which is horrible, it's a horrible experience."

Not *too* horrible, since she laughs that full-bodied, throaty gargle which was so sexy in her second movie, *Valmont*, with director Milos Forman, who tactfully never mentioned *The Great Outdoors* when he cast her as the scheming Marquise de Merteuil. Stephen Frears had turned down Bening for his own *Dangerous Liaisons* (based on the same novel as *Valmont*), but he later hired her as Myra Langtry, one of a trio in *The Grifters* who barters her body for whatever she wants, be it free rent or a partner in crime.

Bening archly suggests that libidinous Warren Beatty go out and jerk himself a soda in *Bugsy*, the movie on which they met.

The Great Outdoors is not a complete washout, however. If you watch carefully, you can see intimations of the tart comic timing that Bening used to great effect in *Bugsy*, and to steal her scene with Meryl Streep in *Postcards From the Edge* as a starlet who shares Streep's lover. There is also a scene where Kate's O-mouthed shock over something echoes Virginia Hill's reaction in *Bugsy* when told that her lover is dead.

"I know the Heimlich Manuever," boasts Aykroyd at one point, and Kate laughs a delicious, sparkling laugh, one that speaks of the special sexual knowledge that has made Bening's characters so intriguing.

The Great Outdoors, 1987
Valmont, 1990
Postcards From the Edge, 1990
The Grifters, 1990
Guilty By Suspicion, 1991
Regarding Henry, 1991
Bugsy, 1991

MEL GIBSON

Actor
First Film: *Summer City* (1977), d. Christopher Fraser
Video Availability: Video City Productions
Role: Scollop

Looking for the "effervescent façade"

*T*hose who dismiss Mel Gibson as simply an action hero for lowbrows or a pinup for fluttering hearts are missing out on his versatility. It's easy to think of him simply as a Mad Max or a Lethal Weapon—but remember, he was a Hamlet too.

And that's why the low-budget Australian surfing flick *Summer City* is a false start, with Gibson as a good-time Charlie—or, in this case, a good-time Scollop—with as little acquaintance with responsibility as with big words.

Gibson, though thought of as Australian, was actually born in Peekskill, New York, and moved Down Under at age twelve—which accounts for the lack of a heavy accent. He attended the National Institute of Dramatic Art in Sydney and had already been onstage in several productions (including Shakespeare) when he was reportedly paid twenty dollars to play one of four bachelors on a last spree in *Summer City*.

The production was plagued with problems from the start. There were power failures and a near-fatal car crash, and the cast and crew had to pitch in to put out nearby brush fires.

Mel Gibson in the sweet Australian movie *Tim* (1979). If only Gibson hadn't made *Summer City* two years previously, he would have had a great debut.

119

Gibson's next film would have made a more interesting debut. In *Tim* he plays a retarded handyman with a crush on an older woman. But *Mad Max* in the same year (1979) was such a hit in Australia that its American-designed sequels, *The Road Warrior* and *Mad Max Beyond Thunderdome*, crossed over and forever made Gibson associated with ultramacho wish fulfillment.

He's not the way he appears on film, however, and nothing at all like those gung-ho actors who go for the glory. "I never do my own stunts," he says, trying to jump-start his day at 11:00 A.M. with endless cappuccinos and Maalox tablets.

Scollop's only cares in the world were finding the perfect wave and the perfect girl. But Mel is a much more stressed-out individual. He has taken to seeing a New Age reflexologist to "find those points" of stress and work them out. "I know it sounds kinda weird and alternative, but his trick is to switch you off. It's impossible to describe. It's amazing. It's kind of hooked up to points and energies and things. It sounds a bit cosmic and weird, but it works. And I wouldn't have given it much credence a few years ago. Sometimes you need someone else to switch the 'off' button, and then what happens is your body kicks in and revitalizes all those places. And about three or four days later you feel like a dancing bear."

Also in 1979, Gibson made *Mad Max*, a popular Australian movie that didn't go anywhere in the States until its two sequels became fashionable.

He likes to transport his wife and six kids with him to wherever he's filming, both for their company and to provide the occasional reality check. And although he has bared his own bottom in a couple of movies (and he is so hairy they had to shave him), he dislikes doing sex scenes. "It has to do with getting the right tone and not turning people off. You don't want to see too much of that. Once you get too gritty on certain levels, especially in action comedies, you lose that effervescent facade that you hope to create. You want to pull back a little from that."

He thinks sex should be confined "to your bed. Or somewhere else. On the kitchen table, I don't care. But sex on the screen makes me uncomfortable, and it's always being forced at you. Nudity itself doesn't bother me, that's all right. I mean, what's nudity?"

Australian cinema gave Gibson his rousing start; in addition to *Tim* and *Mad Max*, there was *Gallipoli*, in which he meets his Waterloo during World War I. He says he has nothing against returning to Australia for more movies, it's just that "I go where the money is."

Summer City, 1977
Tim, 1979
Mad Max, 1979
Attack Force Z, 1981
Gallipoli, 1981
The Road Warrior, 1981
The Year of Living Dangerously, 1982
The Bounty, 1984
Mrs. Soffel, 1984
The River, 1984

Mad Max Beyond Thunderdome, 1985
Lethal Weapon, 1987
Tequila Sunrise, 1988
Lethal Weapon 2, 1989
Air America, 1990
Bird on a Wire, 1990
Hamlet, 1990
Forever Young, 1992
Lethal Weapon 3, 1992
The Man Without a Face, 1993

DIANE KEATON

Actress, director
First Film: *Lovers and Other Strangers* (1970), d. Cy
   Howard
Video Availability: Fox Video (currently on
   "moratorium")
Role: Joan

"It's no big deal anymore to feel him or smell him."

*I*t is only fair that the actress who would aid and abet Woody Allen in his comic studies of
neurotic relationships should have started her career playing a woman whose marriage is
on the rocks because her husband's hair "stopped smelling like raisins."

In the homey comedy *Lovers and Other Strangers*, Diane Keaton has a small role as a
member of an extended family trying to come to terms with the nature of love and
relationships as they prepare for the wedding of Susan and Mike (Bonnie Bedelia and
Michael Brandon). Mike's brother, Richie, is having a hard time explaining why his

Diane Keaton (right) relegated to the fringe of things in the 1992 remake of *Father of the Bride*. She
and Steve Martin look on with parental concern as their daughter (Kimberly Williams) gets ready to
walk down the aisle with George Newbern.

marriage of six years to Joan (Keaton) is unraveling. "What's the story?" his dad keeps demanding in one of the film's running gags.

The movie, released in 1970, puts a comic spin on some of the anxieties aroused by the revolution in sexual mores at the end of the sixties.

Joan arrives late to the wedding—and late in the movie, although we have been hearing about her for some time—and explains to her mother-in-law that the divorce is a result of "all the hurts and disillusionments built up over the years." She complains that Richie never buys her any books: "A book to me means love," certainly something Allen understands in his films. (In *Annie Hall*, Keaton and Allen fight over who gets custody of morbidly titled books in their communal library.)

Although Keaton is slightly giggly and self-conscious, endearing traits that would stay with her through most of her movies and certainly all of her comedies, her role in *Lovers and Other Strangers* doesn't give her any room to play. Later Woody Allen would bring out the best in Keaton by encouraging her to improvise with him—for instance, in the "nose-cloning" scene in *Sleeper* where she and Allen pretend to be doctors who can clone a whole person starting with just a nose, or in the bedroom disputes of *Annie Hall*, a movie based on their real-life relationship.

As Keaton matures, her talents are still not being tapped fully. Witness the compassionate wife in the remake of *Father of the Bride* or the reprisal of her role as long-suffering ex-spouse of Al Pacino in *The Godfather, Part III*. The only good thing about Woody's much-publicized breakup with Mia Farrow is that Keaton returned as leading lady in *Manhattan Murder Mystery*.

Lovers and Other Strangers, 1970
The Godfather, 1972
Play It Again, Sam, 1972
Sleeper, 1973
The Godfather, Part II, 1974
I Will...I Will...for Now, 1975
Love and Death, 1975
Harry and Walter Go to New York, 1976
Annie Hall, 1977

Looking for Mr. Goodbar, 1977
Interiors, 1978
Manhattan, 1979
Reds, 1981
Shoot the Moon, 1981
The Little Drummer Girl, 1984
Mrs. Soffel, 1984
Crimes of the Heart, 1986
Baby Boom, 1987
Heaven, 1987 (director)
Radio Days, 1987
The Good Mother, 1988
The Lemon Sisters, 1990
The Godfather, Part III, 1990
Father of the Bride, 1991
Manhattan Murder Mystery, 1993
Daddy's Little Dividend, 1993

Author's collection

Keaton explains why she's leaving her husband in her first film, *Lovers and Other Strangers*

JEREMY IRONS

Actor
First Film: *Nijinsky* (1980), d. Herbert Ross
Availability: Paramount Home Video
Role: Mikhail Fokine

"Maybe I should...just rehearse the costumes!"

*F*ilthy pederast's whore!" spits Jeremy Irons not once, but twice, in *Nijinsky,* a bold but
failed attempt to depict the chaotic homosexual relationship between the doomed dancer
Vaslov Nijinsky (George de la Pena) and his Svengali mentor and lover Sergei Diaghilev
(Alan Bates). Naturally, "filthy pederast's whore" refers to Nijinsky.

As Mikhail Fokine, proud choreographer of the Ballet Russe, Irons has the beginnings of
a kind of role at which he would excel—a sniffy upper-class sort who cannot tolerate
improprieties. Later he would play that type with some bizarre shadings, most notably in
Reversal of Fortune as Claus von Bulow, for whom social standing was everything even when
faced with charges that he attempted to kill his rich wife with an overdose of insulin. But in
his uninspired debut, he plays it straight, which is why most people can't remember Irons
being in the movie at all.

Jeremy Irons is doubly good at playing interdependent twin gynecologists who bed the same women
for sport in David Cronenberg's *Dead Ringers* (1988).

Misha the choreographer—"the most talented, celebrated choreographer in the world," as Diaghilev puts it—can barely contain his ire as he is gradually supplanted by impresario Diaghilev's madness-prone protégé, whose subsequent choreographies would prove to be as scandalous as they were memorable, such as the *Afternoon of a Faun* in which the faun masturbates. "To try to make a choreographer out of a simple little Polish peasant," sputters Misha to the doting Diaghilev. "You're blinding yourself, you're humiliating the company."

Irons's entire dialogue in the movie—from which he departs in a huff after two reels—consists of a series of escalating rants. "Really, you've gone too far. I consider that costume in abominable taste," he says at a rehearsal. "Maybe I should dispense with the dancers altogether and just rehearse the costumes." Once Irons is gone, the movie bogs down in soap opera and some bad acting.

Irons is somewhat emasculated in *Nijinsky*, but emerged from its ashes to a very successful career. In his early films, he was a romantic type (as Meryl Streep's French lieutenant; in the TV miniseries "Brideshead Revisited"). He tried light comedy in *A Chorus of Disapproval*, in which the distaff members of a neighborhood theater group try to get their hooks in him, but social and sexual naïveté don't seem to sit well on him.

What he's *really* good at is playing warped aristocrats, like Claus von Bulow, a role that won him an Oscar. He was a Kafka on the run in Steven Soderbergh's movie of the same name. Perhaps his most stunning role was as the twin gynecologists in David Cronenberg's deliciously pathological *Dead Ringers*.

"One tends to accept interesting roles when they are offered," said Irons cautiously from behind a pair of movie-star sunglasses at the Toronto Festival of Festivals, after *Reversal of Fortune* met with wild approbation. "I do love romantic stories, because you get to play with great ladies. But I do like the dark side."

For playing "snooty," another thing he does so well and which began back in *Nijinsky*, Irons says that sometimes accent helps. His carefully articulated British accent—he was born on the Isle of Wight—already lends him an air of authority. Here is how he describes preparing to play von Bulow: "To me, the voice was a more important component of the character than normal. The Dane who is pretending to be an upper-class Englishman, the first step in the charade of a man who enjoys creating a charade rather than being alive. He was once described to me as being an actor, not a very good one. It seems that truth was not high on his agenda, and he enjoyed the mystery and mischief of charade of the English gentleman. The accent therefore is overdone, the vowels are too long, the consonants he has trouble with. It was an important hook for me, that voice."

Nijinsky, 1980
The French Lieutenant's Woman, 1981
The Masterbuilders, 1982
Moonlighting, 1982
The Wild Duck, 1982
Betrayal, 1983
Swann in Love, 1984

The Mission, 1986
Dead Ringers, 1988
Australia, 1989
A Chorus of Disapproval, 1989
Danny, the Champion of the World, 1989
Reversal of Fortune, 1990
Kafka, 1991
The Beggar's Opera, 1991
Waterland, 1992
Damage, 1992
M. Butterfly, 1993

Author's collection

A miffed Jeremy Irons raises his eyebrows on finding that the dancer Nijinsky is taking over more of his choreography duties than he would care to relinquish, in his debut in *Nijinsky* (1980).

SCOTT GLENN

Actor
First Film: *The Baby Maker* (1970), d. James Bridges
Available: Warner Home Video
Role: Tad

"Didja know [plants] feel pain?"

A t the age of twenty-eight, a shaggy and gentle-looking Scott Glenn played the easygoing hippie boyfriend of the even easier-going Barbara Hershey in *The Baby Maker*, a movie that was shocking at the time and that predicted the emotional, moral, and legal dilemmas of surrogate motherhood that would crop up in the eighties.

Hershey plays Tish, a free spirit who blithely enters into a contract with a bourgeois couple ("They're the enemy," as Tish's antiestablishment best friend points out) to sleep with the husband and bear them a baby. Back at home, Tad (Glenn) is aimlessly plucking his guitar, tripping on "organic" drugs in the bathtub, giggling, grooving, and looking like a wounded puppy over Tish's bizarre business arrangement.

Although the movie is pro-hippie in terms of the likable casting of Hershey and Glenn, its ultimate message is a dismal one—that the stuffy bourgeois life is ultimately more rewarding than the alternative. Hershey loses both the baby and Tad, the latter of whom she had described as "beautiful... he makes fantastic things out of leather."

Courtesy New York Post

Scott Glenn, in the years before his macho image kicked in, sings a little ditty to describe his idyllic life with fellow free spirit Barbara Hershey in *The Baby-Maker* (1970).

127

He may be beautiful, his leather-work without peer, yet he is not quite a counterculture Einstein. "I got into this whole plant thing while you were gone. Didja know they feel pain?" is Tad's idea of enlightened conversation. When he asks how his lovemaking compares to that of the man who paid Tish five hundred dollars down to conceive a baby together, Tish tells him the other man is older, and Tad's tongue hangs thickly and dejectedly between his teeth. (You'll need the frame-by-frame advance to see it.)

Later, miffed that the baby isn't his and that the pregnancy is cutting down on the number of motorbike trips he and Tish can take, Tad takes up with another woman in a brief nude scene that shows what an admirable job a prior stint in the Marines did on Glenn's lean, mean body.

"I have more brushes and more colors at my disposal now than I did then," says Glenn today of his film debut. "When I made *The Baby Maker* I didn't really understand the differences in modulation in the way of working between being onstage and working with the camera. But the sort of quest of doing what I'm doing is the same, even today."

Glenn compares his work in his first movie to being "in the fourth grade, and now I feel like maybe I've just graduated from high school, ready to go to freshman year of college, in terms of knowing what there is to know and doing what you can do as an actor."

The sensitive, caring-about-plants side of Glenn was never again exploited to the extent that his rugged looks and hard body were. In movie after movie, such as *Urban Cowboy, The Right Stuff,* and *Silverado,* Glenn is the strong, silent, enigmatic type. In *The Silence of the Lambs,* he is Jodie Foster's brooding supervisor at the FBI.

In *Backdraft* he's a firefighter who along with the rest of the cast did his own stunts, and in *My Heroes Have Always Been Cowboys,* he's a rodeo cowboy—"blue-collar people who live by a chivalrous code, in which physical courage is an important ingredient," as he puts it.

The Babymaker, 1970
Angels Hard as they Come, 1971
Hex, 1972
Nashville, 1975
Fighting Mad, 1976
Apocalypse Now, 1979
More American Graffiti, 1979
She Came to the Valley, 1979
Urban Cowboy, 1980
Cattle Annie and Little Britches, 1981
The Challenge, 1982
Personal Best, 1982
The Keep, 1983
The Right Stuff, 1983
The River, 1984
Silverado, 1985

Wild Geese II, 1985
Gangland, 1987
Man on Fire, 1987
Off Limits, 1988
Miss Firecracker, 1989
The Hunt for Red October, 1990
My Heroes Have Always Been Cowboys, 1991
The Silence of the Lambs, 1991
Backdraft, 1991
The Player, 1992
Rope of Sand, 1993
S.I.J., 1993
Slaughtering of the Innocents, 1993

SLOW BURNS

Warm-ups That Led to Long, Steady Careers

JODIE FOSTER

Actress, director
First Film: *Napoleon and Samantha* (1972), d. Ber-
 nard McEveety
Video Availability: Buena Vista
Role: Samantha Connally

The lion bit her

*W*hen Napoleon (Johnny Whitaker) falls down a ravine, Samantha (Jodie Foster) throws
 him a leash that is attached at the other end to the pet lion that kids have run away with.
The lion, Major McTavish, pulls Napoleon to safety. And thus another crisis is averted by
the bright-eyed little girl whose hair was as shaggy as the lion's. Even at age eight, Jodie
Foster had a head on her shoulders.

Jodie Foster and Johnny Whitaker out walking their pet lion—all three with similar haircuts—in
Napoleon and Samantha (1972). The lion may look cute, but it bit Jodie during filming.

Years later, she would make her directing debut on *Little Man Tate*, a story about a child prodigy not unlike herself, torn between matters of the head and heart. "I suppose there are autobiographical elements in *Little Man Tate*. I really love working with kids, there's something about their purity. You can't bribe them with money or something, they don't care. If they don't want to throw the spaghetti, they just don't throw it. There's something actually kind of beautiful in that."

Foster was born Alicia Christian Foster. Her parents divorced when she was a few months old; her mom, Brandy, has always acted as her manager. Jodie made her professional debut when she was still a baby—she was the famous Coppertone billboard tot whose tanline is being exposed by a persistent terrier. She worked in TV commercials and did occasional sitcom work "for about a hundred years," she reckons, until her feature film debut in *Napoleon and Samantha.*

The Disney family movie follows the mild adventures of a couple of kids who run away with an abandoned lion, with whom Foster had "a mishap...It was just one of those accidents that happens all the time. He bit me."

She was also bitten by the acting bug. "Making that first movie was a great experience, it was terrific. Getting a start in movies was a way of going to different countries and learning different languages"—Foster delivered her high school graduation valedictory address in French. "There was a real adolescent feeling on movie sets, and at the same time a real seriousness. You play when you play, but you work when you work. And all the bag of tricks that I have, bits and pieces are certainly taken from all those early years."

Foster's career has been varied, which is one of the reasons she survived the hazardous transition from child actor. Among the stranger things she has done was provide the voice for Pugsley Addams on the TV series "The Addams Family." In the same year that she made the comedy *Freaky Friday*, she also played her second most famous role—next to FBI trainee Clarice Starling in *The Silence of the Lambs*—as the teenage prostitute who sets off Robert De Niro's rampage in Martin Scorsese's *Taxi Driver.*

Those "hundred years" of early work helped to make Foster completely comfortable both in front of a camera and behind it—even with journalists ("Maybe I'm sick, but I like talking to reporters"). She's guarded when you get her alone, but she positively blossoms at press conferences where she's the center of attention.

This sense of security was hard-won, and she can see that when she compares her younger self to the child actor she directed in *Little Man Tate.*

"What's extraordinary about Adam [Hann-Byrd], is a friend was doing a photo shoot, and they had popcorn, and they wanted him to go like this"—Foster grins widely. "And he said, 'I'm not doing this, that's not who I am, it looks stupid, and I don't wanna have any part of it.' When I was a kid, they gave me the popcorn box, and I did whatever I was told, because I thought I couldn't rebel. Now I realize that as professional as that might have been, that it really amounted to other people exerting authority, and me not having the personality to stand up and say, forget it, I don't wanna do that. Adam isn't so set on pleasing people as I was as a child, so I think he's more evolved."

She has made up for lost time by dubbing herself the "Bossy Little Thang," and had jackets printed up with "BLT" when making *Little Man Tate*. She no longer smiles for the popcorn when she doesn't feel like it.

Despite the extreme variety of roles Foster has played—including the rape victim in *The Accused* and Clarice in *The Silence of the Lambs*, both of which won her Oscars—there is a unifying thread. "I try to play true characters. They don't all have to be brilliant law school graduates. What I try to do is play characters that have been sheltered from the mainstream, they are subsets in some ways, misfits too. People who heretofore have been judged and been cast out as Other, not human, not valuable for our society. Sort of recognizing them and redeeming them in some ways. Women who have survived."

Survival is a subject dear to Foster's heart. "That's one of those thing that I like in people, courage and survival. And sometimes I see that in characters who in other ways are not your average cheerleaders."

That may be why some of the characters she has chosen to play appear at first to be victims, trapped in situations nearly as bizarre as the one she found herself in when a fan, intrigued by *Taxi Driver*, shot then-President Reagan to get her attention.

"What really excited me about having Jodie play Clarice," says Jonathan Demme, director of *The Silence of the Lambs*, "is that this is the first part Jodie has ever played where she hasn't had to mask her intelligence, where she is allowed to be every bit as smart as this exceptionally bright person actually is. And she manages to make that kind of erotic, I think. There might be something dry in a way about intelligence, but watching her use that mind of hers is very intoxicating."

Napoleon and Samantha, 1972
Kansas City Bomber, 1972
One Little Indian, 1973
Tom Sawyer, 1973
Alice Doesn't Live Here Anymore, 1974
Bugsy Malone, 1976
Echoes of a Summer, 1976
Freaky Friday, 1976
Taxi Driver, 1976
Candleshoe, 1977
Il Casotto, 1977
The Little Girl Who Lives Down the Lane, 1977
Moi, Fleur Bleu, 1977
Movies Are My Life, 1978
Carny, 1980

Foxes, 1980
O'Hara's Wife, 1982
The Hotel New Hampshire, 1984
The Blood of Others, 1984
Mesmerized, 1986
Five Corners, 1987
Siesta, 1987
The Accused, 1988
Stealing Home, 1988
Backtrack, 1990
Little Man Tate, 1991 (also director)
The Silence of the Lambs, 1991
Shadows and Fog, 1992
Sommersby, 1993

Foster in one other Oscar-winning roles, as FBI trainee Clarice Starling matching wits with Anthony Hopkins in *The Silence of the Lambs* (1991).

ROBERT DE NIRO

Actor, director
First Film: *The Wedding Party* (1963), d. Brian De Palma
Video Availability: VidAmerica
Role: Cecil

"Take those walls, rip them off."

*A*lthough *Greetings* (1968) came out first, an earlier pairing of Robert De Niro and
director Brian De Palma—the first movie for each, and for Jill Clayburgh, there is, too.
The Wedding Party was shot in 1963 but not released until 1969. It is a strange, messy,
peripatetic little movie that is more interesting for the early technical capabilities and
inventiveness of director De Palma than for anything else.

The comedy, occasionally shot with the speeded-up jerkiness of a silent movie (the effect
is garnished with intertitle cards), is about the gathering of the families and friends of a
couple on the eve of their marriage. Clayburgh as the bride with a reluctant groom is in great
need of a voice coach. And De Niro—whose name is misspelled as De Nero twice in the
credits—looks extremely ordinary with short hair and conservative clothing, playing one of
the groom's two pals. He hangs back during his scenes.

Copyright © MCA Home Video

Robert De Niro is a study in tattoos as an ex-
con with divine retribution on his mind in
Martin Scorsese's *Cape Fear* (1991).

The role calls for De Niro as "Cecil" to help talk the groom out of marriage, then to talk him back into it. "You don't want someone to take care of you?" he asks during the second half of his task. "Someone to wash your clothes? Wash your dishes? Cook for you?"

De Niro is perhaps the most revered actor in film today, a "method" actor who becomes what he plays. He can do gangsters (*GoodFellas*), comedy (*Midnight Run*), romance (*Falling in Love*), physical impairment (*Awakenings*). From *Taxi Driver* ("Are you lookin' at *me*?") to *The King of Comedy* to the remake of *Cape Fear*, he does psychos better than anyone.

Maybe the only thing he can't do is grammar. That he would make his start in such a talky movie as *The Wedding Party* is interesting, since in person he can barely finish a sentence. "You just do the movie," he says of how he chooses his roles, "and you see what the beauty of it, or whatever it is, the things about it that appeal to you... You can do a movie that has to be made and no one will want to see it, and it doesn't work—this, that, and the other."

Huh, Bob?

He is asked what kind of image he thinks he projects. "Well, whatever. One day it's... it depends. There are many different sides to people, so..."

But friends say Bob is shy, one of the shyest men on the planet—or anyway, in Manhattan's trendy TriBeCa neighborhood, where he lives and where he has converted an old coffee factory into his Tribeca film production facility, with a restaurant on the ground floor. The man who as Al Capone in *The Untouchables* whacked a baseball bat across the head of an unsuspecting underling is sometimes too meek to make his way through a crowded party.

At interviews, De Niro tends to sit next to someone who has a big mouth, usually his director. Penny Marshall, for example, directed De Niro in *Awakenings* as a patient who overcomes years of a rare comatose state with the aid of an experimental drug. Marshall is quick to fill in De Niro's blanks. When he is intimidated by the row of microphones, mumbling, "It looks like a...," Marshall chimes in helpfully, "A Sony sale?" When De Niro cannot recall whether Robin Williams, who played his doctor in *Awakenings*, was ever funny on the set, Marshall prods him. "Between takes, though?" "Between takes, though," he agrees, thankfully.

A year later, De Niro was slightly more comfortable when questioned about *Cape Fear*— although he was still trailing his sentences off with a sound that is a cross between a small word and a gulp.

In *The Wedding Party*, De Niro is billed as one of the groom's friends, a friendly supporting role. By his second film, *Greetings*, as an inventive draft dodger, he was already getting into the kind of fringe-of-society characters he would excel at. By the time of *Cape Fear*, De Niro is playing a vengeful ex-convict with delusions of religious grandeur. When asked about where divine justice crosses swords with our system of legal justice, De Niro says something like "Hunm," a little sound that dies a lonely death in the stillness.

Director Martin Scorsese nods vehemently to everything De Niro says. He first worked with the actor on *Mean Streets* back in 1973; they have since made a total of seven films together, including *Raging Bull*, for which De Niro famously gained and then lost fifty pounds to play the boxer Jake LaMotta at different times in his life. De Niro and Scorsese understand each other the way twin babies do, nonverbally yet implicitly.

A bland-looking Robert De Niro—or "De Nero" as he is listed in the credits—gestures to the house where his friend's wedding is about to take place and announces he'd like to tear it down in his debut in Brian De Palma's *The Wedding Party*.

More than 20 years later, De Palma and De Niro are reteamed—all spellings correct—for *The Untouchables* (1987).

Penny Marshall is another who understands De Niro. "Thank God Bobby's a mumbler too," she says. "I'd mumble to him, he'd mumble to me, and no one else would understand what we were saying."

Just because he's shy in public doesn't mean De Niro doesn't know what he wants and isn't willing to go the distance to get it. A man who will work out daily for eight months for *Cape Fear* until his back had more ripples than a potato chip is not someone to be trifled with. "I felt that this guy had been in prison so long, so he had been obsessed, working out every day. And I felt I should have gotten further too, I mean I always envisioned him as being like, not like Arnold Schwarzenegger, but sort of, in a sense, really like, this guy is like a rock, and so, anyway, this was as far as I could get."

De Niro trails off with that little sound in the throat that he makes when he feels he has got his point across, no matter where in the middle of a sentence he is stuck.

De Niro was about to make his directorial debut on *A Bronx Tale*. He was also to star in it, which would certainly make communication between actor and director more efficient.

"The point is, indirectly, it'll be what it'll be," says De Niro of the movies he makes. "To make the movie and feel good about what you want to do, what you're doing is enough. If you feel that it's a movie that should have been made, that had to be made, then it's good. Does that make sense?"

Yes, Bob, in its own special way.

The Wedding Party, 1963
Greetings, 1968
Sam's Song, 1969
Bloody Mama, 1970
Hi, Mom!, 1970
Born to Win, 1971
The Gang That Couldn't Shoot Straight, 1971
Bang the Drum Slowly, 1973
Mean Streets, 1973
The Godfather, Part II, 1974
The Last Tycoon, 1976
1900, 1976
Taxi Driver, 1976
New York, New York, 1977
The Deer Hunter, 1978
Raging Bull, 1980
The Swap, 1980
Acting: Lee Strasberg and the Actors Studio, 1981
True Confessions, 1981
The King of Comedy, 1983
Falling in Love, 1984
Once Upon a Time in America, 1984
Brazil, 1985

The Mission, 1986
Angel Heart, 1987
Dear America, 1987
Hello Actors Studio, 1987
The Untouchables, 1987
Midnight Run, 1988
Jacknife, 1989
We're No Angels, 1989 (also executive producer)
Awakenings, 1990
GoodFellas, 1990
Hollywood Mavericks, 1990
Stanley and Iris, 1990
Guilty by Suspicion, 1991
Cape Fear, 1991
Hearts of Darkness A Filmmaker's Apocalypse (docu), 1991
Mistress, 1992
Night and the City, 1992
This Boy's Life, 1992
Blast 'Em (docu), 1992
A Bronx Tale, 1993 (also director)
Mad Dog and Glory, 1993

JERRY LEWIS

Actor, director, producer, screenwriter, comedian
First Film: *My Friend Irma* (1949), d. George
   Marshall
Video Availability: Paramount Home Video
Role: Seymour

"All temperamental artists are nervous on opening night."

*T*he first jerk Jerry Lewis ever played on film was in his first movie, where he was a soda jerk at an Orange Glorious stand. Make that an orange jerk—he and Dean Martin play countermen who only serve orange juice to their customers in 1949's *My Friend Irma.* Jerry presses the oranges and Dean croons to him, "Here's to life with you!"

   Life together started out on a good note for the comedy team, who made sixteen light formula comedies together before breaking up the act in 1956 and rarely (possibly never) tolerating each other again. Although billed way beneath Marie Wilson, who plays the nutty New York ingenue Irma, the love-hate patter between Lewis and Martin is the best thing in *My Friend Irma.* "Remember when the doctor gave you thirty days to live?" Lewis reminds Martin. "Didn't I go out and get you a calendar?"

Jerry Lewis and Dean Martin fight over sleeping quarters in *My Friend Irma* (1949), the beginning of their long screen partnership.

Today, Lewis is more known for his teary Labor Day weekend muscular dystrophy telethons and for the fact that the French embraced him as an artistic genius even when the United States found his juvenile comedy unbearable. "The French read too much into things," is the thanks that nation got when Lewis addressed an audience of adoring fans at the 1991 Fort Lauderdale Film Festival, where the organizers were showing 1963's *The Nutty Professor.*

"Is there something I wish I had known when I made my first film?" asks Lewis rhetorically, in the kind of preachy, charismatic-leader stance he adopts in public. "No. I can tell you right off the top of my head, you don't want to know what you should have known when you did your first film. That's what makes you an artist. You've got to fall on your ass, you've got to make mistakes, and you've got to do some stuff wrong. Then you'll know what's right. You'll never know what tall is until you meet short, you don't know what fat is until you see thin, and you don't know what happy is until you see misery. A specific example of that? My first eight or nine films."

Original poster for *My Friend Irma* touts the new comedy team in town, and in fact, they're the best thing in the movie.

He further dismisses his teamings with Martin as "commercial films, made specifically to make a lot of money. The only one film Dean and I did that had any substance was *The Stooge*, which was made in our third year of the film business, which really was the story of our lives and our breakup that happened ten years later. But the quality of film wasn't the key years ago. It was—how much can we make it for, how much money can we make doing that. Dean and I were in that trap."

He counts *The Nutty Professor*, which he wrote, starred in, and directed, as his favorite movie. He plays a gangly, buck-toothed professor named Julius who develops a potion that turns him into a slick lounge lizard—a caricature of the Dean Martin persona that inhabited all Lewis's early films and provided a foil for his bumbling characters. When Julius drinks the potion, he becomes his alter ego, Buddy Love, a man who drinks too much, croons too much, and woos the girls relentlessly.

Naturally, Lewis has denied that Buddy Love is a manifestation of his missing partner. And yet his comments reveal more about his relationship with Martin than several years on the analyst's couch.

"When you want to know about a writer, read his work," intones Lewis, pausing for effect. "I repeat, if you want to know about a writer, read his work. There were moments in 1961 when I was writing the script that I was terribly troubled that I knew this kind of ugliness, that I knew this kind of coarseness, that I knew this kind of caustic conduct. I was troubled that I was able to write that character, so much so that I flew to the Mayo Clinic and sat with one of the Mayo brothers, who were running the most comprehensive psychiatric unit other than Meninger. He sent me to see Karl Meninger, and I flew to Kansas and sat with Karl Meninger to find out if I was losing my mind, was I indeed that character Buddy Love, how did I know about him.

"Karl's answer to me was a simple one—we know there are people who are child molesters, that doesn't mean we are. We know there are people that will fire six shells into a lady's head, that doesn't mean that we would. Karl Meninger helped me understand I was writing about fantasy, about the kind of a man who is out there—ugly, sardonic, caustic, abrasive, nasty. I wanted Buddy Love to be the comprehensive ugly human being, to play against who I adore, Julius. I needed to have that kind of an ugly human being.

"The thing that shattered me was, when the film was released, we were getting fan mail for Buddy Love. That's when I called Edward McDermott, who has been my casting director for years, and I said—get me somebody to replace this son of a bitch."

My Friend Irma, 1949
At War With the Army, 1950
My Friend Irma Goes West, 1950
Sailor Beware, 1951
That's My Boy, 1951
Jumping Jacks, 1952
Road to Bali, 1952
The Stooge, 1952
The Caddy, 1953
Money From Home, 1953
Scared Stiff, 1953
Living It Up, 1954
Three Ring Circus, 1954
Artists and Models, 1955
You're Never Too Young, 1955
Hollywood or Bust, 1956
Pardners, 1956
The Delicate Delinquent, 1957 (also producer)
The Sad Sack, 1957
The Geisha Boy, 1958 (also producer)
Rock-a-Bye Baby, 1958 (also producer)
Don't Give Up the Ship, 1959
Li'l Abner, 1959
The Bellboy, 1960 (also director, screenwriter)
Cinderfella, 1960 (also producer)
Raymie, 1960 (song)
Visit to a Small Planet, 1960
The Errand Boy, 1961 (also director, screenwriter)
The Ladies' Man, 1961

It's Only Money, 1962 (also director)
It's a Mad, Mad, Mad, Mad World, 1963
The Nutty Professor, 1963 (also director, screenwriter)
Who's Minding the Store?, 1963
The Disorderly Orderly, 1964 (also executive producer)
The Patsy, 1964 (also director, screenwriter)
Boeing Boeing, 1965
The Family Jewels, 1965 (also director, producer, screenwriter)
Three on a Couch, 1966 (also director, producer)
Way...Way Out, 1966
The Big Mouth, 1967 (also director, producer, screenwriter)
Don't Raise the Bridge, Lower the River, 1968
Hook, Line and Sinker, 1968 (also producer)
One More Time, 1970 (director)
Which Way to the Front? 1970 (also director, producer)
The Day The Clown Cried (1972, unreleased)
Hardly Working, 1981 (also director, screenwriter)
Smorgasbord, *(a.k.a. Cracking Up)*, (also director, screenwriter)
The King of Comedy, 1983
Retenez moi...ou je fais un malheur, 1983
Par ou t'es rentre? On t'as vu sortir, 1984
Slapstick of Another Kind, 1984
Cookie, 1989
Mr. Saturday Night, 1992
American Dreamers, 1993

MARTIN SHEEN

Actor
First Film: *The Incident* (1967), d. Larry Peerce
Video Availability: Fox Video
Role: Artie Connors

"Don't be afraid, baby, I dig your jugs, that's all!"

*Y*ou touch that switch and I'll tear your arm off," is Martin Sheen's first line in his first film, *The Incident,* spoken to a pool hall operator trying to get him and his pal to leave at closing time.

Sheen made a commanding film debut as Artie Connors, one of a pair of punks who terrorize a No. 6 Lexington Avenue line subway car full of decent people as it makes its tortuous way down from The Bronx to Grand Central. During the trip, which takes the whole movie, nobody is allowed off the train.

Sheen was twenty-seven and had made his mark in *The Subject Was Roses* on Broadway when he landed this role, paired with newcomer Tony Musante as Joe Ferrone. Of the two, Musante is the meaner one, Sheen the more unpredictable. They leave the pool hall, beat up an old man for money, harass a couple on the street ("Don't be afraid, baby, I dig your jugs, that's all!" calls out Sheen), then hop aboard a subway car with a stuck door and a bunch of people whose stories have been introduced gradually via vignettes. Among the passengers is military man Beau Bridges and Ed McMahon (*yes!*) as a heel of a husband, carrying his sleeping daughter because he's too cheap to take a cab at two in the morning.

Filmed in black and white for that feeling of gritty, urban intensity, *The Incident* arrived in theaters at a time when people felt the social contract was breaking down in cities. Compared to hoodlums today, Sheen and Musante were relatively harmless hell-raisers; the worst thing Sheen does is to "hotfoot" a bum by sticking lighted matches in his shoe while he sleeps and to win a closeted gay man's trust and then humiliate him loudly.

The last scene, in which the shaky passengers carefully sidestep the fallen homeless man on their way to safety, underscores the movie's theme about how apathy weakens the fabric of society and brings degradation upon everyone.

No one could be any more the opposite of Artie Connors than Martin Sheen, or at least than the man Sheen turned out to be. After the famous heart attack that almost sunk the filming of *Apocalypse Now,* during a time when "I hated myself," Sheen pulled himself together, returned to the Catholic faith, and became an avid demonstrator down in the trenches for worthy causes, like environmental concerns and the plight of the homeless. "In the final twilight, we will be judged by love, and by love alone," he says with the evangelical fervor he gets in those intense eyes whenever he's on one of his favorite subjects.

Sheen is constantly reevaluating himself in relation to his faith, his family, and society. "I accept all my brokenness, and this makes me receptive to change," he says, radiating so much empathy you'd like to be adopted by him. As great a believer in reincarnation as Shirley MacLaine, Sheen claims to have been "hundreds and hundreds of people" in past lives, and names as his actual or spiritual teachers and mentors such disparate types as JFK, Mother Teresa, Francis Coppola, and Marlon Brando.

In *The Incident*, Sheen looks remarkably like his son Charlie; all the Sheen children have gone into show business in one way or another, and Martin says he "chose 'em" to be his kids. "It's not an accident. Our children come back to us to make up for past life indiscretions."

It wasn't exactly an indiscretion, but Sheen turned down many film roles that would have made him a star like his son, either through bad judgment or to spend more time with his family. He's proud of son Charlie, the most successful of his children, but "my heart goes

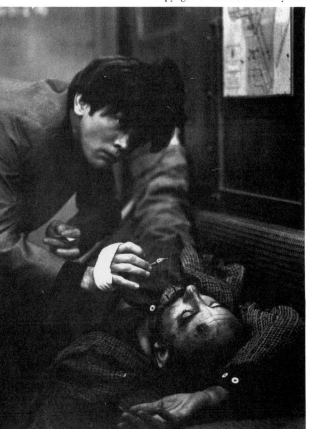

One day Martin Sheen would turn activist and fight for the rights of the homeless. But in his film debut in *The Incident* (1967), he plays a punk who terrorizes a subway car full of people. Here he puts matches in the mouth of a snoozing bum and threatens to light them.

143

out to him. My, my, my, if I had that kind of success at twenty-one it would have destroyed me. Success like that doesn't allow you to grow. There's a lot of noise around Charlie."

But a son in the business can be helpful. In 1987 he played Charlie's father in Oliver Stone's *Wall Street*—"Charlie got me the job"—providing a moral counterbalance to the ruthless Wall Street trader played by Michael Douglas who takes Charlie's character under his wing. When he began his career, Martin Sheen was a rogue; in middle age, he is the voice of reason and compassion.

The Incident, 1967
The Subject Was Roses, 1968
Catch-22, 1970
No Drums, No Bugles, 1971
Pickup on 101, 1972
Rage, 1972
Badlands, 1973
The Legend of Earl Durand, 1975
The Cassandra Crossing, 1977
The Little Girl Who Lives Down the Lane, 1977
Eagle's Wing, 1978
Apocalypse Now, 1979
The Final Countdown, 1980
Loophole, 1981
Enigma, 1982
Gandhi, 1982
In the King of Prussia, 1982
Man, Woman and Child, 1982
That Championship Season, 1982
The Dead Zone, 1983
Firestarter, 1984
In the Name of the People, 1984

Broken Rainbow, 1985
A State of Emergency, 1986
The Believers, 1987
Dear America, 1987
Siesta, 1987
Wall Street, 1987
Da, 1988 (also executive producer)
Judgment in Berlin, 1988 (also executive producer)
Just One Step: The Great Peace March (docu), 1988
Personal Choice, 1988
Promises to Keep, 1988
Walking After Midnight, 1988
Beverly Hills Brats, 1989
Cold Front, 1989
Cadence, 1990 (also director, screenwriter)
Marked for Murder, 1990
The Maid, 1991
Hearts of Darkness: A Filmmaker's Apocalypse (docu), 1991
Fixing the Shadow, 1993
Danger Sign, 1993
Finnegan's Wake, 1993

ANTHONY HOPKINS

Actor
First Film: *The Lion in Winter* (1968), d. Anthony
  Harvey
Video Availability: New Line
Role: Richard

"I will be king!"

*P*eter O'Toole and Katharine Hepburn quibble over which of their three vile sons will be
the next king of England. The most likely choice: Richard the Lionheart, mummy's
favorite, played by Anthony Hopkins in his film debut. "I'm a constant soldier, a sometime
poet, and I *will be king!*" Richard vows to his siblings. "Don't scowl, it makes your eyes go
sullen and piggy and your chin go weak," chides mom.

The Welsh actor had excellent stage credits under his belt by the time he came before the
cameras at age thirty-one in this highly visible role. Hepburn won an Oscar for her portrayal
of Eleanor of Aquitaine; Oscars also went to the writer and composer.

Anthony Hopkins (left) is one of three sons vying to the death to succeed their dad (Peter O'Toole,
right) as king of England in *The Lion in Winter* (1968). Hopkins later drew on the voice of
Katharine Hepburn, who plays his mother, when playing Hannibal "the Cannibal" Lecter in *The
Silence of the Lambs* (1991).

Jerry Ohlinger

Hopkins wanted to be an actor when he saw fellow Welshman Richard Burton returning home triumphant in a Jaguar and with a beautiful woman on his arm. He decided then that was the life for him, and for a while, it seemed he would drown his good fortune in too much liquor.

He has since dried out, and says he is a different kind of actor today than he was back when making *The Lion in Winter.* "I used to take things very seriously, not anymore," he says. "My advice to my daughter, who wants to be an actress, is—you just learn the lines, that's all the information you need, then you put that away into your subconscious mind, let it cook, and then it comes up."

No method actor he. "I don't want to diminish acting, but I keep it simple, I go in, learn my lines. It's taken a long time to develop that system, and I take it seriously. I learn the lines, I show up on time. I have learned to trust my own inner voice. I don't understand it, it still puzzles me, what and how I work."

Hopkins, with his eerie sense of focus, has played a variety of repressed and troubled characters, the most spectacular of which was serial killer Hannibal "the Cannibal" Lecter in Jonathan Demme's *The Silence of the Lambs.*

"Heavies are better, more exciting, to play," he says. "But I've played a range of people in mid-life crisis; as long as you're relaxed, they're very easy to play."

Even Lecter was a snap. "I thought of a man who lives in the sewer of his own mind, and I wanted to sense the kind of subterranean creature that he is. A highly civilized subterranean creature in the darkness," says Hopkins.

In fact, he reached back to his very first film experience for one major aspect of Hannibal Lecter. "You have to get a very strong image before you go in front of a camera, and for Lecter, I decided on the voice first, and the rest was easy. As I read the screenplay, I heard a combination of two voices in my head, and that was what I used."

The voices belonged to the late writer Truman Capote and to his first-film mom, Katharine Hepburn.

BEAU BRIDGES

Actor, director
First Film: *The Red Pony* (1949), d. Lewis Milestone
Video Availability: Republic
Role: Schoolboy

"Might's ain't gettin's."

*A*lthough *Force of Evil* made it into the theaters a little over a month earlier, *The Red Pony* was the first time in the saddle for former child actor Beau Bridges, part of the Bridges acting dynasty. (In *Force of Evil*, he is one of some children playing in the street and cannot be recognized.)

He was born Lloyd Vernet Bridges III, and went on to do much of his early work on his dad's TV series, "Sea Hunt." It was one of the elder Lloyd's beachhouse neighbors, director Lewis Milestone, who cast the blond-haired boy as the smallest of the schoolchildren in his film based on the John Steinbeck novel.

"I started when I was about six. *The Red Pony* was a real classic, and I had two or three lines," says the amiable Bridges, whose star has since been eclipsed by his younger brother, Jeff, to whom he is very close. (Jeff's first film was the 1970 highschool diatribe *Halls of Anger*, before he made a splash in *The Last Picture Show*, in 1971. That is, if you don't count his appearance at four months as a crying baby in the arms of Jane Greer in 1950's *The Company She Keeps*, as a result of a visit to the studio that day by his mom.)

Beau Bridges is the anxious little 'un, far left, swinging his lunch pail and wondering whether it's possible to "brush the hide right off" the little red pony in the 1949 movie of the same name. He swears he made this before *Force of Evil*, which hit theaters more than a month earlier.

"The beach down around Ventura was nothing back in the forties, it was a wasteland, no electricity or water. My dad had gone in with a bunch of other actors, seven of them, to buy this property down on the beach for nothing, and they would spend time down there together. At the end of it was this cliff, since there was no road down to the beach, and only one other stretch south of it where this wonderful director, Lewis Milestone, stayed. I met him there as a little boy, and he put me in his movie."

In *The Red Pony,* a boy's concern for his first pony disrupts his family and close relationship with easygoing ranchhand Robert Mitchum. The kid's school friends first taunt Tom, then admire him for owning a pony, then turn on him again when the pony dies. Beau is the smallest of the kids, and we first see him marching resolutely out of the mist of Tom's broken daydreams of glory.

Beau was not the most agile talker, but at that age, he looks cute fumbling his lines, his lip curled upward. He strains so hard to say "Yer gonna brush the hide right off him!" and the strange homily "Mights ain't gettin's," that he screws up his face and squints at the camera.

"I did a few films as a kid, including one called *Zamba,* where I had to parachute out of a burning plane over Africa, into the trees, and this gorilla named Zamba comes out. I can still hear the guy grunting in his gorilla suit."

Beau quickly learned to be at ease on film, helped no doubt by the Bridges gene pool and by the family's unaffected ways. "Jeff and I have never been interested in the social, so-called 'Hollywood' style of life, never went to parties. We stayed in the neighborhood. My father financially didn't get his success until I was a senior in high school. I was nervous about the fact that he got a big car, so I made him drop me off a few blocks from school; I was nervous about the transition to fame."

Bridges has developed as a strong character actor, and he still draws on his early years for emotional sustenance. "It's hard as I get older to hold on to that child that I was, that makes me unique from everybody else, my essence, what you were like as a little boy, what makes you special. The older you get, the more life takes out of you, the harder it is to remember."

Although very family-oriented, with four children and several future actors among them, Bridges says that leading a normal life after an acting childhood is "a bit of a challenge, because you certainly have that touch of the gypsy when you come from a family in the entertainment business. My dad was always on the road, and we joined him when school was not a factor."

Beau and Jeff teamed memorably as a third-rate family lounge act in *The Fabulous Baker Boys;* Beau doesn't mind that Jeff got Michelle Pfeiffer. "Through a lot of my career I played a lot of guest roles on TV, and got to play the villain a lot," he says. "But I'd like to play more villains."

Michelle Pfeiffer gets the brothers Bridges (Beau, left, and Jeff) all hot and bothered in *The Fabulous Baker Boys* (1989).

The Red Pony, (made in 1948, released in 1949)
Force of Evil, 1948
No Minor Vices, 1948
Zamba, 1949
The Explosive Generation, 1961
Village of the Giants, 1961
The Incident, 1967
For Love of Ivy, 1968
Gaily, Gaily, 1969
Adam's Woman, 1970
The Landlord, 1970
The Christian Licorice Store, 1971
Child's Play, 1972
Hammersmith is Out, 1972
Your Three Minutes Are Up, 1973
Lovin' Molly, 1974
The Other Side of the Mountain, 1974
Dragonfly, 1975
Swashbuckler, 1976
Two-Minute Warning, 1976

Greased Lightning, 1977
Norma Rae, 1978
The 5th Musketeer, 1979
The Runner Stumbles, 1979
Silver Dream Racer, 1980
Honky Tonk Freeway, 1981
Night Crossing, 1981
Heart Like a Wheel, 1982
Love Child, 1982
The Hotel New Hampshire, 1984
The Killing Time, 1987
The Wild Pair, 1987
Seven Hours to Judgment, 1988
The Fabulous Baker Boys, 1989
The Iron Triangle, 1989
Signs of Life, 1989
The Wizard, 1989
Daddy's Dyin'...Who's Got the Will? 1990
Married to It, 1991
Sidekicks, 1993

DUDLEY MOORE

Actor, musician, comedian
First Film: *The Wrong Box* (1966), d. Bryan Forbes
Video Availability: Columbia/TriStar Home Video
Role: John Finsbury

Libidinous; smart too

As befits a man who has mostly made romantic comedies, Dudley Moore can first be seen making out with a chambermaid in the greenhouse in *The Wrong Box*, a 1966 British comedy that holds up well today.

Moore and his stage comedy partner, Peter Cook (it's his debut too, naturally), play greedy nephews who will go to any lengths to ensure they inherit a large fortune. The money is reserved for the survivor of a tontine, and there are only two left of the original group, feuding brothers played by Ralph Richardson and John Mills. Moore and Cook must keep their man alive the longest, even though they think he is already dead.

Of the nephews, Cook is the smart one, Moore the libidinous one. In real life, perhaps Moore was smarter after all; his career has prospered in Hollywood, especially after such movies as *10* and *Arthur,* and despite a string of silly comedies. And he still gets the girl.

The Wrong Box, 1966
Bedazzled, 1967
Inadmissible Evidence, 1968 (songs)
The Bed Sitting Room, 1969
Monte Carlo or Bust! 1969
Staircase, 1969 (music)
Alice's Adventures in Wonderland, 1972
Pleasure at Her Majesty's, 1976
Foul Play, 1978
The Hound of the Baskervilles, 1978
10, 1979
To Russia...With Elton (docu), 1979
Derek and Clive Get the Horn, 1980
Wholly Moses!, 1980

Arthur, 1981
Six Weeks, 1982
Lovesick, 1983
Romantic Comedy, 1983
Unfaithfully Yours, 1983
Best Defense, 1984
Micki and Maude, 1984
Santa Claus: The Movie, 1985
Koneko Monogatari, 1986
Like Father, Like Son, 1987
Arthur 2: on the Rocks, 1988
Crazy People, 1990
Blame It on the Bellboy, 1992

Womanizer Dudley Moore (kneeling) and Peter Cook pay their last respects to what they think is the remains of their uncle in *The Wrong Box* (1966).

CAMEOS

Walk-ons in Need of a Freeze-frame

JEFF GOLDBLUM

Actor
First Film: *Death Wish* (1974), d. Michael Winner
Available: Paramount Home Video
Role: Freak 1

"Don't jive, mother, you know what we want!"

*J*eff Goldblum is so intense that when he first shakes your hand, he holds it just a beat too long, peering at you unblinking with those giant orbs, cocking his head as if trying to sniff you or lock into you through some astral frequency. His ears move sometimes when he talks, adding to the impression that Goldblum is possessed of psychic antennae, and although he can appear gangly on-screen, he is well built and powerfully kept.

That's almost certainly why he eventually played Brundlefly—half-man, half-insect—in David Cronenberg's gooey remake of *The Fly*. His intensity is also what made him so funny as the *People* magazine reporter on the make in *The Big Chill* or as the yuppie who has forgotten his mantra in *Annie Hall*. (Vincent Canby's rave in the *New York Times* about his delivery of his one line in the latter really set his career in motion.) And it's why, as bit-part rapists go, his was particularly memorable in the original *Death Wish*, his first film.

In retrospect, Goldblum's jazzed-up rapist occupies a significant place in film history, because it was that central defiling of all that Charles Bronson held dear that turned Bronson from a bleeding-heart liberal to the vigilante star of three dopey sequels.

Goldblum had been studying acting with Sanford Meisner at the Neighborhood Playhouse in New York, getting the occasional off-Broadway role, "when an agent saw me and sent me up for a movie. *Death Wish* was the first one he sent me up for, and I got that. I played a rapist killer who kills Charles Bronson's wife and rapes his daughter, and there you go! I liked the role back then; I was hungry to act."

Listed in the end credits as "Freak 1," Goldblum plays one of a trio of juvenile delinquents out on what is meant to represent a typical New York City crime spree. At first the guys simply throw food at one another in the aisles of a D'Agostino's supermarket. Then Goldblum waggles his tongue suggestively at a checkout girl. Things escalate when they spy Bronson's wife and daughter, whose address is clearly visible on their grocery delivery bags.

Goldblum has the most stature among the three, at least as far as stature goes among hoodlums. On a street corner, as a group of nuns passes by innocently, Goldblum scopes out his prey like a panther, salivating, legs spread, knees bent, shifting his weight restlessly as if revving his engines. Freak 1 is clearly a man who enjoys his work.

Jeff Goldblum knows how to make a first impression. Here he subdues the wife (Hope Lange) of Charles Bronson before raping his daughter in the first *Death Wish* (1974), and you know how much revenge *that* led to—*Death Wishes* 2, 3, and 4.

"Acting is all about exercising the ability to live truthfully under imaginary circumstances," is Goldblum's philosophy. "To live in an imaginary circumstance as if it were real, that's what we're after."

On the way to the women's apartment, one of the trio brandishes a spray-paint can, the aggressive, methodical shaking and aiming of which serves solely to anticipate the upcoming sexual assault.

Once the trio has burst in upon the hapless women, Goldblum takes the lead in harming and degrading them. Even for a violent movie the dialogue is unusually harsh and pornographic; it is also strangely idiomatic, like bad subtitles to a foreign movie. (The director, Michael Winner, is British, if that makes a difference.) "Don't jive, mother, you know what we want," says Goldblum, who continues to refer to Bronson's wife (Hope Lange) as the generic "mother."

"Goddamn rich cunt!" he yells, kicking her in the face. "I kill rich cunts!"

The women have only seven dollars between them in their purses. Goldblum is so incensed that he pushes aside a pal who has been spray-painting the daughter's bare bottom. "I'll show you how to paint, man!" he says, undoing his trousers and mooning the camera as he forces himself on the daughter, named Carol. "I'm gonna paint her goddamn mouth!"

Since Lange is by now inching her way painfully toward the telephone, Goldblum leaves off what he's doing to stomp her—fatally, as it turns out—and the thugs flee.

The entire ugly scene takes place right after the opening credits, leaving Bronson

155

approximately seventy-five minutes to clean up the streets of New York. He quickly changes his politics, acquires a gun—which he conveniently knows how to use because his father was a hunter—and spends his evenings encouraging the attentions of muggers so he can blast them to bits. He never does get revenge on Goldblum or his consorts, though; Goldblum has done such a thorough job that poor traumatized Carol ends up, according to Bronson's son-in-law, with "catatonia, dementia praecox, passive schizoid paranoia . . . *she's almost a goddamn vegetable!*"

Goldblum is aware of where *Death Wish* stands in the pantheon. "I never went into acting to earn my fortune, I think it's bad odds if you do that," he says. "It was always a matter of following my heart—I had to act, I wanted to act in some way, and it was my appetite and joy for that which allows me to do it. It also obliterates any kind of reasonable sense of career strategy I might have."

Most of Goldblum's bios skip *Death Wish* and go right to his early bit parts in two Robert Altman films, *Nashville* and *California Split*, but Goldblum doesn't shy away from his humble beginnings. "It's tough for me to be critical of movies to begin with. I try not to be an academic expert about anything in life; I think my pursuit of acting has taught me that. But what means most is how I feel about something. If I like it, I like it. And if I've done it, it's done. And I usually have a great time doing it."

Jeff Goldblum wears his birthday suit during teleportation experiments in David Cronenberg's 1986 remake of *The Fly*. His genetic merger with a common housefly wreaks havoc on his love life with Geena Davis.

California Split, 1974
Death Wish, 1974
Nashville, 1975
Next Stop, Greenwich Village, 1976
Special Delivery, 1976
Annie Hall, 1977
Between the Lines, 1977
The Sentinel, 1977
Invasion of the Body Snatchers, 1978
Remember My Name, 1978
Thank God It's Friday, 1978
Threshold, 1981
The Big Chill, 1983
The Right Stuff, 1983
The Adventures of Buckaroo Banzai, 1984
Into the Night, 1985
Silverado, 1985
Transylvania 6-5000, 1985
The Fly, 1986
Beyond Therapy, 1987
Vibes, 1988
Earth Girls Are Easy, 1989
El Mono Loco/The Mad Monkey, 1989
The Tall Guy, 1989
Mister Frost, 1990
Twisted Obsession, 1990
The Favor, the Watch, and the Very Big Fish, 1992
Deep Cover, 1992
Fathers and Sons, 1992
Shooting Elizabeth, 1992
The Player, 1992
Jurassic Park, 1993

NICOLAS CAGE

Actor
First Film: *Fast Times at Ridgemont High* (1982), d.
  Amy Heckerling
Video Availability: MCA Home Video
Role: Brad's Bud

Flipping burgers for chump change

*I*f you take the time to isolate Nicolas Cage in the only clear, full-face sighting of him in *Fast Times at Ridgemont High*, you'll see him looking extremely miserable. Of course, his character is *supposed* to be extremely miserable. He's a high school student making ends meet by flipping patties at All-American Burger, the fast-food joint in which your meal is "100 percent guaranteed," at least until you complain.

This role was so small, the character didn't even have a name of his own—he's listed as "Brad's Bud," meaning he's the buddy of the joint's assistant manager (Judge Reinhold). You can briefly see Cage in several crowd scenes—on line for registration at school, at the football game, at the graduation dance, breaking an egg with one hand into a skillet. And there's that one shot of him looking miserable.

Was Cage reaching deep into his soul to explore the inner misery of Brad's Bud, a boy wasting the best years of his life in an orange uniform and white peaked cap?

Actually, the sixteen-year-old Cage really *was* having a miserable time on the set of *Fast Times at Ridgemont High*. "Young people and young actors can be cruel," remembers Cage. "At that time, I was still Nicolas Coppola"—Cage is the nephew of director Francis Ford Coppola—"and here I was, you know, my first movie, trying to get into this character, and Eric Stoltz is hanging outside my trailer quoting lines from *Apocalypse Now* and *The Godfather*, and just always on my ass. And I said, to hell with this, 'cause I don't need it, and I wanted to be given a fair shot as an actor who could be taken semiseriously. So I changed my name after that."

Cage has worked with his uncle in *Rumble Fish*, *Peggy Sue Got Married*, and *The Cotton Club*, "and I'd work with him again anytime. But I just felt better when I changed the name, because then when I went into a movie I didn't have to talk about twenty years of Francis."

Cage said he had a bigger part that hit the cutting-room floor of *Fast Times*, an energetic and eminently likable slice of high-school mall life. Its vignettes follow the love life and academic crises of a bunch of teenagers, played by an exceptionally bright young cast, including Sean Penn as the long-haired surfer dude Spicoli who washes up to school every once in a while and orders a pizza delivered to history class.

Nicolas Cage (right) looks miserable behind the fast-food counter in *Fast Times at Ridgemont High*. (1982) The rest of his part was cut; no wonder he looks miserable. He changed his last name after this movie to avoid charges of nepotism.

The movie marks the film debuts of Anthony Edwards and Cage's nemesis, Eric Stoltz; also of director Amy Heckerling (*Look Who's Talking*).

"The first idea I had of being an actor was when I was six, and watching TV, and going, how do these little people get inside there? I want to get in there with them," recalls Cage. "When I was about ten, I saw the 'Million Dollar Movie'"—a late-afternoon TV showcase for old movies—"and that theme, ba *bah*, ba *bah*...wow!" Cage sings the opening bars of the *Gone With the Wind* theme, which introduced the TV show.

"But it wasn't until I saw *East of Eden*, where James Dean works so hard to get the money and give it to his father, and he's rejected, that I truly wanted to act. That scene broke my heart. It still does. I was so moved by it, I said, yeah, I want to be able to do that."

Cage quickly established himself as an offbeat, risk-taking, intense young performer. For offbeat, see him croon Elvis songs atop a car roof for the love of Laura Dern in *Wild at Heart*. For risk-taking, see him eat a live cockroach—for real!—in *Vampire's Kiss*. For intense, see him in the bakery inferno smoldering with passion for Cher in the romantic comedy *Moonstruck*.

"I'm not anticommercial, but when I consciously tried to be mainstream because I began worrying about that, it blew up in my face, with *Firebirds*," Cage's most miscast movie. "Mainly, I just want to do things that turn me on. And my taste sometimes is a little bit left-field."

Even the cockroach-eating incident had a precedent in Cage's left-field childhood. "I remember once it was picnic day, and all the kids were supposed to bring an article of food. I bought five cans of fried grasshoppers at the farmer's market, and mixed them into the egg salad. The kids were eating the sandwiches, and someone found a leg, and I got expelled."

He doesn't think having to eat a live cockroach later in life was retribution; in fact, it was his idea. "I really wanted to break the fourth wall and create this super-visceral experience for the audience. I asked them to wrangle me up some cockroaches. I walked on the set, and this bug was about *that* big, and I saw the antennae moving and the legs wiggling, and I rinsed my mouth out with hundred-proof vodka, and I ate it. It was soft, and I spat it out. I couldn't eat or sleep for three days. People refuse to believe that I really ate it; they think they went out and hired a special-effects guy to build a $500,000 remote-controlled cockroach. Think of all the money I saved for the movie."

Fast Times at Ridgemont High, 1982
Valley Girl, 1983
Rumble Fish, 1983
Birdy, 1984
The Cotton Club, 1984
Racing With the Moon, 1984
The Boy in Blue, 1986
Peggy Sue Got Married, 1986
Moonstruck, 1987
Raising Arizona, 1987

Vampire's Kiss, 1988
Never on Tuesday, 1989
Tempo di Uccidere, 1989
Firebirds, 1990
Wild at Heart, 1990
Zandalee, 1991
Honeymoon in Vegas, 1992
Red Rock West, 1993
Amos and Andrew, 1993
Deadfall, 1993

Nicolas Cage is Kathleen Turner's high school sweetheart when she travels back in time in *Peggy Sue Got Married* (1982), one of three movies Cage has made for his uncle, director Francis Coppola.

TOM CRUISE

Actor
First Film: *Endless Love* (1981), d. Franco Zeffirelli
Availability: MCA Home Video
Role: Billy the arsonist

"I was into arson."

As they pray to Tom Cruise pinups on their walls, millions of girls resemble the obsessional teens who inhabit *Endless Love*, Franco Zeffirelli's 1981 movie about crazed puppy love.

Endless Love was a terrific, creepy novel by Scott Spencer about the downside of devotion; a boy sets fire to a girl's house in an attempt to act the hero and win over her family after her father forbids him to see her. His obsession doesn't stop there, either.

The Zeffirelli film adaptation weakened the book, although he effectively shows the kind of starry-eyed first love that he did in *Romeo and Juliet*—a similar story, really, but one in which pathological attachment is ennobled. (Brooke Shields plays the modern Juliet in plenty of lingering close-ups.)

Tom Cruise rolls in the grass, crowing over his arsonist past in *Endless Love* (1981). Director Franco Zeffirelli is known for casting nice-looking lads in his movies.

Author's collection

161

Cruise later gets serious as a paraplegic Vietnam vet who has a change of heart about the war in Oliver Stone's *Born on the Fourth of July* (1989).

Zeffirelli is known for casting beautiful young boys in his movies, and *Endless Love* features two debuts—James Spader as the girl's protective brother and Tom Cruise in a cameo as a teen arsonist. One day, Cruise's looks alone would guarantee him the romantic lead, but here the lovesick role is essayed by Martin Hewitt.

And where does Hewitt get the idea of torching the girl's house and then rushing in to make himself look like a hero? From Cruise, of course, as Billy. He runs sweatily off the soccer field, removes his shirt to reveal a stocky, well-built physique, and rushes his lines in a squeaky voice while rolling on the ground with his legs kicking in the air. It's such an unlovely pose that Zeffirelli cuts away from him for Hewitt's reaction.

"When I was eight years old I was into arson," boasts Billy about a fire that "smoked like crazy... To this day my mother thinks I'm a hero."

No star potential visible there. Cruise quickly followed up *Endless Love* with *Taps*, in which he plays a military academy student described by Sean Penn as "that asshole... the guy's a maniac!" He does display a steely look in the early parade-ground scene, though—the look of a top gun.

The muscles he sported on the soccer field of *Endless Love* have served him well in his movies, many of which feature him as a sports hero—a football player in *All the Right Moves*, a pool hustler in *The Color of Money*, a jet fighter pilot in *Top Gun*, a racecar driver in *Days of Thunder*, a boxer in *Far and Away*. Word has it that he is still concerned about his high-pitched voice; time and career management will tell whether Cruise will be able to stay the "serious" course he charted as Dustin Hoffman's self-centered brother in *Rain Man* and Oliver Stone's anti-Vietnam war hero in *Born on the Fourth of July*.

Endless Love, 1981	*Top Gun*, 1986
Taps, 1981	*Cocktail*, 1988
All the Right Moves, 1983	*Rain Man*, 1988
Losin' It, 1983	*Born on the Fourth of July*, 1989
The Outsiders, 1983	*Days of Thunder*, 1990
Risky Business, 1983	*Far and Away*, 1992
Legend, 1985	*A Few Good Men*, 1992
The Color of Money, 1986	*The Firm*, 1993

Hollywood Book & Poster

James Spader (right) goes ballistic when Martin Hewitt keeps trying to date his sister, played by Brooke Shields. Spader made his debut in *Endless Love* along with Cruise.

GEENA DAVIS

Actress, model
First Film: *Tootsie* (1982), d. Sydney Pollack
Available: Columbia/TriStar Home Video
Role: April Paige

"Hi, I'm April Paige."

"*H*i, I'm April Paige," is Geena Davis's very first line in her very first film, *Tootsie.* She delivers it in skimpy bra and panties to a visibly flustered Dustin Hoffman.

Davis, a former model, is six feet tall, and Hoffman, his face coming up to her bra hook, is considerably shorter—even in the pumps he wore as the frustrated actor who finally gets work by disguising himself as an actress. Backstage at TV's "Southwest General," the cross-dressed Hoffman shares a dressing room with April, whose role on the soap opera is as cardiologist Miss Nyquist, ripe for the pinching. Although Jessica Lange is the main

Dustin Hoffman in drag casts a midward glance at lingerie-clad Geena Davis, who plays a bit-role-within-a-bit-role as a soap opera extra in *Tootsie* (1982).

beneficiary of the new pride that Hoffman's Tootsie instills in the women of the soap cast, it is implied that Davis's more peripheral character also learns to fight off unwanted advances on the set.

Because of her modeling past and those cheekbones carved in granite, Davis was frequently found in similar states of undress in other Tootsie roles in her early films. She was a sexy vampire in the forgettable *Transylvania 6-5000*, where she met her future (and second, and now ex-) husband, Jeff Goldblum, and she wore a bikini for most of *Earth Girls Are Easy* (released in 1989, but made much earlier) as a southern Californian who falls in love with the blue alien (Goldblum) who drops into her pool one fine day and whose sexual powers prove to be out of this world.

"It's not uncomfortable for me to act in a bikini," says Davis with a typically sunny giggle, although her career no longer requires her to.

Another characteristic first glimpsed in *Tootsie* but always found in Geena Davis roles is a quirky, off-kilter sense of humor—and that's even more comfortable for her to slip into. "I must get those parts because there's something in me that I'm able to tap into, parts of myself that are off-center a little bit," she says.

Geena Davis won an Oscar for playing the quirky dog-trainer in *The Accidental Tourist* (1988).

That is why as Veronica, a reporter for *Particles* magazine, Davis agrees to go off with nerdy scientist Seth Brundle (Goldblum again) when he tries to pick her up at a party in *The Fly* by offering her a cappuccino and a look at "something that will change the world, and human life as we know it." "Will it change it a lot? Or just a bit?" asks Veronica, unhooking her stocking for Brundle to inhale and then send through the teleportation machines he invented that will later merge his body with that of an ordinary housefly, making him do push-ups on the ceiling. By that time, Veronica is carrying Brundle's mixed-breed baby, which spawned a sequel *sans* either Davis or Goldblum.

It is a trademark of Davis's beauty that she manages to look alluring and gangly at the same time; *Tootsie* was still drawing on her mannequin exoticism, but by 1988 the camera traveled up those long, long legs in *The Accidental Tourist* to reveal not just a body, but a comic talent so charming and bizarre that she won the best supporting actress Oscar for portraying the frank, sassy dog-trainer Muriel Pritchett, whose persistence and tongue-clicks soon bring the reluctant William Hurt to heel. Free by this point in her career from the limitations that severe beauty can place on an actress, Davis played an unflappable dead housewife whose head gets the full 360-degree *Exorcist* treatment in *Beetlejuice*.

If it took a man dressed as a woman to guide April to personal liberation in *Tootsie*, it is a different Geena Davis who finds her own liberation in *Thelma and Louise*, a bracing road movie told from a female point of view. Costars Davis (as Thelma, a housewife) and Susan Sarandon (as Louise, a waitress) kill a would-be rapist, blow up a lecherous trucker's rig, and find personal freedom without the assistance of any men. "I feel awake. I've never felt so awake," says the exuberant Thelma.

Thelma and Louise put Davis into a select category of female leads, which is how she came to rule the pen in *A League of Their Own* when Debra Winger dropped out. All that's missing in her career, says Davis, is working with the one man her comedian's heart desires. "I'd like to work with Woody Allen," she says. "I just don't know how I get in there." At least she won't be reduced to cross-dressing for the role; no Tootsie she.

Tootsie, 1982
Fletch, 1985
Transylvania 6-5000, 1985
The Fly, 1986
The Accidental Tourist, 1988
Beetlejuice, 1988
Earth Girls Are Easy, 1989
Quick Change, 1990
Thelma and Louise, 1991
A League of Their Own, 1992
Hero, 1992

Davis (right) and Susan Sarandon hit the road in the controversial *Thelma & Louise*, one of the few movies made today where the camera takes a female's point of view.

ROBERT DUVALL

Actor
First Film: *To Kill a Mockingbird* (1962), d. Robert
   Mulligan
Video Availability: MCA Home Video
Role: "Boo" Radley

Out from behind closed doors

*A*ll summer long, six-year-old Scout (Mary Badham) and her brother have been trying to bait Boo Radley into coming out of the haunted house next door, the house where Boo is said to have done all manner of terrible things, including stabbing one of his parents in the leg with a pair of scissors. When he finally does come out—"I'd like you to meet *Mr. Arthur Radley*," dad Gregory Peck gently prods an awed Scout—it is Robert Duvall's first screen appearance, and a memorable one, in the film of Harper Lee's *To Kill a Mockingbird*.

Boo has been cowering behind a door, and as the door slowly swings shuts, he is revealed to be nearly as white as the ghost his nickname suggests, as he has never been out in the sun.

Robert Duvall plays local legend Boo Radley in *To Kill a Mockingbird* (1962). After a lifetime behind shuttered windows, he comes out to save two children's lives and sits on the porch swing with Scout (Mary Badham) as if nothing unusual has happened.

It was playwright Horton Foote who recommended Duvall to director Robert Mulligan, after being impressed by the actor in one of his own stage plays. Foote's *Mockingbird* screenplay won an Oscar.

Duvall has a few brief but shining moments as the mysterious southern neighbor who saves Scout and her brother from a vengeful white-trash bigot who hates the kids' even-tempered lawyer father, Atticus Finch. (The movie is one of Peck's shining moments as well.) "Thank you for my children," Atticus tells Boo as he sits stiffly but contentedly on the porch swing with Scout.

Duvall doesn't have any lines, but through body language he instantly turns Boo from the bogeyman of the children's imaginations to a sympathetic character. He once said it was his thinning hair that steered him toward character acting, since he believed it would keep him from the front ranks of stardom.

To Kill a Mockingbird, 1962
Captain Newman, M.D., 1964
Nightmare in the Sun, 1965
The Chase, 1966
Bullitt, 1968
Countdown, 1968
The Detective, 1968
The Rain People, 1969
True Grit, 1969
M*A*S*H, 1970
The Revolutionary, 1970
Lawman, 1971
THX 1138, 1971
Tomorrow, 1971
The Godfather, 1972
The Great Northfield Minnesota Raid, 1972
Joe Kidd, 1972
Badge 373, 1973
Lady Ice, 1973
The Outfit, 1973
The Conversation, 1974
The Godfather, Part II, 1974
Breakout, 1975
The Killer Elite, 1975
We're Not the Jet Set, 1975 (director)
The Eagle Has Landed, 1976
Network, 1976
The Seven Per-Cent Solution, 1976
The Greatest, 1977

The Betsy, 1978
Invasion of the Body Snatchers, 1978
Apocalypse Now, 1979
The Great Santini, 1979
The Pursuit of D. B. Cooper, 1981
True Confessions, 1981
Angelo, My Love, 1982 (director, producer, screenwriter)
Tender Mercies, 1982 (also producer)
The Stone Boy, 1983
The Natural, 1984
1918, 1985 (song)
Belizaire the Cajun, 1985 (also creative consultant)
The Lightship, 1985
Hotel Colonial, 1986
Let's Get Harry, 1987
Colors, 1988
Lonesome Dove, 1989
The Handmaid's Tale, 1990
Days of Thunder, 1990
A Show of Force, 1990
Convicts, 1991
Rambling Rose, 1991
Hearts of Darkness: A Filmmaker's Apocalypse, (docu), 1991
Newsies, 1992
Stalin, 1992
Falling Down, 1993
Wrestling Ernest Hemingway, 1993

SHARON STONE

Actress
First Film: *Stardust Memories* (1980), d. Woody Allen
Video Availability: MGM/UA Home Video
Role: "Pretty Girl on Train"

Blowing a kiss

*S*haron Stone, the future icepick maiden of *Basic Instinct*, has built her career on tantalizing men—beginning with unlikely suspect Woody Allen.

Stone is billed as the "Pretty Girl on Train" in Allen's bitter satire *Stardust Memories*.

Allen plays a character not unlike himself—a director whose public hounds him to make more comedies, while he wants to make "art." *Stardust Memories* begins with a clip from what is ostensibly the character's latest movie, a lugubrious affair about the unfairness of fate and the meaninglessness of life. Allen is stuck with a bunch of Fellini-esque extras on a train in a garbage dump. Across the track is a similar train, but that one is full of beautiful, joyous people, who clink champagne glasses and laugh merrily; life is good to them. Allen checks his ticket with the conductor to no avail and looks longingly out the window as a

Sharon Stone blows Woody Allen a kiss from the "fun" train across the tracks in *Stardust Memories* (1980).

pretty girl on the other train turns to face him and blow him a kiss. It's Sharon Stone, with her hair swept up and her eyes sparkling. (She also appears briefly in the UFO picnic scene.)

Stone didn't have much of a stellar career between then and *Basic Instinct*. She drank a glass of blood in Wes Craven's *Deadly Blessing*, the only movie of hers in which she goes to bed alone—although it's true that a spider joins her and that she wears sexy lingerie throughout the whole movie, even though everyone else remains dressed. She was particularly ineffective in *King Solomon's Mines*, and played an aggressive photojournalist who blabs too much and wears white into combat zones in *Year of the Gun*.

Finally, a role with some kick—she put her foot squarely in husband Arnold Schwarzenegger's groin in *Total Recall*, but got her comeuppance when he killed her and then announced, "I'm getting a div*awce*."

It wasn't until *Basic Instinct*, playing a sexy mystery novelist who may be trying to kill the detective (Michael Douglas) who is both investigating her and sleeping with her, that the actress *really* got noticed, especially when she crossed and uncrossed her legs. "It was the most exciting and interesting and profoundly moving character I'd ever been offered," she says of the role, in which she is required not to wear panties, or much else. "It's an example of the resurgence of strong parts for women in films."

Stone went on to blow more than kisses as the icepick maiden in *Basic Instinct*, shown here cooperating fully with cop Michael Douglas.

171

Although Stone's roles all call for her to be sexy, "I never thought of myself personally as a 'sex babe.' Now that they're calling me that, I'm trying to just enjoy it and play with it."

The sex scenes with Douglas were so steamy, forty-five seconds of them could only be seen theatrically in more liberated Europe. "To capture eroticism on camera is a very fragile thing," Stone explained at the 1992 Cannes Film Festival, where the extra forty-five seconds were unveiled. She calls those scenes "very choreographed—they had to be because it was a lot of action, so to speak."

Stardust Memories, 1980
Deadly Blessing, 1981
Bolero (France), 1981
Irreconcilable Differences, 1984
King Solomon's Mines, 1985
Allan Quatermain and the Lost City of Gold, 1987
Action Jackson, 1988
Above the Law, 1988
Personal Choice (Beyond the Stars), 1989
Blood and Sand, 1989
Total Recall, 1990
He Said, She Said, 1991
Scissors, 1991
Year of the Gun, 1991
Basic Instinct, 1992
Where Sleeping Dogs Lie, 1992
Diary of a Hitman, 1992
Legends in Light (docu), 1993
Sliver, 1993

WILLEM DAFOE

Actor
First Film: *Heaven's Gate* (1980), d. Michael Cimino
Video Availability: MGM/UA Home Video
Role: Dutch immigrant

A part only a mother could love, or notice

When Willem Dafoe is around, the sap starts rising. At least it does in 1981's *The Loveless*, Dafoe's official first film.

A year earlier, as Dafoe ruefully explains, he can be glimpsed—"probably only by my mother"—as an immigrant extra in Michael Cimino's famous flop, *Heaven's Gate*, about settlers vying for a piece of nineteenth-century Wyoming.

"My part was really inconsequential," says Dafoe, noting that only trivia experts will care. "Cimino had a big core immigrant group, although it was unscripted, so when you saw them die at the end, you can more deeply empathize with the community as a whole. They were extras, but they recur throughout the film."

Willem Dafoe (center) in *The Loveless* brings out the worst in people, including Robert Gordon, as he and his biker friends lay over in a small, uptight town on their way to the Daytona races. Dafoe was an extra before this in *Heaven's Gate* (1980).

Photofest

Dafoe admits that "technically, it was my first job. The funny part was, I ended up spending ten weeks there, but was essentially cut out of the film. The truth is, they shot whole other films"—*Heaven's Gate* has been released with different emphases at varying lengths, all of them too long. "I had whole days where I had scenes, lines, close-ups. Now I don't think I'm even credited on it, it was so inconsequential."

The Loveless makes up for all that. It opens with a camera traveling slowly up Dafoe's lean, leather-clad body. While he and his Daytona-bound biker buddies hang around a southern town drinking beer and fixing one of their motorcycles, sex is on everyone's mind. Soon, and after not a whole lot of dialogue or action, the sleepy town explodes. *The Wild One*, anyone?

Dafoe had already been performing with the Wooster Group, an experimental theater in downtown Manhattan, for several years before he starred as Vance in the movie directed by Kathryn Bigelow and Monty Montgomery. The Wooster Group often incorporates nudity into performances, and in fact there were numerous Dafoe fans before he got into film because of his huge, shall we say, *talent.*

With all that nudity under his belt, Dafoe looks languorously comfortable in *The Loveless* with his clothes off as he beds a teenage girl whose father later threatens to kill him and his buddies in revenge. "I was what you call ragged," he says in voice-over narration. "Way beyond torn up. I wasn't gonna be no man's friend today . . . this endless blacktop is my sweet eternity."

With his late-fifties ducktail and sunglasses, Dafoe looks cooler than cool. The high-flying flame of his cigarette lighter also stands for burning sexuality in David Lynch's 1990 *Wild at Heart,* in which he plays an even scuzzier version of Vance.

Dafoe goes heavy on attitude in *The Loveless,* which—combined with his razor-edged cheekbones—made him a screen villain until Oliver Stone's *Platoon,* in which he is a saintly Vietnam lieutenant, and Martin Scorsese's *The Last Temptation of Christ,* in which he is promoted from saint to Jesus. Since then, he has had varied film roles, and always returns to the Wooster Group between them.

"I enjoy both films and theater," says Dafoe, who is small and compact, but whose cheekbones seem to clear the air around him. "They're very different. At the theater where I work it takes about a year to make a theater piece, it's a collage, cut and paste. Sometimes the process can be very very tedious, but it affords me an opportunity to float with a certain kind of chaos, a lack of control and patience, rather than being a control freak, or being product- or effect-oriented. It allows me to find different ways of thinking and approaching performing, different attitudes about making things."

Dafoe is more articulate about his work now than he was at the start of his fame, but he still doesn't like to describe the characters he plays. "That's a question I don't like to speak about. You know, you do a role, and you do it. And even by the end of it, sometimes you can't really account for it. I much prefer to have people who see the movie tell me what they see and describe the character that way. Because when I approach a character, I don't have a shopping list of things I want to show. I just try to concentrate on the actions in the movie, and then something blossoms from that."

Sex scenes are an issue again in *Body of Evidence*, in which Dafoe's partner is Madonna. "I like action scenes, and love scenes are pure action for the most part," he once said in an interview.

Dafoe defends all his characters, even Vance in *The Loveless*. "All the characters I play are heroes," he argues. "They may be one side of the fence or the other, but they're all heroes."

The lure of moviemaking to Dafoe is gathering "grist for the mill. You're perpetually a dilettante at a lot of different things. You enter different worlds that usually you wouldn't be privy to. Like being put on a cross, in *The Last Temptation of Christ*. When you're on a cross, there's almost a Pavlovian response, no matter what your religious background is. It's a profound experience."

Although the movie was controversial, "they really went after Marty [Scorsese]. I think they cut actors slack and say, ah, they're a bunch of whores, they've gotta make a living. Which is kind of annoying and insulting, because I felt very strongly about that film."

From the role of Vance on up, Dafoe has always played very dramatic roles. "I think I can be a light, fluffy person too," he complains. "I think there's a perception from the work I've done already that there's something dramatic, or heavy or authoritative, about my performing. I don't want a kind of film persona harden on me and stare me back in the face and take all the joy and fun out of what I do. I want different things to remain available to me in the process of a career, always trying to jumble expectations somewhat so people can be more broad-minded in how they see me. In a lot of my roles, I work through something of a mask. There's been a strong physical stamp, a strong condition. Sometimes that's great, it makes you jump off normal behavior and do something a little extraordinary. But I'm really interested in doing something where I look more like myself, where I act more like myself, where there's a little more female energy around."

MERYL STREEP

Actress
First Film: *Julia* (1977), d. Fred Zinnemann
Availability: Fox Video
Role: Anne Marie

"Ooh, you're so famous!"

*Y*ou wouldn't know she was putting on an accent if you didn't know her later work, but Meryl Streep actually trots one out for all of maybe two minutes of screen time in *Julia*. She plays a mutual friend of Jane Fonda's and Vanessa Redgrave's, a haughty, catty, social-climbing, self-absorbed ninny with black crimped hair.

Fonda plays the real-life writer Lillian Hellman, Redgrave the friend Julia about whom Hellman wrote in her book *Pentimento*. Julia is a childhood friend and former rich girl who gives up everything, including one leg, a daughter, and even her life, to help free political prisoners from Nazi Germany. She calls on the unprepared Lillian—who has spent most of

Meryl Streep (middle) cozies up to Jane Fonda at Sardi's in a cameo in *Julia* (1977), cast by a producer who had a feeling she'd become famous.

Author's collection

her adult life wrestling with a play she can't finish writing—to make one semidangerous errand through Berlin, transporting $50,000 in a hat brim.

Much of the movie involves Lillian's fond, romanticized memories of Julia's strength, bravery, beauty, and fearlessness. There are frequent, lingering shots of Redgrave, her eyes shining until she looks nearly maniacal. The purpose of Streep's Anne Marie character is to further underscore how wonderful Julia is by positing her opposite—a cheaply flamboyant society girl with all the wrong values. She's been sleeping with her brother, played by John Glover, since she was sixteen. "Anne Marie is warm and passionate...*I should know!*" says Glover, winking before Fonda overturns a table on him.

We first see Anne Marie at the opening night party at Sardi's for Lillian's newly finished and now smash-hit Broadway play; she is all dolled up and rapaciously interested in being at the right place at the right time. She grabs Lillian's arm and flatters her: "Ooh, you're so famous!"

Later, having lunch with Lillian, she is again overdressed for the occasion, and every compliment is given with the left hand. "Moscow," she marvels with mock-innocence when told Lillian is about to travel there. "What is that, some sort of political thing?...Imagine, Russia, of all places!"

Streep toasts her newfound beauty in *Death Becomes Her* (1992), about an aging actress who has sold her soul for a youth elixir.

And her remarks about Julia are just as calculated. "She's doing something called anti-f...anti-fascist work," she deliberately stammers, before gushing, "You look so slim, Lillian!"

The accent Streep assays in *Julia* is a butter-won't-melt-in-her-mouth snob's voice, full of overbreeding and condescension. Small potatoes next to her later accents—Polish for a woman with a horrible secret in *Sophie's Choice* (see KEVIN KLINE); Danish for the writer Karen Blixen, torn between a no-good husband (Klaus Maria Brandauer) and a handsome veld pilot (Robert Redford) in *Out of Africa;* Australian for a mother who may have let a wild dog kill her baby in *A Cry in the Dark.*

Streep rose quickly to fame. In fact, the producer of *Julia* deliberately cast her, even though it was a small role, because word had already come out of Yale that a major new talent was about to graduate, and the producer wanted to lay claim to Streep's movie debut.

Just one year after *Julia* she was nominated for an Oscar for *The Deer Hunter.* Her movies have never been blockbusters, but her reputation as a fine and serious actress couldn't even be sullied by the ridiculous *She-Devil.* She is most famous for her facility with accents, which is so remarkable that in a different era, she might have been burned at the stake for it. As it is, she gets her head twisted round and round in the special-effects-laden *Death Becomes Her.*

Julia, 1977
The Deer Hunter, 1978
Kramer vs. Kramer, 1979
Manhattan, 1979
The Seduction of Joe Tynan, 1979
The French Lieutenant's Woman, 1981
Sophie's Choice, 1982
Still of the Night, 1982
Silkwood, 1983
Falling in Love, 1984
In Our Hands (docu), 1984
Out of Africa, 1985
Plenty, 1985
Heartburn, 1986
Ironweed, 1987
A Cry in the Dark, 1988
She-Devil, 1989
Postcards From the Edge, 1990
Defending Your Life, 1991
Death Becomes Her, 1992

ROBBY BENSON

Actor
First Film: *Wait Until Dark* (1967), d. Terence Young
Video Availability: Warner Home Video
Role: Extra

Playing hooky, stealing scenes

*A*lthough *Jory,* a pedestrian 1972 Western about a boy who grows up fast when his parents are murdered, is officially listed as Robby Benson's film debut, you can actually see him on-screen—if you squint—as early as 1967 in the thriller *Wait Until Dark.*

"I've always been a ham," says Benson, and he proved it by doing his best to stand out in a crowd of extras during the airport scene, when a doll full of cocaine is being smuggled into New York from Montreal. This will set the stage for three men—one of them Alan Arkin in several disguises—to menace poor blind Audrey Hepburn in her basement apartment, where the doll has been left.

Robby Benson (left) in full Hasidic regalia for *The Chosen* (1981), in which he and less religious pal Barry Miller are divided by their faith. Benson can first be seen on-screen as an extra in *Wait Until Dark* (1967).

"In *Wait Until Dark*, there's this kid in the airport who's throwing this football up in the air, and it really distracts from the entire scene," recalls Benson approvingly.

Actually, it looks more like a basketball, but it's hard to tell, as Benson—age ten at the time and wearing thick, dark-rimmed nerd glasses—is visible for only a few seconds, twice. In any event, the kid is smiling.

"I loved to get out of school so I could go be an extra because I loved to be out of school," says Benson, who managed to be an extra in so many films he can't remember them all. "I was acting since I was about five or six. My father's a writer and my mom was a wonderful actress and a singer, and when my mom did summer stock, I would hand out programs and I would have such a lot of fun doing all kinds of things, and wound up on the stage, and starring on Broadway when I was twelve years old in something called *Zelda*. It seemed like destiny. My career has been blessed; I've done a lot of things." That includes directing, screenwriter, producing and musical scoring.

One of the most unusual things he has done—since he is slight of build and has usually played pleasant young men—is to provide the booming voice of the Beast for Disney's animated feature *Beauty and the Beast*.

"I identify, believe it or not, with the Beast's pain, the torment. I don't know where it comes from, it's either genetic—I'm Jewish—maybe it's parental angst, the second your child is brought into the world things start angering you so deeply. It could've been the economy." He laughs.

More than just empathizing with the Beast, Benson had another attribute that won him the growly role. "I'm actually a bass, not even a baritone; I sing low D-flats for fun, to shake the china at home."

Wait Until Dark, 1967 (extra)
Jory, 1973
Jeremy, 1973
Lucky Lady, 1975
Ode to Billy Joe, 1975
One on One, 1977
The End, 1978
Ice Castles, 1978
Walk Proud, 1979
Die Laughing, 1980
The Chosen, 1981
National Lampoon Goes to the Movies, 1982
Running Brave, 1983
Harry and Son, 1984
The Breakfast Club, 1985 (song)
City Limits, 1985
Rent-A-Cop, 1988
White Hot, 1988 (also director)
Modern Romance, 1990 (also director)
Beauty and the Beast, 1991 (voice)
The Webbers' 15 Minutes, 1993

TONY CURTIS

Actor
First Film: *Criss Cross* (1948), d. Robert Siodmak
Availability: MCA Home Video
Role: Yvonne De Carlo's dance partner

Doing the "mambo-wambo"

"*I* ran around with a lump in my pants, chased all the girls. This is what I reflected on the screen. There wasn't anything deeper or less deep than that," is how Tony Curtis candidly describes his acting method back when he was singled out by director Robert Siodmak to be Yvonne DeCarlo's dance partner in the noir thriller *Criss Cross*.

Tony Curtis isn't kidding when he gives Yvonne DeCarlo those intense looks during their brief but sexy dance number in *Criss Cross* (1948). He says that during his early career, he was guided mostly by testosterone.

If there was a lump in his pants, there wasn't much room for it. Curtis held De Carlo *this close* as he mamboed her across the dance floor of the Roundup bar, with jealous Burt Lancaster looking on. Curtis, whose lifelong womanizing has not been much of a secret, certainly has purpose in his eyes as he swivels his partner.

"About 150 feet from here," Curtis says, pointing beyond the doors of the hotel where he was being interviewed to Universal Studios up the hill, "down on the main strip in 1948 and a half, I was walking to the commissary, and [Robert] Siodmak tapped me and spoke with a very thick European accent. And he said, 'Stop.'"

Curtis does not try to imitate Siodmak even to make the anecdote funnier; he is not exactly the Meryl Streep of accents. In fact, he is famous for sticking by his native Bronx tonalities even when playing a Viking.

"Siodmak says, 'Stop.' And I stopped. He said, 'Can you dance?' I said, 'Yes, sir.' He said, 'Come to my set tomorrow morning.' So I showed up and they said I had to do this mambo-wambo. And they had this really wild music, and I was going to dance with Yvonne DeCarlo. And that's all I needed to know, you know. And I didn't know how to dance that type of music, but I danced it. So that was the first shot at getting in the movies."

Curtis has no lines and isn't billed in the credits of *Criss Cross*, an estimable B thriller in which Lancaster and Dan Duryea try to double-deal each other to the death for the love of a pretty woman and the contents of an armored car. But there's no mistaking Curtis's pretty face and thick lashes, which would define his roles more often than he liked. He was nearly as pretty as Marilyn Monroe when he dressed in drag for *Some Like It Hot*, and you can see the gay subtext in his role as Laurence Olivier's slave boy in the restored scenes in *Spartacus*, now available on video. Curtis had to wage a personal campaign to play the title role of *The Boston Strangler* because no one thought he looked mean enough.

Ironically, Curtis would work with *Criss Cross* star Burt Lancaster again for one of his best roles, that of the slick press agent brownnosing Lancaster's powerful newspaper columnist in *Sweet Smell of Success*. "I had hoped my hair would have been longer, and the suits they gave me, I didn't like the way they were cut," complains Curtis of that movie. "I didn't like the girl that played my secretary, and the scenes with Burt, I felt I could have been more aggressive."

But he is less critical of *Criss Cross*, to which he has an emotional attachment the way most people do to their first sexual partner. "It was a very thrilling and exciting movie for me, because I had not worked in a movie before. And there was Burt Lancaster, brooding, coming through the curtains. And there was Yvonne DeCarlo looking fetching and wanting to dance with me. So, at the end of that thirty-two-second shot, I knew I wanted to be in the movies."

The brevity of his appearance doesn't bother him either. "The contribution we all make to a film, whether it's small or large, has absolutely nothing to do with the film. The film has its own life, its own intent, the author's intent, the director's intent. And we as the actors just progress that story, we kind of shove it along, you know. And so small parts, big parts, all are enjoyable to me."

Now silver-haired and flamboyantly charming—he enters a room with a studied casualness and swoops to kiss the backs of ladies' hands—Curtis talks about his career as if it were one big adventure. "I've made about 105 films. There isn't a performance I would change," he says. "They represent what I was at the time I made them. At twenty-three years old I did the best that a twenty-three-year-old man could do. I felt only so much emotion. At thirty-four, perhaps it was the same thing. In any event I brought to those parts the best that I could do at the time."

Slave-boy Curtis bathes Laurence Olivier *all over* in this suggestive and controversial scene that has only recently been restored to *Spartacus* (1960).

Criss Cross, 1948
City Across the River, 1949
Francis, 1949
Johnny Stool Pigeon, 1949
The Lady Gambles, 1949
I Was a Shoplifter, 1950
Kansas Raiders, 1950
Sierra, 1950
Winchester '73, 1950
The Prince Who Was a Thief, 1951
Flesh and Fury, 1952
Meet Danny Wilson, 1952 (cameo)
No Room for the Groom, 1952
Son of Ali Baba, 1952
The All American, 1953
Forbidden, 1953
Houdini, 1953
Beachhead, 1954
The Black Shield of Falworth, 1954
Johnny Dark, 1954
Six Bridges to Cross, 1954
So This Is Paris, 1954
The Purple Mask, 1955
The Square Jungle, 1955
The Rawhide Years, 1956
Trapeze, 1956
The Midnight Story, 1957
Mister Cory, 1957
Sweet Smell of Success, 1957
The Defiant Ones, 1958
The Vikings, 1958
Kings Go Forth, 1958
Operation Petticoat, 1959
The Perfect Furlough, 1959
Some Like It Hot, 1959
The Great Impostor, 1960
The Rat Race, 1960
Spartacus, 1960
Who Was That Lady? 1960
Pepe (cameo), 1960
The Outsider, 1961
40 Pounds of Trouble, 1962
Taras Bulba, 1962
The List of Adrian Messenger, 1963
Paris When It Sizzles, 1963

Captain Newman, M.D., 1964
Goodbye, Charlie, 1964
Sex and the Single Girl, 1964
Wild and Wonderful, 1964
Boeing Boeing, 1965
The Great Race, 1965
Arrivederci, Baby!, 1966
Not With My Wife, You Don't, 1966
La Cintura di Castita, 1967
Don't Make Waves, 1967
The Boston Strangler, 1968
Rosemary's Baby, 1968
Eye of the Cat, 1969
Monte Carlo or Bust! 1969
Suppose They Gave a War and Nobody Came? 1970
Jennifer on My Mind, 1971
That Man Bolt, 1973
Bucktown, 1975
Lepke, 1975
Trackdown, 1975
The Last Tycoon, 1976
Casanova & Co., 1977
The Manitou, 1977
The Bad News Bears Go to Japan, 1978
Sextette, 1978
Title Shot, 1979
Coal Miner's Daughter, 1980 (producer)
Little Miss Marker, 1980
The Mirror Crack'd, 1980
Road Games, 1981 (exec. producer)
Balboa, 1982
Brain Waves, 1982
Othello, 1982
Psycho II, 1983 (exec. producer)
Where Is Parsifal? 1984
Club Life, 1985
Insignificance, 1985
St. Elmo's Fire, 1985 (exec. producer)
Sweet Dreams, 1985 (producer)
The Fantasy Film World of George Pal, 1986
The Last of Philip Banter, 1986
Midnight, 1988
Welcome to Germany, 1988
Lobster Man From Mars, 1989
Walter and Carlo in Amerika, 1989

STOCKARD CHANNING

Actress
First Film: *The Hospital* (1971), d. Arthur Hiller
Video Availability: MGM/UA Home Video
Role: Emergency room nurse

"Sally, would you get the hell out of here?"

"*I* only had one day's work in *The Hospital*", says theater and film performer Stockard Channing. "There were a hundred speaking parts in that movie, and in the scene I was in, there were about fifty. I don't know if the director knew I was even in it."

Apparently the director did know, because Arthur Hiller used Channing again twenty years later when he made *Married to It*, about three sets of couples grappling with friendship and marriage.

Director Arthur Hiller reteams with Stockard Channing for the relationship comedy *Married to It* in 1991, 20 years after he directed her in her first film, *The Hospital*.

The Hospital is a well-crafted black comedy, screenplay by Paddy Chayevsky, about a medical institution that does more harm than good due to bureaucracy, incompetence, and compounded errors. "A man comes into this hospital in perfect health, and in the space of one week, we chop out one kidney, damage another, reduce him to a coma, and damn near kill him!" is how a disgruntled doctor, played by George C. Scott, sums things up.

Channing's part is so small, she's not listed in the credits. She only has a few lines, as a harried emergency room nurse trying to fend off a pesky woman from the accounting department. "Sally, would you get the hell out of here?" she says. "The patient's in the holding room. If you want his Blue Cross number, you go in and you get his Blue Cross number."

Channing plays the nurse as being extremely irritated, and in fact, irritation is the main emotion she conveys when asked about it. "Doing interviews on a Sunday morning isn't my favorite thing," she says.

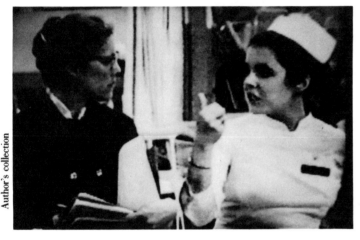

Channing (right) shows the bureaucrats where they can go in her cameo in *The Hospital*.

The Hospital, 1971
Up the Sandbox, 1972
The Fortune, 1975
The Big Bus, 1976
Dandy, The All American Girl, 1976
The Cheap Detective, 1978
Grease, 1978
The Fish That Saved Pittsburgh, 1979
Safari 3000, 1980

Without a Trace, 1983
Heartburn, 1986
The Men's Club, 1986
A Time of Destiny, 1988
Staying Together, 1989
Meet the Applegates, 1991
Married to It, 1991
Blood Law, 1992
Center of the Web, 1992

MEG RYAN

Actress
First Film: *Rich and Famous* (1981), d. George Cukor
Availability: MGM/UA Home Video
Role: "Debby at eighteen"

Touring with Fleetwood Mac

*M*eg Ryan first showed off her chipmunk cuteness in *Rich and Famous* as Candice Bergen's daughter, who has been advised all her life to go ride a horse whenever she feels a sexual urge coming on.

Bergen and Jacqueline Bisset play lifelong pals who manage to stay friendly despite years of competition for men, fame, and fortune. At last Bisset finds love with a handsome young writer (Hart Bochner) from *Rolling Stone* (or the *Stone*, as he calls it). In the meantime, Bergen's daughter, Debby, has grown up to be eighteen and pert, and no longer heeding mom's equestrian advice. Debby dumps her Trinidadian poet boyfriend, who steals

Neither rich nor famous just yet, Meg Ryan makes her debut as trash novelist Candice Bergen's daughter in *Rich and Famous* (1981). She goes on to steal mommy's best friend's beau.

Jerry Ohlinger

cars for a living, and steals Bisset's boyfriend by becoming his assistant as they tour with Fleetwood Mac.

Ryan's chirpy, good-natured humor, the kind you find in *Prelude to a Kiss*, is evident in her first film outing despite her few lines. In fact, you might say she was more adequately used here than as the sanitized girlfriend of Jim Morrison in Oliver Stone's *The Doors* a decade later. In any case, you can see a little of what director Rob Reiner saw when he devised a scene for Ryan in *When Harry Met Sally...* in which she fakes an orgasm in a deli, the scene that made her if not richer, then certainly more famous, than any role she has had.

Rich and Famous, 1981
Amityville 3-D, 1983
Armed and Dangerous, 1986
Top Gun, 1986
Innerspace, 1987
Promised Land, 1987
D.O.A., 1988

The Presidio, 1988
When Harry Met Sally..., 1989
Joe Versus the Volcano, 1990
The Doors, 1991
Prelude to a Kiss, 1992
Sleepless in Seattle, 1993
Flesh and Bone, 1993

Ryan's sparkling personality makes Alec Baldwin fall in love with her in *Prelude to a Kiss* (1992), a movie in which true soulmates find each other no matter what physical form they take.

KEANU REEVES

Actor
First Film: *Youngblood* (1986), d. Peter Markle
Video Availability: MGM/UA Home Video
Role: Heaver

"She do it to me last year, eh?"

*K*eanu Reeves flunked twelfth grade twice; this was several years before *Bill and Ted's Excellent Adventure*, wherein two high schoolers make the grade by importing historical figures through time for a little show 'n' tell. Napoleon is referred to as "the dead dude." Reeves is the Ted dude.

Reeves was apparently spoiling for the part of such a dimwit when he made his first movie, *Youngblood*, in which he played a backwoods teammate on the Hamilton Mustangs, a Canadian junior hockey league. "She do it to me last year, eh?" he remarks in lower-class Canadian about a rooming-house mistress who makes her guests feel welcome in a most excellent way.

Rob Lowe and Patrick Swayze are the stars of this lackluster underdog story in which Lowe learns to fight like a man in his bid to be accepted on the hockey team. Reeves, who spent his formative years in Canada, naturally knew the national pastime well enough to look like a pro on the ice. He appears to be the goalie, although that is not always clear because of the mask.

Among his responsibilities as Heaver are drinking beer, sitting quietly at pep talks, and doing drill practice.

(Incidentally, *Slumber Party Massacre* is playing on a theater marquee in one scene; if only it were *Slumber Party '57*, Debra Winger's unconvincing film debut.)

Reeves hated high school and describes his younger self as being "an apathetic loner" and "the class clown," but he has high aspirations. "When I'm thirty, I'd like to be a Cary Grant dude," he says. "I'll even take deportment classes."

The coltish, floppy-haired Reeves (his Hawaiian first name means "cool breeze over the mountain") quickly went on from *Youngblood* to have a, like, *totally awesome* career, especially in the eyes of his numerous teenage fans. He's done some quality work, as a sensitive teenager numbed by the presence of a classmate's dead body in the woods in *River's Edge*, as the mayor's hustler son in Gus Van Sant's *My Own Private Idaho*, and as the

189

Keanu Reeves (right) and Alex Winter pl
home as the time-traveling dudes of *Bill
Ted's Excellent Adventure* (1989). You can
hardly find Reeves in his first film, the
hockey drama *Youngblood* (1986).

glandular music teacher in eighteenth-century France in *Dangerous Liaisons.*

But mostly—and despite the fact that he originally auditioned for the part of Bill—he is known for being the Ted dude.

Keanu Reeves (left) and fellow hockey
teammate spy on Rob Lowe having sex with
their landlady in "Youngblood," Reeves' first
appearance on film.

Youngblood, 1986
Flying, 1986
River's Edge, 1987
Dangerous Liaisons, 1988
The Night Before, 1988
Permanent Record, 1988
The Prince of Pennsylvania, 1988
Bill and Ted's Excellent Adventure, 1989
Parenthood, 1989
I Love You to Death, 1990

Tune in Tomorrow, 1990
My Own Private Idaho, 1991
Point Break, 1991
Bill and Ted's Bogus Journey, 1991
Bram Stoker's Dracula, 1992
Much Ado About Nothing, 1993
Hideous Mutant Freekz, 1993
Even Cowgirls Get the Blues, 1993
Little Buddha, 1993

FAMILY AFFAIRS

Nepotism, Romantic Couplings, Sibling Rivalry

GOLDIE HAWN

Actress, producer, dancer
First Film: *The One and Only, Genuine, Original
    Family Band* (1968), d. Paul L. Cameron
Video Availability: Disney Home Video
Role: Dancer

Just a few dancing steps from Mr. Right

They didn't have much in common back then—she was twenty-three, he was sixteen—but it's one of life's happy ironies that Goldie Hawn's first movie also featured her future soulmate, Kurt Russell.

"Goldie Jean Hawn" had a bit part as a dancer in *The One and Only, Genuine, Original Family Band*, a sappy Disney effort about a singing Von Trapp–style family that alternately stirs up and calms down the crowds during the 1888 presidential elections. Walter Brennan

Goldie Hawn, to the right of star Leslie Ann Warren, prepares to kick her heels up in *The One and Only, Genuine, Original Family Band* (1968)—little suspecting that fresh-faced Kurt Russell (visible behind Warren's right shoulder) would one day be her real-life partner.

Photofest

plays the fired-up grandpa who enlists the talents of his son, daughter-in-law, and their eight kids—including Kurt Russell as Sidney Bower.

"I didn't meet him, I was not introduced at the time," says Hawn. "But I did see him, and I knew he was there, and"—she giggles the Goldie Giggle—"I *looked* at him."

Kurt and Goldie fell in love sixteen years later when they made *Swing Shift,* and remain together today. ("As far as I'm concerned, we *are* married," says Hawn, whose two previous divorces have made her leery of marriage. "I love him, and he loves me, and we exchanged our own personal vows in the sight of our children.")

Sitting in a hotel room in Boston after finishing the comedy *Housesitter* with Steve Martin, Hawn owns up to her appearance in *The One and Only.* But a couple of years earlier, in a London hotel room after *Bird on a Wire* with Mel Gibson, Hawn declared that her very first movie was Gene Saks's *Cactus Flower* in 1969. Certainly the supporting-actress Oscar she won for that looks better on the résumé than a bit part in a flop. (See TIMOTHY HUTTON.)

"I was right here, in London, when I won that Oscar. I had gone to bed and went to sleep, and I got a phone call at four in the morning, or whatever it was, and they said, You got it! You won it! And I thought, my god, my first movie. I was so young. I thought it was kinda sad that I won my first time out, because I didn't feel that I earned it. And I felt that if I got it that easily, probably it would be a long time before I got another one."

The odd thing about *Cactus Flower* is that it should have been Ingrid Bergman's movie, but the saucer-eyed Hawn stole it out from under her as the ingenue Toni Simmons, in love with a commitment-shy older dentist (Walter Matthau). The movie is actually about the dentist's starchy receptionist (Bergman), who blooms like the cactus plant when she realizes she too is in love with Matthau. But Bergman is *so* starchy in this role that her eventual flowering, or deflowering, is embarrassing, especially when she takes to the disco floor to the strains of ersatz Monkees tunes.

Hawn performed with the Ballet Russe de Monte Carlo at the age of ten. She studied ballet and taught dance while still a teenager, but also took jobs as a go-go dancer to make ends meet. "I never felt frustration about any form of what I've ever done," says Hawn. "All I had then really was hope. I didn't envision anything for myself or my career, but I seemed to get one job after another."

She lists them, practically in one long sentence: "I went to New York, I worked at the World's Fair, then I did summer stock, then I went to Puerto Rico, then I went to L.A. Then I went to Anaheim, then to Vegas, then I came back, then I was dancing on an Andy Griffith special, and then I did a Herb Alpert special, and then I got this TV show ["Rowan and Martin's Laugh-In"], because an agent saw me and introduced me to the producers, and the next thing I knew I was really on my way. So I never had the misfortune of having to sit back in consternation and wonder what I was going to do. The one thing I never wanted to be was an aging, sad person trying to be something I wasn't."

In this rambling résumé, she leaves out *Family Band*. It came out the same year as "Laugh-In," which propelled her to fame as the dumb blonde who fluffs her lines and whose body is a host for graffiti.

"The sixties was a very romantic period, because we had so much ideology then," says Hawn. "But during that time I was a hard-working girl. I wasn't stoned out, I wasn't a hippie. I sweat for a living. And I had goals."

The Giggle, like an aging photograph sensitive to light, is only trotted out occasionally, and has a practiced sound to it. But Hawn insists that it stems from an intrinsically happy nature. "My personality is what it is, it's always been that way. There's a part of me that's very frivolous and very funny, and I don't apologize for it—it's a gift, really. I'm a happy person. I laugh easily. I also have a sadness inside. I must cry four times a day. I write poetry that nobody would ever identify as coming from me. So there is a darkness in me too."

Although she gamely wore a fatsuit in *Death Becomes Her*, Hawn turns quite serious on the subject of looksism in Hollywood. "Women have been judged by their looks, by their age, by their youth most of the time. We've always worked from a deficit, really, so that in itself creates a kind of competitive soil. It's the soil that creates a sort of distorted fruit. I personally never felt that way because I have good self-esteem, and I knew very clearly that no man would ever take care of me financially, even if I had to pick up trash in the street."

Hawn and Russell play house in *Overboard* (1987) to celebrate the years they've been playing house for real, ever since they made *Swing Shift* together.

But she has had moments of worry about her looks fading, and takes comfort in the advice Warren Beatty once gave her: "Eat the right foods, take care of your body, because you're not going to age. *You* have the face that will stay young. It's the women with the cheekbones who won't."

One thing Goldie and Kurt have in common is their mutual inability to remember their first film. When asked about his, Russell gets testy and finally admits to 1964's *It Happened at the World's Fair;* three years before that was a small role in *The Absent-Minded Professor.*

The One and Only, Genuine, Original Family Band,
   1968
Cactus Flower, 1969
There's a Girl in My Soup, 1970
$, 1971
Butterflies Are Free, 1972
The Sugarland Express, 1974
The Girl From Petrovka, 1974
Shampoo, 1975
The Duchess and the Dirtwater Fox, 1976
Foul Play, 1978
Lovers and Liars, 1979
Private Benjamin, 1980
Seems Like Old Times, 1980
Best Friends, 1982
Swing Shift, 1984
Protocol, 1984
Wildcats, 1986
Overboard, 1987
Bird on a Wire, 1990
My Blue Heaven, 1990 (exec. producer)
Deceived, 1991
The Warner Bros. Story (docu), 1991 (co-host)
Criss Cross, 1991
Housesitter, 1992
Death Becomes Her, 1992

MELANIE GRIFFITH

Actress
First Film: *The Harrad Experiment* (1973), d. Ted Post
Video Availability: Wizard (old copies still lying around)
Role: Extra

Group marriage counseling

Get your freeze-frame ready to catch Melanie Griffith in her first screen appearance—opposite none other than her future husband, Don Johnson!

At fourteen, Griffith was too young to play one of the college students toying with opposite-sex roommates in *The Harrad Experiment*, kinky for its time, about a college where the only subjects are nude yoga, nude swimming, "premarital relations," and explorations of the concept of "group marriage."

Melanie Griffith can be glimpsed behind and to the right of Bruno Kriby Jr., in "human values" class in *The Harrad Experiment* (1973). Her mother, Tippi Hedren, plays the professor, and her new boyfriend, Don Johnson, plays the hippest naked guy at the experimental college.

Author's collection

Nevertheless, Griffith stood in for a member of the student body—although not one of the numerous naked student bodies—as an extra in a scene where Johnson and three others play out a partner-swapping scenario in order to come to terms with their innate jealousy. The "human values" professor teaching the class is played by Melanie's mother, Tippi Hedren, which explains why Melanie was on the set.

During the filming of *The Harrad Experiment*, Griffith and the twenty-two-year-old Johnson began seeing each other offscreen, much to the consternation of Hedren, who has a scene with Johnson in which she nearly has sex with him in public to teach him a lesson about the pitfalls of casual relations. Within a few years, Melanie and Don were married. The marriage ended before another year was up; they remarried in 1989.

To find Melanie, freeze-frame the video during the "human values" class every time Bruno Kirby, Jr.—in his own film debut, including scenes involving full-frontal nudity—asks a question. Griffith is seated in a chair behind him and slightly to the right, wearing a black turtleneck and pendant necklace. "Well, I think we're all a liberated group," says Tippi Hedren cheerfully before a cut to a reaction shot from the class, including her smiling, liberated daughter.

Griffith's more formal debut was as a nymphet in Arthur Penn's *Night Moves* (1975), made the same year she appeared in *The Drowning Pool*. Here she is dried off by Gene Hackman and Jennifer Warren.

Griffith's more formal acting debut came in 1975, when she appeared in three movies: as nymphet Delly Grastner in the thriller *Night Moves*, as Miss Simi Valley in *Smile*, and as Schuyler Devereaux in *The Drowning Pool*. With her simulated masturbation in *Body Double*, her bondage-and-discipline teasing in *Something Wild*, her "bod for sin" in *Working Girl*, and her femme fatale in *Bonfire of the Vanities*, Griffith has built her career on roles in which she gets to wear lingerie straight out of the Victoria's Secret catalog.

(In *Shining Through*, she falls down a hamper, which at least is *near* the lingerie, but in *A Stranger Among Us*, as an undercover cop among the Hasidim, she has to cover up more than she has in any other movie.)

The next time Griffith and Johnson appear together on-screen is after their second wedding, playing a battling couple in severe need of marriage counseling in *Paradise*.

Griffith, "key-lighted" around the eyes in old Hollywood style, attempts to diversify her career in *Shining Through* (1992) as a double agent in Nazi Germany.

The Harrad Experiment, 1973
Night Moves, 1975
The Drowning Pool, 1975
Smile, 1975
Joyride, 1977
One on One, 1977
Roar, 1981
Body Double, 1984
Fear City, 1985
Something Wild, 1986
Cherry 2000, 1988
The Milagro Beanfield War, 1988
Stormy Monday, 1988
Working Girl, 1988
The Bonfire of the Vanities, 1990
In the Spirit, 1990
Pacific Heights, 1990
Paradise, 1991
Shining Through, 1992
A Stranger Among Us, 1992
Born Yesterday, 1993

JULIA ROBERTS

Actress
First Film: *Blood Red* (1986), d. Peter Masterson
Available: New Line Home Video
Role: Maria Collogero

"Si, papa."

The shy, pretty daughter with the bow around her virginal white dress looks like Julia Roberts, and yet it's not the Julia Roberts we expect. This Julia has nothing to say, and although she appears watchful, she looks as if she's on the verge of giggling whenever the camera is on her.

Still in her teens, Julia was thrown this scrap of a role because her more famous brother Eric was the star; he got her the part on a lark during the time that Julia, who had left home relatively young, was trying to make a living for herself in New York.

Blood Red is about Italian immigrant winegrowers who fight for their northern California turf in 1895. Eric plays Marco Collogero, the manly son who avenges the death of his father when dad stands up to an aggressive railroad tycoon (Dennis Hopper) and a hired thug (Burt Young). Meanwhile, the less fortunate Julia plays the pathologically demure Maria, one of Marco's two conventional sisters. One of her few lines is, *"Si, papa,"* and one of her few functions is to carry her father's clothing downstairs to him.

In other scenes, she sits quietly with that now-famous wide mouth pursed into a long thin fault line across her face, possibly to keep from nervous laughter. She looks skittish and uncomfortable. In scenes where she is standing next to her brother, the camera's focus is on Eric. Julia's big emotional scene is played standing stick-still next to a tree as her father is by turns dragged by a horse, shot, and strung up. Julia manages to look upset, but not upset enough to get her a listing in the credits.

This is the woman who would soon win an Oscar nomination for playing a southern diabetic in *Steel Magnolias*, who broke the bank as Richard Gere's high-priced hooker in *Pretty Woman*, who made wife-beating look nearly romantic in *Sleeping With the Enemy*, who died and came back to life in *Flatliners*, who made dying young a good way to go if you've got Julia by your side in *Dying Young*, who put the belle in Tinkerbell in *Hook*.

Every now and then someone comes along who is simply stunning on film, whose chemistry ignites the screen. Roberts's early movies make much of her tawny reddish mane (she has since cut it), her bright eyes, and that smile with the Cinemascope spread. Added

202

Prostitute Julia Roberts rests her head cutely
on the shoulder of white knight Richard Gere
in *Pretty Woman* (1990).

to that is a certain innocent effusiveness. In *Blood Red*, she is the heirloom that
inadvertently got mixed in with the everyday china.

Blood Red was made in 1986 but only released in 1988, after Roberts had already parted
the waves in the sweet female-buddy movie *Mystic Pizza*, about small-town pizza girls hoping
for something better in life. In that movie, she was more like herself as the sensual, strong-
willed Daisy. "Daisy was bold and wonderful," says Roberts. "And anyway, nobody wants to
play a wimp."

And yet Maria Collogero of *Blood Red* is most certainly a wimp, a role entirely against Roberts's nature. "I was a rugged individualist at thirteen years old, and it worked out for me," she says. Still, she has no regrets, even about *Blood Red*. "I've had a good life, there's nothing that happened in my life that didn't lead me to be right here, right now, so that's not a bad thing."

If there is a moment in *Blood Red* where there is a glimmer of the insouciant Julia Roberts to come, of the Julia who will blissfully sing off-key in the bubble bath in *Pretty Woman* with her headphones on, it is in one small, nearly wordless scene she plays with her brother. As the only witness to their father's murder, Maria accompanies Marco to the saloon to identify the culprit. Hooded so she won't be recognized, and walking a step behind her brother for protection, Julia sort of hops along in Eric's shadow with her chin practically resting on his shoulder. It's an endearing and almost comical pose, one immortalized in publicity stills from *Pretty Woman*, with Roberts's chin now on Gere's shoulder.

As for the nervousness she displays in her first film outing, she says being on any set is a trial by fire that prepares her for the next step up. "I learn a lot of personal stuff doing movies. I'm a lot stronger a person than I thought I was."

She'll need that strength, since Roberts—with her mood-swing of a love life and a mysterious rest-cure in a hospital—could serve as a poster child for one of those Freudian monographs on people who are wrecked by success. "For better or worse I'll always be just like this," she claims. Let's hope not.

It was thanks to Eric Roberts, shown here making his debut as the reluctant *King of the Gypsies* (1978), [that sister Julia got her start in *Blood Red*, a movie so bad it didn't come out until after Julia achieved some fame of her own.] Eric's career was considered the one to watch.

Roberts achieves similar cuteness with her brother Eric's shoulder in *Blood Red* (1986), her first movie.

Blood Red, 1986
Satisfaction, 1988
Mystic Pizza, 1988
Steel Magnolias, 1989
Flatliners, 1990
Pretty Woman, 1990
Sleeping With the Enemy, 1991
Dying Young, 1991
Hook, 1991
The Player, 1992

ANJELICA HUSTON

Actress, model
First Film: *Sinful Davey* (1969), d. John Huston
Video Availability: N/A
Role: Extra

In the shadow of the stars

The year 1969 was not a very auspicious one for the eighteen-year-old Anjelica Huston. It was the year that her mother died and she moved from her childhood home in Ireland to the United States. It was also the year in which she made her film debut, first in an uncredited bit part in the period highway-robbery movie *Sinful Davey*, then in a leading role (for which she was unprepared) in the hellacious period romance *A Walk With Love and Death*, in which two young people fight to keep their relationship going during rocky times in fourteenth-century France. Both of those films were directed by the fledgling actress's fearful and demanding father, John Huston (who had a more spectacular debut of his own when he directed *The Maltese Falcon*, 1941).

In her early movies, Huston sports the long hair and exotic features that would later make her one of the most fascinating-looking leading ladies in Hollywood. She radiated none of the sense of security, concentration, and inner calm that marks her today. Instead, she looked petrified—and in fact, she was.

"Yeah, I was disinclined to work in the film business for some fifteen years following that whole episode," says Huston now, laughing wryly.

It didn't quite take fifteen years to get back into movies, but Huston remembers how painful her early reviews were, and expresses sympathy for Francis Coppola's daughter Sofia, who was similarly subjected as a teenager to rotten reviews in a leading role in *her* father's movie, *The Godfather, Part III*. "I felt very bad for Sofia; I don't know how her day-to-day working life was with her father, but she was sort of unnecessarily ostracized" because of her performance, according to Huston.

"I think that contrary to some criticism, I find her quite beautiful, and she has a lot of charm and a lot of sweetness, and I think it's really unfair to go after someone so young, just because they've had the advantage of a father who is powerful in the business. I don't know whether she'll want to go on with it, or what her plans are, but I certainly felt better after I'd studied acting with Peggy Feury and regained my confidence. That kind of criticism can be very debilitating. When one's that young, I think it's very hard to overcome, it's hard to not

206

be very personally affected by it."

After Huston's bad start, she turned to modeling "because it was lucrative and I was a show-off, but I didn't want to be criticized for a while, and that was okay. I was still very uneasy with my looks. I wasn't a typical American face, not that there is a typical American face, but I felt unusual."

Courtesy *New York Post*

Veteran director John Huston gives his 17-year-old daughter Anjelica some tips while directing her in *A Walk with Love and Death* (1969), considered by many to be her debut. Actually, her father directed her in a small part in *Sinful Davey* earlier that year. It took Anjelica 15 years, by her count, to get over the experience.

Later, she wanted to act again, but was afraid the charges of nepotism would be doubly bad, since she had been living with Jack Nicholson since 1973. "I didn't want handouts, I didn't want to be in an advantageous position in terms of either my father or my boyfriend at the time, so I started working on small parts, and not really because I chose small parts, but at that point that was really the only thing that was coming my way. And I learned a lot from it. *The Cowboy and the Ballerina* might not be everyone's idea of an illuminating thing to do, but on the other hand, the more you work, the more you learn about work, and at that point, it was necessary that I learn. By the time *Prizzi's Honor* came along"—for which she won an Oscar—"I was well ready to take advantage of that situation, and I understood the character and her problems."

The insipid beauty of *A Walk With Love and Death* was just about the last time Huston would be cast in so mediocre and traditional a role. In recent years, her noble looks have been exaggerated for comic effect to play the Grand High Witch of *The Witches* and the sultry Morticia Addams of *The Addams Family*, and her melancholic quality has been used to great advantage dramatically in *The Grifters* and humorously in *Enemies, a Love Story.*

Huston cops an attitude as Morticia Addams in *The Addams Family* (1991) (see BARRY SONNENFELD). It was not evident from her early work that she was such a gifted actress.

Sinful Davey, 1969
A Walk With Love and Death, 1969
Hamlet, 1970
The Last Tycoon, 1976
Swashbuckler, 1976
The Postman Always Rings Twice, 1981
Frances, 1982
The Ice Pirates, 1984
This Is Spinal Tap, 1984
Prizzi's Honor, 1985
Captain Eo (short), 1986
Good to Go, 1986
The Dead, 1987

Gardens of Stone, 1987
John Huston and the Dubliners (docu), 1987
The Cowboy and the Ballerina, 1988
A Handful of Dust, 1988
John Huston, (docu) 1988
Mr. North, 1988
Crimes and Misdemeanors, 1989
Enemies, a Love Story, 1989
The Grifters, 1990
The Witches, 1990
The Addams Family, 1991
The Player, 1992
Manhattan Murder Mystery, 1993

TATUM O'NEAL

Actress
First Film: *Paper Moon* (1973), d. Peter Bogdanovich
Video Availability: Paramount Home Video
Role: Addie Pray

"Are you my daddy?"

*L*ittle Tatum O'Neal stole everyone's heart as the persistent child accomplice to real-life dad Ryan O'Neal, who may or may not be her screen father, in the low-key Depression-era comedy *Paper Moon.*

Little Tatum O'Neal seems to catch on quickly to the Bible-salesman scam pitched by real-life daddy Ryan O'Neal in *Paper Moon* (1973). But director Peter Bogdanovich says he had to feed the child her lines one at a time or she wouldn't remember them.

67-13

Tatum plays Addie Pray, alone in the world after her prostitute mother's death. She gets a lift from the elder O'Neal, a two-bit hustler who fears Addie will interfere with his scam of selling overpriced Bibles to grieving widows. But Addie proves more adept at the hustle than he—which really proves she is her father's daughter.

Among Tatum's best scenes are the ones in which she demands her share of the profits from a beleaguered Ryan; where she balks at playing second banana to a fleshy, floozy Madeline Kahn; and where the tomboy in her stands aside to experiment with femininity in front of the mirror. At age ten, Tatum—dressed in a man's tuxedo with shining lapels that wouldn't stay put—trotted off with a supporting-actress Oscar for her endearing performance.

Director Peter Bogdanovich offers a behind-the-scenes perspective on the filming of *Paper Moon*, made when he was "hot and arrogant, which is a good time to be arrogant, when you're hot."

Bogdanovich, speaking at the Fort Lauderdale Festival to film students and not realizing there was a journalist present, was uncommonly candid about working with Tatum. "Her long scenes were hell to do," he says with particular vehemence. He realizes that "what counts is what's up on the screen," but he says the younger O'Neal was no actress, and it took all his skill as a director and in the editing room to cover for her.

"I'd scare her, bribe her, I screamed at her one time. She ate too much cotton candy and got sick, I had to feed her her lines one at a time," complains Bogdanovich. "I couldn't believe it when she won the Oscar."

Tatum went on to do well in a few juvenile roles, notably as the pitcher in *The Bad News Bears* and as a summer camper experiencing a sexual awakening on a dare in *Little Darlings*. But she dropped out of the industry once she married tennis ace John McEnroe and had children of her own. They are now separated, and O'Neal is just now trying to get back into film.

Paper Moon, 1973
The Bad News Bears, 1976
Nickelodeon, 1976
International Velvet, 1978
Circle of Two, 1980
Little Darlings, 1980
Prisoners, 1983
Certain Fury, 1984
Little Noises, 1991
In Between Days, 1993

Tatum O'Neal, all grown up and able to memorize her lines, in the child's fantasy *Goldilocks and the 3 Bears* for Showtime cable television.

TIMOTHY HUTTON

Actor
First Film: *Never Too Late* (1965), d. Bud Yorkin
Video Availability: N/A
Role: Extra

Bonding on the set

*T*imothy Hutton is barely into his thirties, and yet his memory is failing already. When asked on an airplane—where he graciously consented to an interview in the first class aisle—about his very first film appearance, Hutton talked at length about *Ordinary People* (1980), in which he played the survivor of a boating accident that killed his brother and made things even chillier between him and his already distant parents. Both Hutton and first-time director Robert Redford won Oscars, as did the movie and the screenwriter.

However, fifteen years earlier, Hutton appeared briefly with his dad, actor Jim Hutton, in the uneven comedy *Never Too Late*, about a middle-aged couple facing parenthood.

First-timers Robert Redford and Timothy Hutton discuss a scene in the Redford-directed *Ordinary People* (1980), for which they both won Oscars. Hutton can actually be seen earlier as an extra in *Never Too Late* (1965) with his actor father, Jim Hutton.

As with many actors who select cafeteria-style from their list of credits (see "Inadmissible Evidence"), Hutton stands by *Ordinary People* as his first film, or first "real" film. He described his awe of being on its set with "actors I had watched since childhood," including Donald Sutherland and Mary Tyler Moore as his parents and Judd Hirsch as his user-friendly shrink in a ratty old cardigan. "It was like a circus—there were trucks, cameras, all these people doing different jobs. It was a machine that became more and more involved," says Hutton.

Mainly he was impressed by the relationships that develop on a movie set. "People's barriers every day are broken down. My experience there made me think that it's necessary to be close to everyone on the set, with everyone open and spending time together. But I don't feel that way anymore. Each movie you make takes on its own characteristic. It doesn't *have* to be a family; I'm not there to make friends."

Never Too Late, 1965
Ordinary People, 1980
Taps, 1981
Daniel, 1983
Iceman, 1984
The Falcon and the Snowman, 1985
Turk 182, 1985
Made in Heaven, 1987
Everybody's All-American, 1988
A Time of Destiny, 1988
Torrents of Spring, 1989
Q&A, 1990
The Dark Half, 1991 (unreleased)
The Temp, 1993

LAURA DERN

Actress
First Film: *White Lightning* (1973), d. Joseph Sargent
Video Availability: MGM/UA Home Video
Role: Extra

Mutual admiration society

*B*oth Laura Dern and her mother, Diane Ladd—the first mother-daughter team ever nominated for Oscars the same year, for *Rambling Rose*—claim they are very close. You can see proof of it on film in the early seventies, when the future star of *Smooth Talk* and *Wild at Heart* accompanied her mom on two movie sets and made it into both of them as an extra.

The first one was *White Lightning*, in which Burt Reynolds plays a rum-runner sprung from federal prison in order to avenge his younger brother's murder by a crooked sheriff (Ned Beatty). Diane Ladd (her name misspelled as "Lad" twice in the credits) plays the wife of a frightened liquor hauler (Matt Clark) coerced by Reynolds into helping him.

Laura, aged eight at the time, plays Ladd's daughter, appropriately enough. In most of her scenes, she is playing on a tire swing in the backyard, although you can see her clearly for a moment sitting on her mom's lap in a car on the way to a funeral.

When Laura was nine, she began studying acting at the Lee Strasberg Institute in New York, where she lived for a few years when her mother remarried. (Her father, Bruce Dern, left in a divorce when Laura was a baby.) At around the same time, Laura appears briefly in the final diner scene of Martin Scorsese's *Alice Doesn't Live Here Anymore*, in which Ladd plays a salty-tongued waitress. You can see the very blond Laura sitting at the end of the counter wearing black-rimmed glasses, her eyes following her mom rather than Ellen Burstyn, whose climactic scene it is.

Laura's "legitimate" film debut, the one listed in the sourcebooks, was in Adrian Lyne's *Foxes*, playing a teenager trying to crash Jodie Foster's party. The adolescent Laura was already tall enough for older parts.

"She's a magnificent actress," gushes Diane Ladd about her daughter. "I remember her eating that ice cream cone in *Alice Doesn't Live Here Anymore*, and I'm so glad she turned out the way she did. It's such a joy to do work with someone I love."

The two worked together again in *Wild at Heart*, in which Dern again played her mother's daughter. Ladd describes that experience as working "with one of the most professional actresses I've ever worked with—my own daughter. I raised her to be her own woman."

Laura Dern made a spectacular showing in *Smooth Talk* (1985) as a teenager on the cusp of womanhood. She was still on the cusp of childhood when she tagged along with her actress mother, Diane Ladd, in *White Lightning* (1973).

Dern, in reply, giggles. "Mother, I want to thank you for the genes."

Working with a family member is a family tradition—Diane Ladd's second film, the 1966 bad-boy biker flick *Wild Angels*, costarred Bruce Dern. And Ladd insists that Laura's first screen appearance was in that film, as the tiny bulge in her tummy.

But Ladd did not encourage young Laura to be an actress; she and Dern wanted to spare their daughter the heartbreak. "Face it, only five hundred actors make more than five thousand dollars a year," says Ladd. "Laura complained to me, 'Mom, if I were a piano player, you would tie my hands behind my back and not let me play till I was twenty-one.' I wanted her to be a doctor, a lawyer, anything so that she would not have to be judged by her appearance, which is what they do to actresses. Be a leper missionary, Laura, just don't be an actress. But I have to say, she stuck to it, she gave up her Saturday playtimes, she applied herself."

When Laura didn't win a lead role in *Foxes*, Ladd found her "sobbing on the couch. She said, 'But, Mother, you don't allow me to smoke, I'm too young to drink, all I can do is cry.' And Adrian Lyne said to me, 'Your daughter is going to be a giant star.' I was so humble, I can't tell you."

White Lightning, 1973
Alice Doesn't Live Here Anymore, 1975
Foxes, 1980
Ladies and Gentlemen, the Fabulous Stains, 1982
Teachers, 1984
Mask, 1985
Smooth Talk, 1985

Blue Velvet, 1986
Haunted Summer, 1988
Fat Man and Little Boy, 1989
Wild at Heart, 1990
Rambling Rose, 1991
Jurassic Park, 1993

MARIEL HEMINGWAY

Actress, restaurateur
First Film: *Lipstick* (1976), d. Lamont Johnson
Video Availability: Paramount Home Video
Role: Kathy McCormick

"He raped my sister."

Designed to showcase the slim body and slimmer acting talents of model Margaux Hemingway, *Lipstick* also features a role for her younger sibling Mariel, fifteen. For their twin debuts, the sisters play sisters—which is acting stretch enough.

Margaux is a top fashion model whose sultry poses attract the attention of little sister's music teacher (Chris Sarandon). When Margaux doesn't respond well to tape recordings of the man's atrocious synthesizer compositions, he rapes her in a variety of positions.

Remarkably composed for a rape victim—perhaps because of the limitations of her acting skills or the similarly bad direction—Margaux must break it to young Kathy that her music teacher is a jerk. They take him to court, but despite Anne Bancroft's attempts to prosecute, the guy goes free to perpetrate his two crimes—raping women and making awful music.

Rape is a downer for the elder McCormick sister, but soon she gets that smile back for the cameras. While she is strutting her stuff, Kathy goes wandering off in her girlish denim overalls and encounters the music teacher in another part of the building. He rapes her too.

Margaux is *really* mad now, so she retrieves a shotgun that is unaccountably stored in the trunk of her car and shoots the music teacher while she is wearing an expensive gown. "The failure of justice may be more damaging to society than crime itself," intones the movie, trying to make up for its needless exploitation.

It was Mariel who would go on to have the higher-profile movie career. Although like her sister she never showed a great deal of range, the sweetness and little-girl vulnerability you can see in *Lipstick*—not to mention her striking, strong-boned beauty—made her a standout as Woody Allen's teenage girlfriend in *Manhattan* and as slain Playboy playmate Dorothy Stratten in *Star 80*. (She got her breasts enlarged for the latter part.) A sports enthusiast, this granddaughter of Ernest Hemingway also gave a strong, physically demanding performance in *Personal Best* as a lesbian track star.

In *Lipstick*, Mariel's voice is high, thin, and reedy; she has admitted that it is the aspect about herself she most dislikes.

Although *Lipstick* (1976) was a vehicle for Margaux Hemingway, it served to launch the more bankable career of Mariel, who naturally plays her little sister in the movie.

Bruce Willis steadies the adult Mariel Hemingway at the scene of a murder he plans to solve in *Sunset*.

Margaux plays a cosmetics model who is raped by her little sister's music teacher in *Lipstick*. If there was an acting stretch involved for the elder Hemingway, it was that she allowed her beautiful hair to be pulled by Chris Sarandon during the rape scene.

Lipstick, 1976
Manhattan, 1979
Personal Best, 1982
Star 80, 1983
Creator, 1985
The Mean Season, 1985
The Suicide Club, 1987
Superman IV: The Quest for Peace, 1987
Sunset, 1988
Fire, Ice and Dynamite, 1990
Delirious, 1991
Falling From Grace, 1992

INADMISSIBLE EVIDENCE

THEY Won't Admit It, But We Can Prove It

ARNOLD SCHWARZENEGGER

Actor, bodybuilder
First Film: *Hercules in New York* (1969), d. Arthur
  Allan Seidelman
Video Availability: MPI Home Video
Role: Hercules

"I'm a Democrat."

*I*f you guessed that in Arnold Schwarzenegger's first film, he played a mythically indestructible figure who spoke few lines and found many occasions to reveal his muscular physique, you'd be right. But Arnold's first movie was *not* George Butler's seminal weight-lifting documentary *Pumping Iron* (1976), which served as his springboard to Hollywood. And it wasn't his walk-on as a goon in *The Long Goodbye* (1975). And it wasn't even the little-known and hardly missed *Stay Hungry* (1975), in which Sally Field is a bodybuilder groupie at a gym where Arnold wears a bat mask while he works out.

No, Arnold's introduction to the medium he would come to dominate with an iron bicep was back in 1969, in the execrable *Hercules in New York*, sometimes known as *Hercules Goes Bananas*. It makes his later movies look like masterpieces.

Although the MPI video release has changed the credits to cash in on the Arnold mystique, Arnold was originally billed as "Arnold Strong" in opposition to his spindly costar, Arnold Stang, a sort of poor man's Woody Allen. Only twenty-two at the time, the young and finely chiseled Arnold plays the Greek god Hercules with a towel wrapped around his waist. Most of the scenes were shot in New York's Central Park, including the one where he turns a taxi on its side and rides a chariot across the Great Lawn. (No wonder they had to reseed in the eighties.)

Hercules is the illegitimate son of Zeus and a human, which makes Zeus's jealous wife, Juno, hate the "insolent young whelp." Even Zeus is fed up: "If I'd known what trouble he would cause me, I'd have thought twice when I met his mother on vacation."

Arnold's Austrian accent is so impenetrable that his entire role is dubbed, from his simple opening line, "I'm bored," to such marble-mouthed speeches as when he is asked for bucks or dough to pay his cab fare and he responds: "Bucks? Doe? What is all this zoological talk about the male and female species?"

Made for little dough and fewer bucks, *Hercules in New York* was clearly meant to satirize those cheap Italian he-man flicks. Instead, it is the butt of its own joke.

Illustration for Arnold Schwarzenegger's not very illustrious first movie, *Hercules in New York* (1969). He descends from Mt. Olympus for some flexing and thesping, only to lose a weightlifting contest to Monstro the Magnificent.

There is a scene in which Arnold is beaten in a weight-lifting contest by Monstro the Magnificent after Juno has slipped him some weakness-inducing powder. "I like the chance to play vulnerability," said Arnold years later, after making *Predator*, which was his idea of playing a vulnerable character. "To play that you're frightened that this is your last second on earth kind of thing."

Highlights of his first film include Arnold beating up an escaped grizzly bear (actually a man in a moth-eaten bear suit) and pumping up his accordion-like pectorals one breast at a time in quick succession.

One notable line: When Arnold is picked up by a navy ship (played by a cruise ship, whose deckside shuffleboard court cannot be masked), he tells the crew he is a Democrat.

The surprise of this stinker is that Arnold shows exactly the kind of magnetism to which he owes his career. He is far less stiff than the typical amateur and earnestly puts his heart into the role. Even his skin tone looks better on camera than the pallor of those around him.

Arnold's strength continued to be his strong suit as he heroically muscled his way through the *Conan*" movies. Eventually he toned down both the muscle mass and the Austrian accent and became the highest paid star in Hollywood.

"Challenges inspire me," says Arnold, who is preternaturally charming and relaxed in interviews. "I pick them in the first place. I look forward to tremendous obstacles, taking tremendous risks. Some of the films come out not as successful as you hoped. There is no such thing as a smooth ride. It's one step back, two to the front."

He likens his film career to the jagged lines of a stock chart; Arnold in his spare time is a smart investor, especially in real estate.

Anyway, *Hercules in New York* was not as much a step back as it might at first appear. It got Arnold in front of the cameras, and even in his toga by Fieldcrest he never seems as goofy as he does later in *Stay Hungry*, where he wears a shiny cowboy shirt that he calls "the height of elegance" and strums a banjo.

What Arnold does in movies may not be acting in the Lord Olivier sense of the word, but what he does, he does with energy and a sense of humor that carried him through the ignominy of the Conan movies to the Olympian heights of fame he enjoys today.

In *Pumping Iron*, you get a better sense of the master plan Arnold mapped out for himself. It included training himself "to be cold," worshiping the great dictators, and getting off on power. Pumping up his muscles "is as satisfying to me as coming," he says in one memorable interview in the movie. "I'm coming day and night, so I'm in heaven."

Hercules in New York, 1969
Stay Hungry, 1975
Pumping Iron, 1976
The Villain, 1979
Conan the Barbarian, 1982
Conan the Destroyer, 1984
The Terminator, 1984
Commando, 1985
Red Sonja, 1985
Raw Deal, 1986
Predator, 1987
The Running Man, 1987
Red Heat, 1989
Twins, 1988
Kindergarten Cop, 1990
Total Recall, 1990
Terminator 2: Judgment Day, 1991
Feed (docu), 1992
The Last Action Hero, 1993

WILLIAM SHATNER

Actor
First Film: *The Brothers Karamazov* (1958), d. Richard
   Brooks
Video Availability: MGM/UA Home Video
Role: Alexey Karamazov

"Dmitri, we all need love."

S tar date: 1958. William Shatner makes his film debut in *The Brothers Karamazov.*
Director Richard Brooks adapted the screenplay from the great Dostoyevsky novel about greed, missed opportunities, murder, and suicide in the lives of a tyrannical father (Lee J. Cobb) and his four sons during czarist Russia.

Which son is Shatner? He's Alexey, the religious one in the monk's cloak and a fringe of shiny, neat bangs on his forehead—just like a certain Vulcan we know.

Monk William Shatner tries to calm excitable older brother Yul Brynner in *The Brothers Karamazov* (1958), a movie which calls upon him to be the statesman between warring family members, much the way he would become the intergalactic statesman in the various *Star Trek* enterprises.

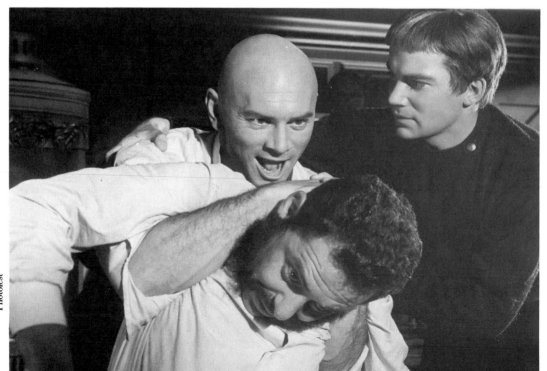

Shatner is still the peacekeeper he was back in *The Brothers Karamazov* as he and Spock (Leonard Nimoy) handle a diplomatic crisis in outer space in *Star Trek VI* (1991).

The stiff line readings, noble eye squint, wooden movements, and simplistic homilies that later made Shatner such a favorite among comedy impressionists are all beamed aboard the actor's first film. "Dmitri, we all need love," he chastises his more interesting brother, played by Yul Brynner in the movie's only intelligent performance.

This peculiar rendering of Dostoyevsky has not stood the test of time. In its day, it was nominated for an Oscar for Cobb, whose first scene has him tying up a willing maiden and tickling her toes with a feather. By today's standards, the movie has a claustrophobic feeling, with its fake snow, sanctimony, and mismatched brothers—each with a different accent. (Shatner's is American, although he was born in Canada.)

Interestingly, Shatner's stiff style is perfect for the engaging *Star Trek* movies—which is just as well, since the starship has been his most visible and valuable movie enterprise.

The Brothers Karamazov, 1958
The Explosive Generation, 1961
Judgment at Nuremberg, 1961
The Intruder, 1962
The Outrage, 1964
Incubus, 1965
Big Bad Mama, 1974
The Devil's Rain, 1975
Impulse, 1975
A Whale of a Tale, 1976
Kingdom of the Spiders, 1977
The Land of No Return, 1978
Star Trek: The Motion Picture, 1979

The Kidnapping of the President, 1980
Visiting Hours, 1981
Airplane II: The Sequel, 1982
Star Trek II: The Wrath of Khan, 1982
Star Trek III: The Search for Spock, 1984
The Bradbury Trilogy, 1985
The Canadian Conspiracy, 1986
Star Trek IV: The Voyage Home, 1986
Star Trek V: The Final Frontier, 1989 (also director)
Star Trek VI: The Undiscovered Country, 1991
Bill and Ted's Bogus Journey, 1991 (in film clip)
National Lampoon's Loaded Weapon 1, 1993

CHER

Actress, singer
First Film: *Wild on the Beach* (1965), d. Maury Dexter
Video Availability: N/A
Role: Half of Sonny and Cher duo

"I got you, babe."

*W*hen Cher won her Oscar for *Moonstruck* in 1987, she thanked "Mary Louise Streep, who I feel...so unbelievable...that I did my first movie with her and now I was nominated with her and I feel really thankful." Meryl Streep had costarred with Cher in *Silkwood* in 1983.

Cher is Chastity personified in the 1969 movie of the same name. She and then-partner Sonny appeared in two previous movies; *Wild on the Beach* (1965) was their first.

691

Cher plays a quiet Italian girl who finds love with her fiancé's passionate younger brother in the romantic comedy *Moonstruck* (1987). Cher herself was moonstruck when she accepted her Oscar and conveniently forgot about all her early movies in her acceptance speech.

It's a good thing Cher's acting abilities, singing voice, and surgically reconstructed body far surpass her memory. Only one year before *Silkwood*, Cher had starred in *Come Back to the Five and Dime Jimmy Dean, Jimmy Dean*, and that's not all. Not only did she name her daughter after *Chastity*, the movie she made in 1969 about a teenage girl with wanderlust (and lust), but Cher also appeared in two prior movies, *Good Times* (1967), which is listed in most reference books as her first, and *Wild on the Beach* (1965), her *real* first film. In her first two, she and singing partner (and former husband) Sonny essentially appear as themselves.

Wild on the Beach is about a battle of the sexes over a rooming house. The local college is experiencing a housing crunch and accepts students only if they can prove they have an address. The boys and girls decide to share the house, divided by an "iron curtain"; it's no Wall of Jericho. Tensions relax when Sonny and Cher drop in at the house to sing.

So a long memory is not Cher's strong suit. Still, she's the only woman in the world who can truly carry off a Bob Mackie gown, even as she approaches fifty. She has also proven herself a fine dramatic and comic actress in every one of her movies—at least those she can remember.

Wild on the Beach, 1965
Good Times, 1967
Chastity, 1969
Come Back to the Five and Dime Jimmy Dean, Jimmy Dean, 1982
Silkwood, 1983

Mask, 1985
Moonstruck, 1987
Suspect, 1987
The Witches of Eastwick, 1987
Mermaids, 1990
The Player, 1992

227

AL PACINO

Actor
First Film: *Me, Natalie* (1969), d. Fred Coe
Video Availability: N/A
Role: Dance partner

"Do you put out, or don't you?"

Al Pacino nearly had a great film debut with *The Panic in Needle Park* (1971), which usually passes as his first film. Unfortunately, there is the little matter of *Me, Natalie*, an annoying 1969 Patty Duke vehicle in which Pacino comes on gangbusters in a walk-on.

Me, Natalie is about a supposedly ugly girl's lifelong quest to feel pretty and attract a guy.

Al Pacino helps girlfriend Kitty Winn shoot heroin on the roof of their hotel in *The Panic in Needle Park* (1971), the movie everyone *thinks* is Pacino's debut. Actually, he propositioned Patty Duke in *Me, Natalie* (1969) in a scene that won him this role.

Photofest

She eventually "finds herself," and James Farentino too. He plays an artist who paints nudes for a living but—how ironic!—appreciates inner beauty as well.

Luckily, you don't have to endure the entire movie, because Pacino is right there in the first twenty minutes, in the scene where she, Natalie, spends a blind date sitting forlornly at a dance hall. As she tries to leave, Pacino comes out of nowhere and whooshes her onto the dance floor, with an aggressive "Wanna dance?" He's wearing overgrown sideburns, the style of the time.

"You have a nice body . . . do you put out?" he asks roughly. "Do you put out, or don't you?"

"No," says Natalie.

"I don't know what I'm doin' talkin' to you. Somebody like *you* should be asking *me*." And he's gone.

His self-assurance in that bit part won him *The Panic in Needle Park*, and you can even see that interesting Pacino habit of looking fixedly away from someone who is answering him and making a motion with his mouth as if he is tasting what the person is saying.

The Bronx-born Pacino considers himself a real New York actor, by which he means "someone who works more on the stage than in films, who's worked more on Off- and Off-Off-Broadway and has been around the acting schools, and has been influenced by the kind of temper, the temperature of the Method. In California, they're more oriented toward mood than Method. I was acting on my roof at age three, in the South Bronx. I lived in [Greenwich] Village at sixteen, seventeen, working at the Living Theater, at café theaters, where we'd pass the hat around. I think that scene no longer exists the same way; television and movies have altered it."

Pacino in *The Godfather Part 3*, a mobster with a lot on his mind.

Pacino is easily forgiven his failures because of his spectacular successes in such movies as *Serpico* and *Dog Day Afternoon* and as the reluctant new godfather in the *Godfather* series. Although he winces to hear it called a "comeback," Pacino's lonelyhearts cop in *Sea of Love* brought him out of mothballs in 1989; his previous film of note had been 1983's *Scarface*.

The elegantly groomed, Italian-silk-clad Pacino is so soft-spoken that the air conditioning has to be turned down so he can be heard over the hum. "When success in movies first came, I found myself going back to the theater without even knowing why, and not because I held it up in any ideal, but because it seemed to me something I was most familiar with, something where I could be more myself. I had a kind of aloof relationship to what was happening in movies. But I think it only appeared to be aloof, that it was really a precaution for me. I worried about being taken up in it. It's only recently that I have started to come closer to movies."

Me, Natalie, 1969
The Panic in Needle Park, 1971
The Godfather, 1972
Scarecrow, 1973
Serpico, 1973
The Godfather Part II, 1974
Dog Day Afternoon, 1975
Bobby Deerfield, 1977
...And Justice for All, 1979
Cruising, 1980
Acting: Lee Strasberg and the Actors Studio (docu), 1981

Author! Author!, 1982
Scarface, 1983
Revolution, 1985
Sea of Love, 1989
Dick Tracy, 1990
The Godfather, Part III, 1990
The Local Stigmatic (short), 1990
Frankie and Johnny, 1991
Glengarry Glen Ross, 1992
Scent of a Woman, 1992

DREW BARRYMORE

Actress
First Film: *Altered States* (1980), d. Ken Russell
Video Availability: Warner Home Video
Role: Margaret Jessup

Tawdry things to come

When little Drew Barrymore as Gertie came face-to-face with E.T. for the first time, she let out a scream heard 'round the world and at the box office. She was only seven and already calling her movie-brother things like "penis breath."

But the youngest member of the Barrymore acting dynasty can be seen plying the family trade even earlier, at age five, in *Altered States*. (See WILLIAM HURT)

As Maggie Jessup, the youngest daughter of scientists William Hurt and Blair Brown, Barrymore faced such acting challenges as being put to bed by her daddy, riding on Hurt's shoulders, fighting with her sister to answer the phone first, and entering a room with her little roller-bubble toy while mommy and daddy are having a fight.

Jerry Ohlinger

Innocent little Drew Barrymore on the set of *Altered States* (1980), where she played one of the children of William Hurt, a scientist more interested in isolation tanks than fatherhood.

231

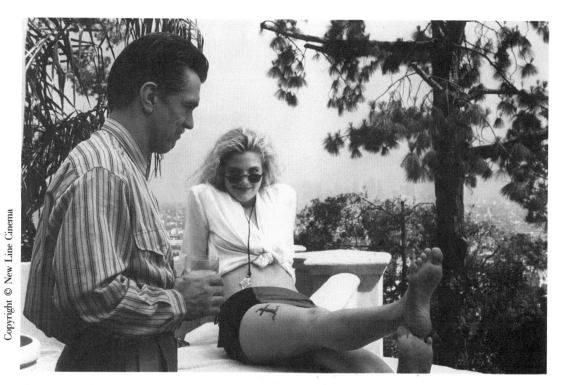

Innocent no longer, a languorous Barrymore eyes Tom Skerritt, father of her best friend, in the pleasantly trashy *Poison Ivy* (1992).

Playing cute-as-a-button Gertie in *E.T.: the Extra-Terrestrial* however, is what crystallized Barrymore's image as a sweet, sparkling child, even though she followed up that movie with *Firestarter*, in which her special powers enable her to spark fires at will.

In fact, the *E.T.* image is so indelible, and Barrymore so firmly associated with it, that it was all the more astonishing when she blossomed into an overripe sex kitten—first in *Far From Home*, in which her sluttish ways attract all the wrong elements in a small town, then more spectacularly in *Poison Ivy*, in which she spiritedly seduces and disables all the members of her best friend's family so that she can ultimately have the daddy all to herself.

After a well-publicized bout of drug addiction, Barrymore has emerged as a teenage sex goddess. Maybe saying "penis breath" was an indication of tawdry things to come.

Altered States, 1980
E.T., the Extra-Terrestrial, 1982
Firestarter, 1984
Irreconcilable Differences, 1984
Stephen King's Cat's Eye, 1985
Far From Home, 1989
See You in the Morning, 1989

Poison Ivy, 1992
Motorama, 1992
Gun Crazy, 1992
Sketch Artist, 1992
Doppelganger, 1993
No Place to Hide, 1993

JENNIFER BEALS

Actress
First Film: *My Bodyguard* (1980), d. Tony Bill
Video Availability: Fox Video
Role: Student

In the lull before fame

*J*ennifer Beals made such an impression in *Flashdance* as the welder by day, semiexotic dancer by night, that some of the images from that movie are permanently etched into the national pop-culture consciousness. The late John Belushi satirized Beals's aerobic dancing in a bit on "Saturday Night Live" in which he sprawled back on a chair, pulled a shower cord, and had a bucket of water dumped on his head, then pumped his legs up and down while erotically massaging his thighs. Oh, what a feeling.

Jennifer Beals (to the left of Matt Dillon) is a classmate in *My Bodyguard* (1980). Of course, everyone thinks she began her career as the welder-turned-exotic-dancer in *Flashdance* (1983).

Everyone hailed *Flashdance* as a stunning debut for Jennifer Beals, a silky-skinned Yale student whose dance sequences were mostly enacted by a body double. The soundtrack album went through the roof, even though the song "Maniac" (*"She's a maniac, maniac on the floor/ And she's dancing like she never danced before"*) was originally written with lyrics about a homicidal killer, not a determined young woman with aspirations to learn ballet.

And yet, *Flashdance* was not the first time you could see Beals on film. Three years earlier, she was one of the high school students menaced for her lunch money by bully Matt Dillon in Tony Bill's directorial debut, the undemandingly amusing *My Bodyguard*.

That movie also marks the debut of Adam Baldwin (no relation to Alec) as the hulking Ricky Linderman, perceived to be a psychopath by everyone at the school except Clifford (Chris Makepeace), who hires the misunderstood youth to be his personal bodyguard. Frizzy-haired Joan Cusack also has a small role as a girl with an unrequited crush on Dillon.

Beals doesn't have a speaking part and therefore is not listed in the credits. But you can see her sitting in homeroom behind Dillon, and sitting around the picnic table with the other students when it is discovered that the beefy Linderman apparently doesn't know how to fight, and therefore makes a lousy bodyguard.

Beals went on to wear white as the Frankenstein monster's bride in *The Bride,* which was sent back to the graveyard at the box office. Despite her initial splash in *Flashdance,* she was never able to jump-start her career. Partly it was because she took time out to finish at Yale, where she studied English literature. She appears occasionally in low-rent movies as she struggles to get back on track, which may occur after starring in her husband Alexandre Rockwell's low-budget critical hit *In the Soup.*

My Bodyguard, 1980
Flashdance, 1983
The Bride, 1985
La Partita, 1988
Split Decisions, 1988
Vampire's Kiss, 1988
Sons, 1989
Docteur M. (Club Extinction), 1990
The Gamble, 1990
Blood and Concrete, a Love Story, 1991
In the Soup, 1992
Day of Atonement, 1993
Sons, 1993

REBECCA DeMORNAY

Actress
First Film: *One From the Heart* (1982), d. Francis
   Coppola
Video Availability: Columbia TriStar Home Video
Role: Diner patron

There's always take 2

"*T*hat's right, yeah, *Risky Business* was my first role," says Rebecca DeMornay, her chain-smoking creating a fog that must have clouded her memory of her actual first film, *One From the Heart*, made a year before *Risky Business*.

It was *Risky Business* that put her and her costar, Tom Cruise, on the map, while her single scene in *One From the Heart* as a diner patron impatiently awaiting waiter Raul Julia to serve her requires careful freeze-framing to verify her identity.

Rebecca DeMornay is barely visible as a diner at the next table in *One From the Heart* (1982), where she has to cool her heels and have her food cool too while waiting for Teri Garr and waiter Raul Julia to finish flirting.

Author's collection

Francis Coppola's failed romantic comedy is notable for its striking, imaginative cinematography and for its re-creation of a glossy, dreamlike Las Vegas filmed entirely on the soundstages of the director's Zoetrope Studios. It is not, however, remembered for its story—about Teri Garr and Frederic Forrest's shaky relationship. Each of them has an affair with a stranger—Forrest with circus girl Nastassia Kinski, Garr with singing waiter Raul Julia—before they realize that they were better off with each other.

Garr meets Julia at a diner where he is about to serve the couple at the next table, but he gets so caught up in flirting with Garr that he sets all the plates down at his own table. DeMornay wants her waffles, her companion wants his club sandwich, and they spend the scene looking peeved and trying to get Julia's attention.

The blond, icy-blue-eyed DeMornay got a better deal out of *Risky Business*, in which she played the prostitute Lana who helps teenager Tom Cruise spend a wild weekend while his parents are out of town. "I tested for the role," she says. "The director, Paul Brickman, had looked for this character of Lana in New York, L.A., and Chicago, and had been unable to find her. The studios were pressuring him to go with a name, he didn't like any of the names who were around. He couldn't find the girl. He was all set to go to Paris—maybe there was a French girl who could play the role—and I walked in. I was basically the last person out of eight hundred women that walked in, and he liked me."

DeMornay and Tom Cruise share a moment in *Risky Business*, the movie De Mornay says is her first. The moment they shared must have been really something, because they lived together for **several years** after.

Cruise was shooting *The Outsiders*, so to work around his schedule, he and DeMornay screen-tested together at 6:00 A.M. "This was the famous Chemistry Test, and the chemistry worked," recalls DeMornay. Not only did it work, but the two lived together for two and a half years after making the film.

"We shot the movie, we had a ball, nobody interfered with us, there were no studio people down with us, it was really a very closed unit. I was very scared, it was my first movie"— well, not quite—"but I was dead sure of who the character was, and even with no experience I really was able to put my foot down about decisions about the character because I understood her completely. Then the movie came out, it made a ton of money, both of us went on, and that's how it goes."

And Cruise became a mega-star, and that's how *that* goes.

DeMornay resurfaced as the nanny from hell in *The Hand That Rocks the Cradle*. "What I've learned since my first movie is that there's always take two, so I don't feel as much pressure on each take, because there's always another take."

One From the Heart, 1982
Risky Business, 1983
Testament, 1983
Runaway Train, 1985
The Slugger's Wife, 1985
The Trip to Bountiful, 1986
Beauty and the Beast, 1987
And God Created Woman, 1988
Feds, 1988
Dealers, 1989
Backdraft, 1991
The Hand That Rocks the Cradle, 1992
Beyond Innocence, 1993

MARTIN SHORT

Actor, writer, comic
First Film: *Lost and Found* (1979), d. Melvin Frank
Video Availability: Columbia/TriStar Home Video
Role: Engel

"It's, uh...it's Emily Dickinson!"

*I*t's understandable why Martin Short has taken the liberty of editing 1979's *Lost and Found* out of his bio; after all, that leaves him with a film debut opposite his buddies Steve Martin and Chevy Chase in *Three Amigos!* (1986).

Lost and Found is *A Touch of Class*, except without the class, but similarly starring Glenda Jackson and George Segal. A youthful-looking Short plays Engel, one of professor Segal's English-lit students, who is embarrassed when he doesn't know the answer to a question about Emily Dickinson, and who in turn embarrasses Segal when *he* doesn't know the name of another student.

Martin Short (right) trades pleasantries with fellow amigos Chevy Chase (left) and Steve Martin as they head down Mexico way to earn some "real money...*amigo* money." Short insists— repeatedly—that *The Three Amigos* is his very first movie. Must be that amigo amnesia.

Still, Short maintains that *Three Amigos!* is his very first film, and drops frequent references to that in interviews.

Three Amigos! bombed, although it is a guilty pleasure for some. The three amigos are silent-action film stars who are called to Mexico for what they believe is a movie job that will pay "*real* money. *Amigo* money." It turns out that some trusting villagers are hoping the amigos will rid them of actual banditos.

"How I got that role was that in the spring of 1985, Lorne Michaels—and I didn't really know Lorne, I had met him once or twice—invited me to his home to talk about this script he was producing. He said he felt I'd be great for it. I mean, they didn't *really* want me to do it at that point; I think if Bill Murray had wanted it, then Bill Murray would have done it. At that time, I hadn't made a movie"—Short's short memory kicking in again—"so that was the first conversation. I agreed to do it in November '85, and we started shooting in January of '86. I had never met Steve, I had never met Chevy, I had never met [director] John Landis. It was a total first, on every level."

Short is still close with Martin and Chase. "To this day, we have our Amigo dinners, we take our Amigo-ettes. It was an instant chemistry."

Not as much chemistry between him and director Landis, however. "I think that was the only movie I can honestly say in which I kept thinking that because it was the movies I should maybe do something different. And because John Landis doesn't allow actors into dailies, it was hard to see what I was doing. To be quite honest, I don't think that John was tremendously familiar with my career. And so I think that what he wanted was what he got— a very sweet, lovable Ned Nederlander. Near the end of shooting, he was a little surprised to see that I could also improvise."

Lost and Found, 1979
The Outsider, 1979
The Canadian Conspiracy, 1986
Three Amigos!, 1986
Cross My Heart, 1987
Innerspace, 1987
Three Fugitives, 1989
The Big Picture, 1989 (unbilled)
Clifford, 1991 (unreleased)
Pure Luck, 1991
Father of the Bride, 1991
Captain Ron, 1992
We're Back, 1993 (voice)
The Pebble and the Penguin, 1993 (voice)

DIRECTORS

Earliest Signs of Auteurism

PETER BOGDANOVICH

Director
First Film (as director): *Targets* (1968)
Video Availability: Paramount Home Video
(Role: Sammy)

Making movies on the run

*T*aking a page from his mentor Roger Corman, Peter Bogdanovich "borrowed" the star of
a Corman film in progress to make parts of *Targets*, virtually the last movie for Boris
Karloff.

Karloff owed Corman three and a half days of shooting on *The Terror*, so Bogdanovich took
both Karloff and portions of *The Terror* to fill out his movie, in which he also has a role as a
young screenwriter named Sammy who is rebuffed by aging horror star Byron Orlok
(Karloff).

Orlok is threatening to retire from the business before making Sammy's next picture,
reasoning that there is no call for a "painted monster" in a time when real-life violence is
scarier. And anyway, "all the good movies have been made."

Although Bogdanovich was the additional sequence director (as "Derek Thomas") on
Voyage to the Planet of Prehistoric Women in 1965, *Targets* is his full directorial debut. "This
motion picture tells a story that sheds a little light on a very dark and very deep topic,"
claims a blurb at the start of the video.

That dark and deep topic is the issue of gun control, or the lack thereof. *Targets* features a
mild-mannered fellow who snaps one day, shoots his family, then goes out on the highway to
snipe at cars. After killing a few passersby, he moves on to a drive-in theater where an Orlok
film is in progress.

In a clever touch, Bogdanovich has the sniper aim through the screen from the back to
shoot randomly at the spectators; in the denouement, the sniper is confused by Karloff
apparently approaching him from two directions—the screen, and real life.

Targets is an example of what the lanky, slightly graying director refers to affectionately as
"guerrilla moviemaking." "It was shot in twenty-three days, and was a lot of fun—if you
think of blind terror as being fun," he says. "Of all my pictures, it was the most consuming,
on top of which we were doing it so fast."

He had already been writing scripts for Corman, undoubtedly the master of guerrilla
moviemaking, but *Targets* offered first-hand experience at the helm: "Unless you're on a

242

soundstage or in a studio, making a picture in real life is extremely difficult. You're trying to bend reality."

Later, when he made *The Last Picture Show* in 1971 with then-girlfriend Cybill Shepherd, Bogdanovich experienced similar real-life frustrations. "Some kids were playing in the yard a block and half away. I said to the AD [assistant director], get those kids out of the yard. And he said, *Hey, you kids, get out of your yard!*" Today, citizens are more apt to offer resistance.

"For the initial sniper scene in *Targets*, we weren't allowed to shoot on the freeway, there were no permits, but we did it anyway. It was a little dangerous, I don't advise it. We had two cameras going at the same time to stage a sequence on the freeway, directed through walkie-talkies. You can never get away with that sort of thing with a big company, but we did it. If there was a car coming down the freeway, I'd yell—shoot it!"

Bogdanovich says he has tried to "re-create those days on other films. It's important not to be too comfortable. The director Leo McCarey once told me that the perfect way to get into pictures was with a little bit of larceny."

Peter Bogdanovich directs the comedy *Noises Off* (1992), based on the Broadway hit. He began his career in what he calls "guerrilla moviemaking" with *Targets* (1968), working by the seat of his pants.

The son of a painter (his dad) and a frame-maker (his mom), Bogdanovich was acting in theater as early as age fifteen. "I tried to get on the free screening lists at studios; that way I thought I could meet some of those great directors and actors. I got to meet John Wayne, Orson Welles, Cary Grant. It was my way of putting myself through the university of training in pictures. I believed that the way to learn was to ask the people who'd done it, and most were very happy to share their secrets. They're all dead now, but I owe those people a tremendous debt."

Although Bogdanovich has made films in many different styles—including the comedies *What's Up, Doc? Paper Moon*, and *Noises Off*—he feels most strongly about the construction of suspense movies. "One of the biggest mistakes in pictures today is mystifying the audience when you should be giving them information," he chides, illustrating with references to Hitchcock and crosscutting devices to build an audience's expectations.

Of all his work, *They All Laughed* is his favorite, probably because it starred his lover Dorothy Stratten, the *Playboy* Playmate who was murdered by her ex-husband, and to whose younger sister Bogdanovich is now married.

Looking back over his career, which he began as a film critic and writer, Bogdanovich says, "I'd like to reshoot *Targets*, not recut it. But I learned early you can't beat your head against the wall if you want to reshoot. Part of the tension that should communicate itself on the screen is the sense that it's fresh, it just happened. It shouldn't seem rehearsed."

Another reason for Bogdanovich to love the guerrilla form of moviemaking comes from an insight Orson Welles once shared with him: "You could almost say a director is a person who presides over accidents."

Voyage to the Planet of Prehistoric Women, 1965 (directed a few scenes)
Targets, 1968 (also actor, producer, screenplay)
Directed by John Ford, 1971 (also screenplay)
The Last Picture Show, 1971 (also screenplay)
What's Up Doc? 1972 (also producer)
Paper Moon, 1973 (also producer)
Verites et Mensonges/F for Fake, 1973 (actor only)
Daisy Miller, 1974 (also producer)
At Long Last Love, 1975 (also producer and screenplay)
Diaries, Notes and Sketches—Volume 1, Reels 1–6; Lost Lost Lost, 1975 (actor)

Nickelodeon, 1976 (also screenplay)
Opening Night, 1977 (actor)
Saint Jack, 1979 (also actor and screenplay)
They All Laughed, 1981
The City Girl, 1983 (exec. producer)
Mask, 1985
Illegally Yours, 1988 (also director)
Hollywood Mavericks, 1990 (actor)
Texasville, 1990 (also producer and screenplay)
Noises Off, 1992
The Thing Called Love, 1993

KENNETH BRANAGH

Director, actor
First Film (as director): *Henry V* (1989)
Video Availability: Fox Video
(Role: Henry V)

Riding Shakespeare's coattails

*W*hile still in his twenties, the stage actor and director Kenneth Branagh had the nerve to write his autobiography, the purpose of which was to raise money for his Renaissance Theatre Company. Before he would turn thirty, this precocious heir to the Olivier mantle would adapt, direct, and star in an exciting new film version of *Henry V*, for which he won numerous awards and was nominated for directing and acting Oscars.

Henry V was in fact only the third theatrical film Branagh had ever worked in. He made *High Season* and *A Month in the Country* in 1987, although he was already well known in England for TV, including his miniseries "Fortunes of War," which costarred his future wife and frequent leading lady, Emma Thompson.

The Belfast-born, English-raised Branagh is a little embarrassed by the inevitable comparisons to Lord Olivier, but "I'm sure other people get tired of it before I do," he jokes.

Kenneth Branagh and wife Emma Thompson watch dailies on the set of the Hitchcockian thriller *Dead Again*, the first Hollywood movie Branagh accepted after his powerful debut as a director with *Henry V*. In both movies, he starred opposite Thompson.

"It's meaningless, of course. I'm not Laurence Olivier and never will be. He's the giant of the century and I've been doing this for two minutes. I'm happily in the tradition of someone who was bold and brave and courageous in the choice of work that he did."

Smart, quick, and amiable, Branagh can expound equally on Shakespeare or Hitchcock, the latter of whom influenced him for his next directing assignment, the witty and accomplished Hollywood thriller *Dead Again*. It was two years after *Henry V* that he made *Dead Again*, because although Hollywood wanted him, it didn't quite know what to do with him.

"Battle scenes, definitely battle scenes," is what it offered him, because of his spectacular handling of the battlefield in *Henry V*. "And I tended to get some of the Vietnam movies that hadn't got made, some American Marine pictures. Anything with water in it seemed to be sent to me. I also received various literary bio-pics, the life of Tolstoy—a movie that the world is waiting to see—and several lives of William Shakespeare. I was sent specialized material that they guessed would be rather less boring in my hands."

Branagh says he was surprised by the success of what he calls *Henry Five*. "I always hoped it would cross over to the kind of audience that might otherwise be frightened of it. The [Oscar] nominations signaled to people to see it. Essentially, I didn't care if people were dragged to see it or not. I know lots of people were—kids dragged by their teachers. No skin off my nose. I'm glad if they went and had some sort of experience they enjoyed, instead of passing some sort of exam or intelligence test. So that was very rewarding. As I go around the world, I've met so many people of different backgrounds and ages for whom it's blown a few cobwebs off the notion of what would be entertaining, and made them not necessarily equate something like Shakespeare with just being good for you. It got to more people than I ever imagined."

Branagh grew up watching old movies, paying particular attention to the end credits. "I could never fathom it at the time, but I realize now it must have been some deep, unconscious attraction," he says. "I wanted to know why there were so many people involved, who they could possibly be. I'd see all these names recur—who *are* these people? What's this 'continuity' thing? Where is Burbank? Now I know."

He used his memory of old films to make *Dead Again*, which features a mansion right out of *Rebecca*. "I loved the look and mood of those movies. When we found the mansion, I said, 'Towers on it, please. Gorgons and gargoyles. Let's get those gates.' We really Gothiced it up. We Edgar Allan Poed it. That was something that was right out of the sort of deliciousness those movies had."

One of the first movies that made a big impression on young Kenneth was "that incredible Raquel Welch movie, *One Million Years B.C.*, one of those *grunt* movies. Then they go light the fire, and there's the first half of the film," says Branagh in an impressive grunt. "Then the second half of the film, they go and hunt something, grrr, grrr. Then they bring the bloody deer over the fire. And in between, it's got a lot of running, scantily clad people. All the men are ugly, and all the women are well endowed. In today's movies, the grunting is just slightly clearer."

Branagh's reasonable attitude about stardom is thanks to the grounding in harsh reality given him by his first drama school teacher.

"I went to audition for Hugh Cruttwell when I was seventeen, and he called me up on a Saturday night, and said, 'I saw you the other day, everybody wanted to give you a place [in the school]. I thought it was ten-a-penny—that kind of acting—didn't interest me at all. So you'll have to come and do it again.' So I came in on a Wednesday and did a piece from *The Glass Menagerie*. He stopped me again and said, no no, that's rubbish, dreadful, absolutely dreadful. And then for half an hour he explained the difference between performing and acting. The difference between, you know, you start at school and find you have a facility for showing off, as opposed to presenting a character, in which you can submerge some elements of your performing instinct in order to serve a character that may not have them in quite the same ways. And that means serving a character instead of serving your sense of being a performer."

Cruttwell stood by on the set of *Henry V* to offer advice, because "he has no awe or fear or intimidation of me. Because people can have an image of you at a distance, that you're some genius because you're in a Shakespeare film. They confuse Shakespeare's genius with yours, which is sometimes helpful, but nevertheless is a trick. And I'm happily riding his coattails four hundred years off."

High Season, 1987 (actor)
A Month in the Country, 1987 (actor)
Henry V, 1989 (also actor)
Dead Again, 1991 (also actor)
Peter's Friends, 1992 (also actor)
Much Ado About Nothing, 1993
Swing Kids, 1993 (actor)

TIM BURTON

Director
First Film: *Frankenweenie* (1982)
Video Availability: Disney Home Video

Pop culture, comics, Vincent Price

*A*lthough nowhere else in this book are short movies considered a filmmaker's "first" effort, it was just too hard to resist including *Frankenweenie*, a tantalizing twenty-nine-minute Gothic short by Tim Burton, future director of such black comedies as *Beetlejuice* and *Edward Scissorhands*—not to mention the two *Batman* movies.

Anyone familiar with Burton's work—an off-kilter scramble of pop references, comics, the surreal, and Vincent Price—will recognize *Frankenweenie* as his. In it, a kid resurrects his pet dog from the cemetery, stitches him together, and jolts him back to life with a microwave and toaster in a crude mad-scientist laboratory. The rejuvenated dog terrorizes the nicely-nice neighborhood.

It is the same kind of cookie-cutter suburb that will one day be visited by Edward Scissorhands, a razor-fingered boy stitched together by Vincent Price—who, by the way, was the subject of an animated short Burton made while working at the Disney animation studio when he was fresh out of art school.

Burton's official first film is *Pee-wee's Big Adventure*, a sort of funhouse *Bicycle Thief* starring Pee-wee Herman. *Frankenweenie* got him that gig at age twenty-five and it was finally released on video in 1992.

Frankenweenie (short), 1982
Vincent, (short), 1982
Pee-wee's Big Adventure, 1985
Beetlejuice, 1988
Batman, 1989
Edward Scissorhands, 1990
Batman Returns, 1992
Singles, 1992 (actor)
Nightmare Before Christmas, 1993 (producer)

Director Tim Burton hedging on the well-manicured set of Edward *Scissorhands* (1990).

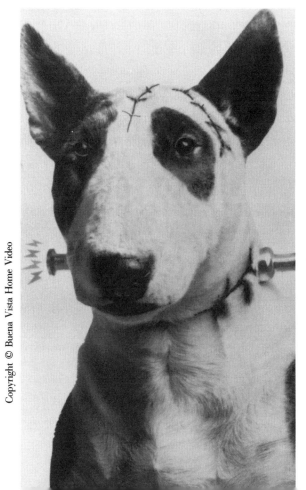

The star of Tim Burton's first movie, *Frankenweenie* (1982), had to suffer the indignities of the makeup chair in order to look effectively like a dog brought back from the dead.

249

FRANCIS FORD COPPOLA

Director
First Film: *Tonight for Sure* (1962)
Video Availability: Video Yesteryear

A man and his dream

Eleanor Coppola likes to tell how she met her husband, Francis, in 1963 on the set of *Dementia 13*, where she was a set designer and he was making his directorial debut.

"He was young and enthusiastic, and wanted to make any film he could," she recalls of the Roger Corman production. Coppola had been working in Europe on another picture with Corman, who went home, leaving Coppola in Ireland with $22,000, a few leftover stars from *The Young Racers*, and a mandate to film Francis's own script. With those materials, he made a creepy black-and-white horror picture about axe murders, insanity, and a tug-of-war over a family inheritance.

"Roger would call from the States and yell into the phone, 'More sex and violence!'" laughs Eleanor.

Actually, Coppola was making good on Corman's call for more sex way before *Dementia 13*, which is erroneously considered his first movie.

While still a student at UCLA, he made a nudie called "The Peeper," about an inept peeping Tom whose clumsy attempts to spy on a nearby photo session end in disaster. He peeps through a telescope and sees only a bellybutton, or some other minor body part. Or, he peeps and trips himself up.

Coppola's footage was combined with another budding filmmaker's giggly nudie, this one with a Western theme. The two stories were vaguely linked with a contrived storyline and two men who are trying to get rid of strip joints because their lives have been ruined by strippers, and then released together with the title *Tonight for Sure*.

Although sex scenes have rarely graced Coppola's multiple-Oscar-winning career, he had a second filmmaking stint in 1962, the same year as *Tonight for Sure*, in which bosoms again figure all too prominently. He filled out a 1958 German picture called *Mit Eva Fing die Sunde* with 3-D segments about a bellboy who dons disguises to infiltrate a roomful of lingerie models.

There is a good amount of Coppola footage in the mix, retitled either *The Playgirls and the Bellboy*, or *The Bellboy and the Playgirls*, depending on the version you find. It's easy to

An importuning Francis Ford Coppola tries to coach one of his actresses on the finer points of her next scene in his first movie, the nudie *Tonight for Sure* (1962). It's a long, long way to *The Godfather*.

locate Coppola's material—it's in color. June Wilkinson is one of the starlets who take every opportunity, or none at all, to remove their bras and giggle while the bellboy does slapstick routines around them, like falling into a tub of water or dressing in drag. Michael Weldon reports in his *Psychotronic Encyclopedia of Film* that ads described Wilkinson as "Staggering—Magnificent—Mighty—Sensational (43-22-36)!"

Unfortunately, Coppola was very shy about directing naked women, and still is. "I have great trepidations about approaching erotic scenes in movies. I think it is a shortcoming, and I think the answer to it is that people like me who feel sexuality is like a mysterious, sacred thing, have a tough time in an industrial setting asking women to take their clothes off," said Coppola after making *Dracula*, in which the occasional bare breast can be glimpsed.

"My mother was sort of a fanatic about having to respect women, and I was brought up believing that if you like a girl, if you make some kind of little pass at her, you'll be disrespecting her. So if the actress said, Oh, I'm going to do it, that's okay; but if I have to ask her, I feel like I'm some dirty old man or something. *One From the Heart* was conceived as having these very hot love scenes, and I just could never ask Teri Garr to take her clothes off, she's so sweet and so nice. And she has a beautiful figure, too."

Coppola recalls the ordeal of shooting naked footage for his second nudie. "There was a 3-D scene where we had to have five girls sitting at their dressers, and they were hired and paid to do this. One of the girls came to me and said, 'I'm only seventeen and my father is going to kill me.' So I said, 'Well, okay, leave your brassiere on.' So there were these four girls, plus one who has a bra on, and I got fired because they were complaining they paid the girls $500. So this has been one of the themes in my life. Maybe when I'm eighty I'll break through the nudity barrier."

Tonight for Sure, 1962
Mit Eva Fingdie Sunde, 1962 (directed segments)
Tower of London, 1962
Dementia 13, 1963
Battle Beyond the Sun, 1963 (as "Thomas Colchart")
The Terror, 1963 (asst. director)
Is Paris Burning?, 1966 (screenplay)
This Property Is Condemned, 1966 (screenplay)
You're a Big Boy Now, 1966
Finian's Rainbow, 1968
The Rain People, 1969
Patton, 1970 (screenplay)
TXH 1138, 1971 (exec. producer)
The Godfather, 1972
American Graffiti, 1973
The Conversation, 1974
The Godfather, Part II, 1974
The Great Gatsby, 1974 (screenplay)
Apocalypse Now, 1979
The Black Stallion, 1979 (exec. producer)
The Escape Artist, 1982 (exec. producer)
Hammett, 1982 (exec. producer)
One From the Heart, 1982
The Black Stallion Returns, 1983 (exec. producer)
The Outsiders, 1983
Rumble Fish, 1983
Mishima: A Life in Four Chapters, 1985 (exec.
    producer)
Captain Eo (short), 1986
Peggy Sue Got Married, 1986
Gardens of Stone, 1987
Lionheart, 1987 (exec. producer)
Tough Guys Don't Dance, 1987 (exec. producer)
Powaqqatsi, 1988 (producer)
Tucker: The Man and his Dream, 1988
New York Stories, "Life Without Zoe," 1989
The Godfather Part III, 1990
Hollywood Mavericks, 1990 (actor)
Central Park (docu), 1990 (actor)
Wind, 1992 (exec. producer)
Bram Stoker's Dracula, 1992
The Secret Garden, 1993 (exec. producer)

WES CRAVEN

Director, Screenwriter
First Film: *Last House on the Left* (1972)
Video availability: Vestron

Reflecting the unseen world

"To avoid fainting," read the apt if not particularly original ad line for *Last House on the Left*, "keep repeating: It's only a movie ... It's only a movie."

Wes Craven's directorial debut, *Last House on the Left*, broke new ground in realistic gore pictures—graphic emasculation scenes weren't so plentiful back in 1972—and is still shocking, primarily because it doesn't have the audience-winking humor his later films developed. The low-budget, unstoryboarded movie includes rape, torture, humiliation, nudity, stabbings, disembowelment, castration, chainsaw murders—and that's only the stuff they left in.

Teenager Mari Collingwood is late coming home for her birthday party, and that's because she and a female friend, while trying to score some marijuana for a night of fun, have been kidnapped, raped, and tortured by escaped convicts. Before killing the girls, they force one to "piss her pants" and both of them to fondle each other. One rapist's saliva clings stickily to Mari's cheek; drool and sticky goo are important components of the Craven oeuvre.

Although Craven and his producer, Sean Cunningham, were deliberately going for shock value, former humanities teacher Craven has said that even he was appalled by some of the stuff in their fly-by-night project. (Portions were filmed in Cunningham's driveway and at Craven's parents' house to save money.)

The movie is notorious for the many scenes—some only hinted at, such as a lesbian scene—that got lost in the transition to an R rating. In fact, Cunningham has admitted that when the movie opened, he merely pasted the Motion Picture Association of America's R rating symbol on the ads instead of submitting it for review.

By now the movie has appeared in so many different forms that it's impossible to reconstruct the original. But the MPAA has had its revenge on Craven. The director's entire career has been spent in one ratings battle after another in a system he feels is prejudiced against the horror genre.

"I am in the business of making intense films and reflecting the unseen world," says the well-spoken Craven. "How can I make my movie less intense just for an R rating, and do I want to? After my experience with *Nightmare on Elm Street*, I wrote the MPAA an impassioned letter, claiming that Bunuel wouldn't have been able to make *The Andalusian Dog*. Lots of artists are interested in bloody and intense subjects, going back to Homer's *Odyssey* with people's eyes being put out by monsters. It's part of the human experience. We should stop that because of some sensitive soul someplace? That's an argument for blandness. I think it's very dangerous."

The hullabaloo over content happens just about every time Craven makes a movie, but he notes that only adults seem to get upset. "The audience I address in my films is teenage, in that volcanic stage of their lives. Older people have squelched those impulses. It's almost like an adult listening to rock music—of course it sounds abrasive, coarse to the ears. But for its audience, it's not. These teens are on the brink of adulthood, of wars, of leaving their parents. They're reevaluating the entire way things are run."

Of all his films, only *The Serpent and the Rainbow* wasn't stamped with an X rating during its first pass through the MPAA. Of the others, Craven's worst experience was with *Deadly Friend*, about a boy who keeps a dead neighbor girl in his garage and brings her back to life, sort of. "I resubmitted that movie thirteen times before we got an R. It was real hell, because the cuts affected a key scene in which Anne Ramsey [playing a cranky old lady across the street] is killed with a basketball. It was grotesque humor and silly. The audience laughed. The scene had to be chopped up, and the movie ended up so painfully cut and hacked, it made me look bad as a filmmaker. You spend a lifetime trying to be a good filmmaker and editor. In the end, they're literally not my films anymore."

One of the MPAA's objections to Craven's work has been its "intensity," an argument originally applied to *A Nightmare on Elm Street*, the first of the series that spawned the long-taloned Freddy Krueger, who stalked teenagers in collective dreams, and who represents, according to Australian filmmaker Philip Brophy, the archetypal child molester, with his wizened face and probing fingers. "There's a scene where Johnny Depp is being pulled into a bed and then a geyser of blood comes out of the bed, similar to what was in *The Shining*, where blood comes out of the elevator. I cut sixteen seconds off of that shot, even though there was no person in it."

Horror filmmakers, according to Craven, actually censor themselves in anticipation of controversy, "all the while being haunted by the feeling that you're cutting more than you have to. It's a very excruciating period for a filmmaker. I'd almost rather cut something they find offensive entirely, even though it's like cutting off my own finger, than tone it down. I'll go down in history as that much less of an intense, less accomplished director."

Therefore, Craven defends *Last House on the Left*. "Horror filmmakers are looked at as wild-eyed exploiters," he says. "I think it's because our culture tends to segregate and deny its own impulses toward violence. We forget about Vietnam and what we did to the Native American Indian. We tend to glorify wars, rather than see them as bloody and political. The culture does not like to take a very hard look at itself. The idea that horror films are legitimate reflections of society, instead of products of a disturbed mind, is too discomforting.

"There are scenes I imagine that I can never put on film, because they'll never get past

Wes Craven directs Amanda Wyss to dream of long-taloned Freddie Krueger in his breakthrough *A Nightmare on Elm Street* (1984). His first film, *Last House on the Left* (1972), was a breakthrough in a different way—it was considered so vile, even Craven had problems with it.

the rating board. Whenever a scene is doing great in the preliminary screening, you figure, oh my god, the MPAA will cut it. I'm always waking up in a cold sweat in the middle of the night, thinking, *I forgot the MPAA!* And my blood runs cold."

Together, 1971 (asst. producer)
You've Got to Walk It Like You Talk It or You'll Lose That Beat, 1971 (editor)
Last House on the Left, 1972 (also screenplay)
The Hills Have Eyes, 1977 (also screenplay)
Summer of Fear, 1978
Deadly Blessing, 1981 (also screenplay)
Swamp Thing, 1982 (also screenplay)
A Nightmare on Elm Street, 1984
The Hills Have Eyes Part II, 1985 (also screenplay)
Deadly Friend, 1986
Flowers in the Attic, 1987 (screenplay)
A Nightmare on Elm Street Part III: Dream Warriors, 1987 (exec. producer, screenplay)
The Serpent and the Rainbow, 1988
Shocker, 1989 (and actor, screenplay, exec. producer)
Bloodfist II, 1990 (advisor)
The People Under the Stairs, 1991

DAVID CRONENBERG

Director, actor, screenwriter
First Film (as director): *They Came From Within*
  (a.k.a. *Shivers*, *The Parasite Murders*, *Frisson*)
  (1975)
Video Availability: Vestron

Body consciousness

*D*irector David Cronenberg's horror movies prey on the frailty of the human body and the deviousness of the human mind. Most of them can be seen as containing metaphors for society's twisted perception of social mores and human nature.

In *The Fly*, made while Cronenberg's father was dying of cancer, Jeff Goldblum's humanity gives way to his baser nature as a housefly's genetic makeup gradually overtakes his body. In *Dead Ringers*, Jeremy Irons plays twin gynecologists who are attached psychologically until death do them part. *Videodrome*, where TV images literally suck

David Cronenberg checks out some special effects for *Scanners* (1981), a movie in which heads explode.

viewers in, is a brilliant satire on media dominance in our culture. In *Naked Lunch*, the William Burroughs–based character has a writer's block so strong that he perceives his typewriter as a gooey, imperious insect.

These movies can all trace their ancestry back to *They Came From Within*, one of the many titles given to Cronenberg's first feature. Set in a sterile, self-contained apartment complex, the movie shows Cronenberg's career-long penchant for disintegrating body parts and slimy special effects.

A phallic-looking parasite invades residents while they are going about the banalities of everyday life—one woman gets it between her legs while in the bathtub, another is infected when the parasite jumps up at her from a washing machine.

The parasite is a combination aphrodisiac and venereal disease, playing on the ambivalence brought about by the sexual revolution. As in *The Fly*, base human nature cannot be kept under wraps, and the more you try to squelch it, the more virulent it becomes. As isolated as the housing complex is, no one is safe—the last shot in the movie is of the residents carpooling into the nearby city to infect the populace at large.

Cronenberg, whose base of operations is still his native Toronto, is by his own account a sensitive, "thin-skinned" person who is "always amazed when people don't like my movies. You know of course that it may happen, but I always show my movies with the utmost naïveté. Because I love them, I expect you to love them. To me, they're not shocking. It's not the Oliver Stone approach to filmmaking."

At first, Cronenberg was loathe to let people see his early work—"my absolutely first films, the shorts, which I rigorously try to kind of suppress." But a retrospective at the Rotterdam Film Festival a few years back was so well received that he changed his mind. "People liked them because they're funny and short. It's really seeing me learning how to make films, since I'm completely self-taught, so those films were really the most primitive and awkward, and I was doing everything myself, from cutting the negative to recording the sound."

Those shorts are *Transfer* and *From the Dream*; after that were two sixty-five-minute films shot in 35-mm, *Stereo* and *Crimes of the Future*. "By that time I was branching out," says Cronenberg, "but I don't watch them now. I can't."

He agrees that everything that can be seen in his later work can be seen in embryo in his early work. "Yeah, I think it's all there. I remember seeing Fellini's directorial debut, a film called *Variety Lights*, when he was considered a neorealist. A character comes onstage, one of those kind of sexually ambivalent amazing grotesques, and that's all *Fellini Satyricon*. All his films can be glimpsed in that early film, just in different proportions. The same is probably true of mine—certainly in *Stereo* and *Crimes of the Future*, and I'd say in *Shivers* too."

Shivers is one of the alternate names for *They Came From Within*, a work that Cronenberg considers "my first *movie*, as opposed to my first *film*. Because it was commercial in the sense that I was being paid to make it, and everybody was a professional. Whereas my earlier short films were very much underground."

Resident of pristine apartment complex comes cheek to jowl with parasite trouble in *They Came From Within* (1975), Cronenberg's first feature film.

Although he doesn't like to play critic after the fact, Cronenberg cites "a real body consciousness" as one of the elements you can find in *Shivers* that is applicable to all his later work. "There's humor, genuine humor within the film, not send-up humor, but black humor. Then there's that body consciousness, a feeling that reality is physical, and I think that's certainly one aspect of my films that is always there in different proportions."

The director says he has always been body-conscious, something that is very natural in childhood. "You'll notice kids very obsessed with their bodies, coming to terms with them. They get a cut and it's a major big deal—the Band-Aids, the blood. And people grow up and later suppress this amazement that they are a physical being. I'm not very paranoid about my physical health—I race cars, and if I were worried about my body's integrity, I wouldn't be doing that. The trick you have as an artist or writer is to allow yourself to tap into things that most people suppressed. When people respond to my movies, at least for the duration of the screening of the film, they have also allowed themselves to relax those inhibitions or sanctions or whatever, and connect with what I'm doing."

As for other images that dominate his movies, Cronenberg is not crazy about needles and finds getting a shot a "freaky" experience, but "I happen to like bugs. I'm amazed when people are repulsed. I swear, it is not my intention to disgust or shock people. The insect world is an incredible and fascinating one. It always amazes me that people think we have to go to outer space to see alien life forms, when we've got them right here. Insects are alive, and yet so totally nonhuman. It's easy to project humanness onto seals and pussycats, but we can't do that with insects, and I suppose that's why I find them so fascinating."

Stereo (short), 1969 (also screenplay)
Crimes of the Future (short), 1970 (also screenplay)
They Came From Within, 1975 (also screenplay)
Rabid, 1977 (also screenplay)
The Brood, 1979 (also screenplay)
Fast Company, 1979 (also screenplay)
Scanners, 1981 (also screenplay)
The Dead Zone, 1983
Videodrome, 1983 (also screenplay)
Into the Night, 1985
The Fly, 1986 (also screenplay)
Dead Ringers, 1988 (also screenplay)
Nightbreed, 1990 (actor)
Naked Lunch, 1991 (also screenplay)
Naked Making Lunch (docu), 1991 (actor)
M. Butterfly, 1993

JONATHAN DEMME

Director, producer, screenwriter
First Film (as director): *Caged Heat* (1974)
Video Availability: New World

An ongoing relationship with "screen violence"

"You're in a house of desperate women here and a long way from home," is the plight of several women at the Connorville Maximum Security Prison, where CPT (Corrective Physical Therapy) is administered by a sadistic doctor. But not before he cops a few feels.

Caged Heat is grade-Z standard issue from the Roger Corman school of genre flicks, with one exception—Jonathan Demme at the helm. Just before he made it, he met Bertolucci for the first time, and according to *Projection: A Forum for Filmmakers*, the master asked Demme whether he was planning to use a lot of long shots, "You know, scenes that don't need editing." It gave Demme pause.

Director Jonathan Demme adjusts the restraints on Anthony Hopkins before filming the part of *The Silence of the Lambs* that was lampooned on the 1992 Oscar show, when emcee Billy Crystal was wheeled onstage wearing a mouthguard. Demme's first effort, *Caged Heat* (1974), wasn't nearly as memorable.

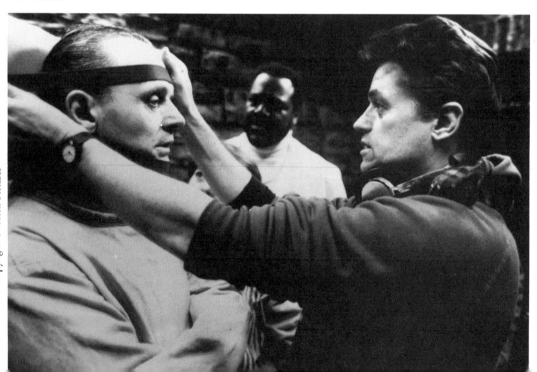

Not that you'd know he consulted with Bertolucci before making *Caged Heat*. With the faintest of exceptions, you'd never be able to tell it was a work by Demme, accompanied by his future cinematographer Tak Fujimoto. The movie features bare breasts, female wrestling, nude solitary confinement, molestation, shoot-outs—plus a few funny lines in Demme's script. ("Correcting human behavior with drugs and surgery...," muses the stony, wheelchair-bound prison matron. "Perhaps I'm just old-fashioned.")

"The only true consistency with the movies I've done so far is hopefully they were done from good scripts," says Demme, reflecting on his career. "As you know, the vast majority of movies are dreadful, mostly because of so few good screenplays. There is a terrible crisis of writing in the motion picture industry. It's laden with talent in all categories except writing."

Demme has retained his gratitude to Corman for giving him his directing start, and gave Corman a cameo in *The Silence of the Lambs* as an FBI chief. "Roger is always in charge. You may be the one directing, but he's still in charge. He's a great guy. I'm very very fond of him. I never get to see him, and one of the few ways to see the tycoon is to cast him in a movie. Roger is always looking for another way to make a little money. When you go to make a deal with him, and tell him, 'Minimum plus a little bit,' he says, 'That's okay, the residuals add up.'"

Making *Caged Heat* wasn't just a foot in the door to Demme. "I learned from Corman. He talks about how good it is to struggle for ways to find good motivation to move the camera, when to slow down. He teaches you a lot of good stuff—basic, important stuff about how to make a movie that audiences will like."

Caged Heat was the last time the feminist director would be unkind to women, but many of his movies, including essentially comic ones like *Something Wild* and *Married to the Mob*, have *Caged Heat*–style streaks of violence. "On the violence front, I do have this ongoing relationship with screen violence, and if you care about violence in society, you inevitably wind up in some conflicts, some dialogue within yourself about it," he explains, his sentences losing focus only when he gets nervous or excited, as anyone knows who watched his Oscar acceptance speech for *The Silence of the Lambs*.

"My big struggle is wanting to be very responsible and show violence when it's called for in a piece, as something horrifying, demeaning, and something which must be prevented by any means necessary. The little-kid moviegoer in me, that grew up loving Westerns and war movies—even though I now know better—still sticks his head out from time to time and gets carried away with a thrilling action scene. I don't get thrilled anymore if there's orgiastic, pornographic, bullet-spraying kind of violence, violence for violence's sake. But a movie professing to have a theme of integrity and has one of those big show-down kind of moments, I can get swept up in that as I have for the past thirty or forty years. I wanted to do that as a filmmaker. I failed at that a lot in *Married to the Mob*, trying to do some exciting, thrilling gunfights. I think I'm a lot more successful in *Silence of the Lambs* because that picture really is antiviolence, clearly antiviolence. It's not a movie that invites you to cheer at violence, it's a movie that makes you dread violence, and when it rears its head, it wants to confirm to you that violence is awful."

Searching in vain for a link from *Caged Heat* to any of Demme's later work turned up one very small item. There is an initial tracking shot down the corridor of jail cells that is the same staging as our first meeting with serial killer Hannibal Lecter in *The Silence of the Lambs*.

Otherwise, the voyeurism and histrionics of *Caged Heat* quickly disappeared from the Demme oeuvre, as if he had endured some Corrective Physical Therapy himself. "With a single twist of the drill, you'll see a mellowing effect," promised the prison doctor of the movie, and sure enough, Demme mellowed and became a masterful, socially and politically conscious artist.

Angels Hard as They Come, 1971 (producer, screenplay)
Black Mama, White Mama, 1972 (story)
The Hot Box, 1972 (producer, screenplay)
Caged Heat, 1974 (also screenplay)
Crazy Mama, 1975
Fighting Mad, 1976 (also screenplay)
Citizens Band/Handle With Care, 1977
The Incredible Melting Man, 1977 (actor)
Roger Corman: Hollywood's Wild Angel, 1978 (actor)
Last Embrace, 1979
Melvin and Howard, 1980
Ladies and Gentlemen, The Fabulous Stains, 1982 (screenplay)
Stop Making Sense, 1984
Swing Shift, 1984 (also screenplay)
Into the Night, 1985 (actor)
Perfect Kiss (short), 1985
Something Wild, 1986 (also screenplay)
Swimming to Cambodia, 1987
Haiti Dreams of Democracy, 1988 (also producer and screenplay)
Married to the Mob, 1988
Miami Blues, 1990 (producer)
Cousin Bobby (docu), 1991 (also actor)
The Silence of the Lambs, 1991

HERK HARVEY

Director, actor
First Film (as director): *Carnival of Souls* (1962)
Video Availability: VidAmerica
(Role: Ghoul)

When you can't fathom what's happening to you

C arnival of Souls opened in 1962 on a double bill at drive-ins with *The Devil's Messenger.*
First-time feature director Herk Harvey, a maker of industrial and educational films, felt confident enough about the film's viability to go off to South America on a shoot. On his return, his small-time distributor reluctantly gave him a check. It bounced.

"That's when I knew I was in trouble," says Harvey, a college film professor who had such a bad experience with distribution on *Carnival of Souls* that he has never made another film to this day, and in fact didn't make any money from it until its "restored" video release a quarter century later.

In the interim, *Carnival of Souls* wouldn't let him rest. Even in the chopped versions that showed up on late-night television or the pirated versions that circulated on video, the horror movie—shot for $30,000 mostly in Harvey's hometown of Lawrence, Kansas—became a cult classic.

It's about a lonely church organist, Mary Henry (Candace Hilligoss, the only professional actor in the cast), who survives a car crash into a river on her way to her new job. She emerges dripping from the watery grave where everyone else in the car died, but from then on, reality seems increasingly unreal. She believes she is being pursued by a phantom figure with a chalk-white face and dark circles under his eyes.

The dark circles may have been justified, since Harvey pulled double duty to direct and also play the ghoul so as to save money on his measly budget. "The makeup I intended to use was eggwhite," recalls Harvey. "What I had hoped to do was put on elaborate makeup that would flake so it looked like it had been in salt water, so when you're walking around and it's drying, the thing is peeling off. But there were restrictions of time, so finally it came down to using regular white greasepaint and darkening the eyes."

The organist finds herself less attracted by the holy church she works in than by a deserted carnival out on the highway; one of the simply spookiest scenes on film is the whirling dance of the ghouls in that empty pleasure palace.

Candace Hilligoss stumbles from the wreckage of a watery grave that claimed the lives of her friends in *Carnival of Souls* (1962), the only movie director Herk Harvey ever made. The eerie outlines of the carnival were superimposed on this publicity still.

"I was driving back home from California one time and as I went past Salt Lake, I saw this place Saltaire, just about the way Mary Henry sees it out the car window in the film. I stopped the car and walked about half a mile to get there, and couldn't believe that this old deserted amusement park was there. The lake had receded from it so it was sitting there just on the salt. It was a fantastic place, it made you feel spooky. The state of Utah let us use it for free, and we hired students from the dance troupe at the university to come do the 'Danse Macabre' and the chase under the pilings; we did that in one afternoon." (The elegant Saltaire later burned down and was completely submerged by the rising water table in the seventies.)

One of the ways in which Harvey creates the sense of Mary's dislocation is to film small scenes without any soundtrack; it enhances the metaphor about a single woman's feeling of isolation in society. When she tries to buy a dress, the sales help ignore her, a common enough experience. And the analysand's greatest fears are confirmed by the scenes in which Mary's entire therapy sessions are conducted with the psychiatrist's back turned.

The mood, enhanced by the black-and-white cinematography and the dismal landscape, is one of unrelenting melancholy. The movie works not only because it is so economical in its use of character and budget, but because it plays on common feelings of insignificance and helplessness.

"The thing to me that's really scary is when something happens in the real world and you're not aware or can't fathom what's happening to you," says Harvey. "It's like someone in the early stages of Alzheimer's disease, thinking something is weird here but I don't know what's going on."

Carnival of Souls, 1962

264

HENRY JAGLOM

Director, actor, editor
First Film (as director): *A Safe Place* (1971)
Video Availability: N/A

It's all in the editing

*H*enry Jaglom says he inherited his arrogance from his father, tempered by his mother's optimistic nature. You might say the first sign of his arrogance shows up on film in *Splendor in the Grass* (1963), the first film in which he had a bit part—"I sat behind Natalie Wood in the classroom, and whenever the camera was on her I'd be busy doing something so I could steal the scene."

Jaglom's arrogance as a director is hated by some and championed by others, because unlike most filmmakers, Jaglom works completely independently of the studios, never makes a movie for more than a million bucks, takes his time—sometimes several years—cutting his films, and encourages his actors to leave the script behind. (And he's his own screenwriter!)

A Safe Place was Jaglom's directorial debut, the only time he would work with a studio and with a predetermined script. Starring Jack Nicholson and Tuesday Weld, it's about a girl who lives in a world where she can't grow up. "That movie spoiled me, because my producer said to me, 'The only person more indulgent than you for making this movie is me for letting you. I'm not going to make you cut it. And I can't possibly make a penny.'"

That last part was certainly true. *A Safe Place* bombed in America and has never been put on video—"it's too expensive to pay for the music rights," says Jaglom. "I didn't make another movie for five years. But I've always made them my way, and I get a lot of pleasure out of it."

Jaglom was an actor, mostly on TV shows, when he helped edit a movie for his friends Dennis Hopper and Jack Nicholson. *Easy Rider* became a counterculture hit, and anyone associated with the movie was considered a potential gold mine. "They let Jack direct *Drive, He Said*, and they let me direct *A Safe Place*. Jack and I had always promised each other we'd be in each other's movies when we became directors. So I was in *Drive, He Said*. But when it came time to make my movie, Jack had just made about a million dollars from *Carnal Knowledge*, and that was the budget of my entire movie. He knew I couldn't afford to pay him, and he didn't want to take a pay cut, so he said, 'Well, you know, I need a new color TV set.' So that's what he was paid for making my movie."

In order to get Columbia's backing, Jaglom showed the studio a tailored script, "very Neil Simonish. But in the middle of the movie, it occurred to me that actors are always being restricted in what they can do, and they have all this wonderful imagination and memory and language. That's how I invented the form of moviemaking I use today. I had Jack and Tuesday Weld in a sex scene, and they were wonderful, but I knew them very well, and I knew they were more interesting than what I wrote for them. So I told them to just continue the scene in their own words. That's improvisation."

Jaglom found then and now that by casting his movie with actors who come from improv— or even just from Alcoholics Anonymous or other self-help groups that encourage confession—he is able to take a theme, shape it into a format, and let his actors run with the ball.

"It's in the editing room that you create the rhythms, sounds, the energy of the movie, the dynamic, and then make it entertaining. I'm getting better at it; when I made *A Safe Place*, I was defiant. I thought nobody's going to let me make a movie again. It's my first movie, and I've gotta put in everything I know about life on this planet."

It's emotions that Jaglom is after, and he will go to great lengths to get them. In *Always*, he detailed the breakup of his marriage and had his real ex-wife play herself opposite him. In *Someone to Love* and *New Year's Day*, he detailed loneliness and fear of starting over. In *Eating*, one of the rare Jaglom films in which he does not appear, women at a birthday party talk about their problems with food and body image, often speaking directly, heart-breakingly, into the camera. In *Venice/Venice*, about a film director's search for a wife, Jaglom actually found his future second wife, Victoria Foyt, among his talking-head interviewees.

"I encourage my actors to open up because I make them feel safe"—he gives them a safe place—"and they know I won't let them look foolish in the finished film. It's not like trying to render on film what you've predetermined, and that's what I discovered while making *A Safe Place*, that in a conventional film, you eliminate yourself. People who love my movies and who hate my movies say the same thing: It's so intimate they feel almost like they're eavesdropping."

Jaglom's closest male friend was the great Orson Welles, who has appeared in several Jaglom films and who gave him three pieces of important advice while he was making *A Safe Place*. First—"the enemy of art is the absence of limitations," a phrase that Jaglom has pasted up on the wall of his editing room. "If you have all the money in the world, you become Steven Spielberg, you go for special effects, you blow up a bridge," says Jaglom. "Without the money, you are forced to create; it creates a kind of nervous creative tension."

Second piece of advice: "Don't listen to anybody, don't let them tell you what to do, don't worry about the audience. You're going to have to live with this movie for the rest of your life. Make it for yourself, and at least you'll never be embarrassed."

And finally: "If the cinematographer doesn't want to do a shot because it's not in the script, if the continuity editor protests and the actors and the producer rebel, just tell them it's a dream sequence. That they understand."

Director Henry Jaglom has always worked independently of the major studios to make the kind of personal, relationship-oriented films he prefers.

Splendor in the Grass, 1963 (actor)
Psych-Out, 1968 (actor)
Easy Rider, 1969 (consultant)
Drive, He Said, 1971 (actor)
The Last Movie, 1971 (actor)
A Safe Place, 1971 (also screenwriter)
The Other Side of the Wind, 1972 (actor) (unreleased)
Hearts and Minds, 1974 (producer)
Lily Aime-Moi, 1974 (actor)
Tracks, 1976 (also screenplay)
Sitting Ducks, 1979 (also actor, screenplay)
National Lampoon Goes to the Movies, 1982

Can She Bake a Cherry Pie? 1983 (also actor)
Always, 1985 (also actor, producer, screenwriter)
Someone to Love, 1987 (also actor, producer, screenwriter)
New Year's Day, 1989 (also actor, producer, screenwriter)
Eating, 1990 (also screenwriter)
Little Noises, 1991 (exec. producer)
Venice/Venice, 1992 (also actor)
Happy Endings, 1993
Lucky Ducks, 1993

SPIKE LEE

Director, actor
First Film (as director): *She's Gotta Have It* (1986)
Video Availability: Island
(Role: Mars Blackmon)

The personal is political

*O*ne of the most deliberately controversial directors today, Spike Lee started out being called (a bit condescendingly) "the black Woody Allen" because of *She's Gotta Have It*, a small black-and-white comedy that does for Brooklyn relationships what *Manhattan* did in another borough.

Lee had previously made an excellent hour-long film, *Joe's Bed-Stuy Barbershop: We Cut Heads*, as a thesis for his film course at NYU. In fact, *Joe's Bed-Stuy*, about a neighborhood barber shop plagued by local black racketeers trying to make it into a betting parlor, contains many of the themes Lee would later explore in his films, whereas he never again made the kind of urbanized drawing-room comedy of *She's Gotta Have It*.

That film is about a woman named Nola Darling who cannot and will not decide among her three jealous lovers. Lee plays one of those lovers, Mars Blackmon, a fast-talking ("Please, baby, please, baby," etc.) jokester who never takes his sneakers off, not even in bed.

On the face of it, *She's Gotta Have It* was feminist in its content; Lee argued that for the first time, it is the woman who is allowed to have the more active sex life. However, the misogyny (or at the very least, lack of understanding of women) that would color Lee's subsequent films has a firm toehold in *She's Gotta Have It*. Nola is so infuriatingly indecisive and so feral in her desires that she frustrates the boyfriends, one of whom finally rapes her. A woman who is raped for being sexually demanding is not exactly a feminist prototype of a liberated woman.

As the first black filmmaker since the era of blaxploitation to have a strong presence in Hollywood, Lee has turned his attention both inward and outward to black problems. *School Daze* (1988), a failed musical, is a diatribe against black ambivalence over skin tone. *Jungle Fever* takes the skin-tone problem wider to address the origins and ramifications of interracial relationships, with Wesley Snipes and Annabella Sciorra as the scorned couple; Lee's own father married a Jewish white woman, who is not on Lee's hit parade of favorite relatives.

268

Lee's political films have created unending controversy, first with *Do the Right Thing*, which can be read as an encouragement to blacks to overthrow white society, but which is hampered in that message by the director's own seeming ambivalence about race, class, and the New York social powder keg. And Lee waged a bitter but ultimately successful battle with Warners to finish *Malcolm X* the way he wanted it—including a lengthy running time and a continuation of filming after the budget ran out, thanks to contributions from wealthy blacks in the entertainment community.

All of Lee's movies are individual, stylish, and beautifully photographed by Ernest Dickerson. They are also angry and frequently ambivalent, with strains of racism, sexism, and anti-Semitism. (In an essay in the *New York Times*, Lee partially defended the hateful Jewish stereotypes in *Mo'Better Blues* by saying that since blacks have long been stereotyped in Hollywood films, it was unfair to criticize him.)

"To tell you the truth, stuff like that only makes you stronger," says Lee of the heat he gets. "I do the best I can; that's really all you *can* do. And my heart is in the right place. You just know that there are always going to be detractors out there. But I think that I have more supporters than detractors."

Lee is defensive in interviews, sometimes more so than others. At one of three meetings with him, he was playfully hostile; at another, genuinely hostile. He comes to interviews positive that whatever he is asked, the questions would be different for a white director. "It's not my responsibility to provide an answer or a cure for racism," he says in a preemptive strike to ward off any questions on the subject. "I don't know if you could look to me, or any artist, to provide an answer to social ills that affect us all. As artists, we're there to raise the issues and hold the mirror up. I don't have any answers per se."

In a career based on politically relevant issues, *She's Gotta Have It* stands in stark contrast. "I think there wasn't that much social stuff in *She's Gotta Have It*. But again, this comes to a double standard. Why shouldn't African-American filmmakers be allowed to make films that reflect their experience? After my first two films, I was often asked by many white journalists, when was I going to have white people in my films? I know that is a question they would never ask Woody Allen."

The success of Spike Lee's modest independent feature *She's Gotta Have It* (1986) enabled the controversial director to cross over to the studios, where he commands large budgets and continues to maintain much control over his work.

269

Actually, many would ask Allen that and worse if the filmmaker would just agree to sit for an interview.

"I consider myself a filmmaker and I try to learn my craft, get better command of my craft. The technique of *She's Gotta Have It* was really determined by the budget. I had no money, so I had to cut corners but still make the film cinematic and interesting. One of the quickest ways to light anything is to have somebody stare into a camera; it doesn't take two hours to light that. We shot the film in twelve days."

Actors tactfully note that Lee is not the most communicative director. "I don't think there's any need for actors and directors in the middle of the shoot to go off in the corner for a story conference with a hundred people waiting," says Lee.

And when he's acting in his own movie, he defers to longtime cinematographer Dickerson. "Of all the things I do as a filmmaker, acting is the thing I like the least. When I'm in front of the camera acting, Ernest is really like my director, and he tells me how to be successful at what I'm trying to do."

Lee's success has spawned a whole generation of exciting young black filmmakers, but he says Hollywood needs even more of them before they'll be completely accepted as a group. "It shouldn't be a situation where if you don't like *my* films, there are not other black filmmakers to see. There should be black filmmakers who do animated films, PG-rated films, science fiction, all that. I only make the movies that appeal to me."

Joe's Bed-Stuy Barbershop: We Cut Heads (short), 1982
  (also producer, screenwriter)
She's Gotta Have It, 1986 (also actor, producer,
  screenwriter)
School Daze, 1988 (also actor, producer, screenwriter)
Do the Right Thing, 1989 (also actor, producer,
  screenwriter)
Making "Do the Right Thing," 1989 (actor) docu
Mo' Better Blues, 1990 (also actor, producer,
  screenwriter)
Lonely in America, 1990 (actor)
Jungle Fever, 1991 (also actor, producer, screenwriter)
Malcolm X, 1992 (also actor, producer, screenwriter)
The Last Party, 1993 (actor)

BARRY LEVINSON

Director, screenwriter
First Film (as director): *Diner* (1982)
Video Availability: MGM/UA Home Video

Overlapping dialogue; "the thing you do with the thing"

*I*f you look sharp, there is a brief scene in Barry Levinson's *Avalon* in which the young boy looks out the rear window of a car and notices a diner going up, one of those old-fashioned types that look like a railroad car. The young boy is the future director, who will start his career by making *Diner*, a funny, tender, autobiographical look at a group of guys coming of age in 1950s Baltimore.

The guys hang out at a local diner, where they talk about girls, sex, life, and TV shows. (See ELLEN BARKIN.)

One of the distinctive touches that gives *Diner* its homey feel is the pastiche of overlapping dialogue. Like real people, these characters interrupt each other, dangle sentences, talk with their mouths full, segue from topic to topic.

"You try to bring it out in the actors by creating a fairly loose set, so the actor feels he has

Director Barry Levinson (left) lines up the shots in more ways than one on his first film, *Diner* (1982), here with Steve Guttenberg and Timothy Daly.

a great deal of freedom," says Levinson, whose friendly, open face is framed by graying hair, slightly darker eyebrows, and glasses.

"I'll say, look, don't worry about whatever it may be. Obviously I don't want all these people talking so I can't hear anything and it becomes chaotic. But between it becoming more manicured and where it becomes a little looser, it starts to develop. Once they get used to it, it becomes fairly natural, so it doesn't always have that over professional kind of quality, where everyone says their line in a clean way."

Diner proved a career boost for Mickey Rourke, Daniel Stern, and Kevin Bacon. It was probably the best movie STEVE GUTTENBERG has ever made.

The overlap style is not so noticeable in Levinson's more mainstream movies, like *Good Morning, Vietnam*, in which Robin Williams as a Vietnam disc jockey dominates both the airwaves and the movie; or the Tom Cruise–Dustin Hoffman starrer *Rain Man*, which won four Oscars, including one for directing; or the much-nominated *Bugsy*, with Warren Beatty as the famous gangster gone Hollywood.

But in his trilogy of Baltimore-based films, including *Tin Men* and *Avalon*, Levinson further developed the folksy, Altmanesque dialogue rhythms he began in *Diner*.

"Barry says, 'I didn't write that scene very good, I'm just going to turn on the camera and you ramble,'" explains Elizabeth Perkins, who worked with Levinson on *Avalon*. "People asked why I'd wanted to work with a man who isn't known for good women's roles, but gee, he's known for letting actors do what they do best. Barry is completely about characters and about performances, and still makes a beautifully cinematic movie. And he leaves nothing over on the cutting room floor."

Levinson believes he must turn out a mainstream hit every time he wants to alternate with a small, personal film like *Diner* because otherwise the studios won't advance him the money. Like the moneymen, he has "mixed feelings, because I don't think we are basically used to having movies that are semiautobiographical in America."

At any rate, Levinson seems to have figured out the formula for keeping both himself and Hollywood happy. Perkins says it has to do with the director's abilities with his actors. "He can relate much better to actors than a lot of directors I've worked with," she says. "I know he's not going to con me. He knows what to say. He says, 'Cut! The thing you do with the thing, that's good. The thing you did with that other thing? Don't do that.'"

The Internecine Project, 1974 (screenplay)
Street Girls, 1974 (screenplay, asst. camera)
Silent Movie, 1976 (actor, screenplay)
High Anxiety, 1977 (actor, screenplay)
And Justice for All, 1979 (screenplay)
Inside Moves, 1980 (screenplay)
History of the World Part I, 1981 (actor)
Best Friends, 1982 (screenplay)
Diner, 1982 (also screenplay)
Unfaithfully Yours, 1983 (screenplay)
The Natural, 1984
Young Sherlock Holmes, 1985

Good Morning, Vietnam, 1987
Tin Men, 1987 (also screenplay)
Rain Man, 1988 (also actor)
Avalon, 1990 (also screenplay, producer)
Bugsy, 1991
Journey of Hope, 1991 (co-presenter)
Kafka, 1991 (exec. producer)
Sniper, 1992 (exec. producer)
Bob Roberts, 1992 (co-presenter)
Toys, 1992 (also screenplay)
Wilder Napalm, 1993 (co-producer)

DAVID LYNCH

Director
First Film: *Eraserhead* (1977)
Video Availability: Columbia TriStar Home Video

Open to interpretation

A director who likes to get under the skin of things, David Lynch's first movie features a
baby who is born without a skin, with all of its need and hideousness exposed. The
surreal, black-and-white *Eraserhead* is full of the kind of nightmare imagery and existential
horror that Lynch would use in all his films. Though he frequently claims to have had a
"normal," happy-go-lucky midwestern childhood, his movies are obsessed with the seamy

Jack Nance is having a tough time with fatherhood in the surreal, unpleasant *Eraserhead* (1977),
David Lynch's first film and a cult favorite.

underbelly of ordinary life. *Eraserhead* is the kind of early work that would naturally lead to a *Blue Velvet*.

Jack Nance plays Henry, the man with the famous tilt-topped hairdo, who at one point will imagine his brain and hair being put to use as the rubout end of a pencil. He is forced to marry his epileptic girlfriend, Mary, when her parents discover she has given birth—to a mewling creature that looks like a slimy version of E.T. (Lynch also created the special effects.) The thing's constant need for attention and care sends Mary packing and eventually drives Henry to kill it.

Just as in *Blue Velvet*, which revealed the literal and figurative bugs behind the placid facade of suburban life and sexuality, *Eraserhead* operates on two levels—the normal and the perversion of the normal, the latter of which may be the more realistic. The dialogue is completely banal stuff—"Is there any mail?" "No"—but delivered in such a vacuum of squalor, despair, and eerie pauses that it loses all context and meaning, and in fact begins to sound informally ominous. When Henry comes home to meet Mary's parents, a conversation about his line of work continues without missing a beat even though Mary suffers an epileptic fit during it.

The Kafkaesque daytimes and Bosch-like nightmares of *Eraserhead* can be found again in Lynch's work, particularly in *Twin Peaks: Fire Walk With Me*, the movie that takes his own trendy but short-lived TV series further than television dares to go. Themes of sexual molestation and transmogrification abound.

In interviews, Lynch is politely opaque. "I don't like to give interpretations. I have my own version of everything, and when I'm working, I answer to myself. I'm against a film that makes one interpretation."

He says he doesn't blame audiences for walking out, although he did tone down parts of *Wild at Heart* after test screenings. "Once you've already 'gotten' something, and there's more, it's like shoving something down your throat. That's when you get angry, and you say enough is enough. It goes beyond telling a story into a form of abuse."

Lynch's fascination with the dark side of people gets another cheery rationale. "They're not really sick," muses Lynch. "I think what happens is, like Rodney Dangerfield says, the only normal people are the ones we don't know. You meet somebody, and they seem normal, and then you get to know them, and just like in films the negative things stand out more than the positive things. You're more shocked by discovering something negative in them, and it's upsetting. What's really happening is, there's all sorts of negative things and all sorts of positive things, and a strange kind of war between them."

Lynch on the awful hallucinations to which his characters are in thrall: "Abstractions exist all around us anyway, and they sometimes conjure up a thrilling experience."

He is less benign when defending a filmmaker's right to portray what's vile: "If we didn't want to upset anyone, we could make films about sewing—and even *that* could be dangerous. I believe in very strong films and I don't apologize one bit, as long as there's a balance."

274

The audiences at the Cannes Film Festival, which rewarded Lynch for *Wild at Heart* but were more ambivalent toward the *Twin Peaks* movie, seemed bothered by Lynch's predilection for violence. "I don't know why there's violence in American films, probably because there's a lot of violence everywhere, in the air. I believe in it, but I don't want to champion it. Maybe I'd have to spend a long time with a psychiatrist to know why I like it."

The Alphabet (short), 1968
The Grandmother (short), 1970
Eraserhead, 1977 (also producer, screenplay, special
    effects)
The Elephant Man, 1980 (also screenplay, sound
    design)
Dune, 1985 (also screenplay)
Blue Velvet, 1986
Weeds, 1987 (song)
Zelly and Me, 1988 (actor)
Hollywood Mavericks, 1990 (actor)
Wild at Heart, 1990 (also screenplay)
The Cabinet of Dr. Ramirez 1991 (exec. producer;
    uncredited)
Twin Peaks: Fire Walk With Me, 1992 (also screenplay)
Hugh Hefner: Once Upon a Time (docu), 1992 (co-
    producer)

PENNY MARSHALL

Director, actress
First Film (as director): *Jumpin' Jack Flash* (1986)
Video Availability: Fox Video

The school of negativity and depression

*A*fter being summarily tossed off the set of *Peggy Sue Got Married*, Penny Marshall was summarily dumped onto the set of *Jumpin' Jack Flash*, a lame comedy in which computer operator Whoopi Goldberg helps a spy who has been blackballed by his embassy.

Her close friend Debra Winger had asked Marshall to direct her in *Peggy Sue*, but she was dropped as too inexperienced three weeks into production, and Winger left shortly thereafter with back problems.

Inexperience didn't stand in her way, though, when she was brought aboard *Jumpin' Jack Flash* ten days into shooting. One of the difficulties, aside from the lackluster script, is that Goldberg has entire scenes all by herself, since the spy she is assisting communicates only via computer modem. Goldberg's facility with an empty stage in her own one-woman Broadway show didn't seem to help.

Penny Marshall lines up a shot on *Jumpin' Jack Flash* (1986), a movie she was dumped onto 10 days after shooting commenced. Marshall belongs to the select school of directing by whining; it must be effective, since she is the only female director whose movies have passed the magic $100 million mark at the box office. (Not *this* movie, however.)

Photofest

A worse problem presented itself in the technical arena. Marshall was accustomed to the three-camera setup of TV shows, and the crew quickly saw that she knew little about lenses and lighting. What saved her was her coterie of film heavies—like her pal James L. Brooks (*Broadcast News*) and ex-husband Rob Reiner—who visited the set frequently. The kindest thing one can say about the finished product is that it is adequate—or in the words of WHOOPI GOLDBERG, "It doesn't cure cancer."

"The movie had already been shooting under a different director and Penny had only three days to prepare, and she had never directed before," says longtime friend Jon Lovitz, who had a small role in *Jumpin' Jack Flash* ("It wasn't even a part, it was just filler, but she's very loyal to her friends") and later did another small role as a baseball talent scout in Marshall's *A League of Their Own*.

"It was an impossible job. But she knows what she's doing now, she gets the people she wants, the cast, the crew, she has become a lot more confident. She does a lot of 'coverage' so she can have a lot of choices in the editing room. And that's very fair to the actors—everybody gets their close-up, everybody gets their shot, not just the main characters."

Ironically, Marshall would have a chance at *Peggy Sue* material after all. *Peggy Sue* was about a woman who goes back in time to reexperience her teenage years; Marshall made *Big*, about a boy who experiences manhood overnight. She got the assignment when another pal, Steven Spielberg, discarded it.

Harrison Ford was penciled in for the lead, then Robert DeNiro; ultimately, Tom Hanks made a splash in the role, and *Big* became the first movie made by a woman to top the magical $100-million mark. (Hanks reappeared as a soused baseball coach in *A League of Their Own*.)

Marshall finally snared DeNiro for *Awakenings*, based on a true story about a medical experiment that briefly brought comatose patients back to life. *Awakenings* bears some resemblance to *Big*—both are stories about little boys who awaken to find themselves grown men. "I'm still trying to wake up to adulthood," admits Marshall. "I tend to be interested in things that don't quite fit in, or people who are"—she grimaces, stammers, and fidgets—"*uncomfortable* in their surroundings. I guess part of me feels slightly uncomfortable, so I identify. I'm a female director in a male-dominated business...I always felt a little different, in a sense, because I always wanted to look like everybody else."

She certainly doesn't talk like everybody else. But Marshall insists that her self-effacing style, trailing sentences, and distinctive Bronx whine are not due to lack of conviction. "I'm low-key, almost inaudible sometimes," she says. "Sometimes I don't know the proper words to say, I just say do it again, I'll know it when I see it."

This peculiar style of directing has become as much her trademark as Alfred Hitchcock's intimidation of his leading ladies. Director Garry Marshall (*Pretty Woman*) has described his sibling's technique as, "Penny will go up to an actor and say, 'Please do it this way, I have a headache and I'm gonna throw up.' But she always knows what she's doing."

Marshall too is quick with the jokes. She comes from a funny family, married into a funnier one, and has surrounded herself with funny people. She was born Penny Marscharelli, the youngest of three, in 1943. A dilettantish life led to an early marriage to a college football hero, an early child (Tracy, now a mother herself), an early divorce, and a short-lived stint as a secretary. She arrived on her already famous brother's doorstep, and when she hit rock bottom by playing the "homely girl" opposite Farrah Fawcett in a shampoo ad, Garry and his TV empire rescued her.

Known for her TV comedy roles as Oscar's secretary, Myrna Turner, on "The Odd Couple" and the blue-collar Laverne on "Laverne and Shirley," Marshall had planned to branch out by directing *The Joy of Sex*, but her friend and movie lead John Belushi died of a drug overdose. She did, however, direct four episodes of "Laverne and Shirley."

Crews on her early movies grumbled about Marshall's apparent indecisiveness, but *Big* coproducer Robert Greenhut chalked it up to sexism. By the time *Big* rolled around, Marshall was resisting male pressure to add sex scenes, substituting instead a sweet moment in which Tom Hanks turns the light back on to better appreciate his first view of an adult female breast.

She subsequently turned down *White Palace*, *Mermaids*, and a slew of "high concept" comedies, settling on *Awakenings* and then *A League of Their Own*.

She insists that she spends her spare time in bed, hiding. "I'm from the negativity and depression school," she jokes. "I'm terrified that I'll make mistakes or find out that I don't know anything."

How Sweet It Is, 1968 (actor)
The Savage Seven, 1968 (actor)
How Come Nobody's on Our Side? 1975 (actor)
1941, 1979 (actor)
Movers & Shakers, 1985 (actor)
Jumpin' Jack Flash, 1986
Big, 1988
Awakenings, 1990
The Hard Way, 1991 (actor)
A League of Their Own, 1992
Calendar Girl, 1993 (exec. producer)

MIKE NICHOLS

Director, producer
First Film: *Who's Afraid of Virginia Woolf?* (1966)
Availability: Warner Home Video

Breaking the language barrier

Mike Nichols, who became a hit in cabarets and on Broadway with his comedy partner
Elaine May, was a successful Broadway director in 1966 when he agreed to break into
films with *The Graduate*, which would earn him a directing Oscar. But he held back making
The Graduate in favor of *Who's Afraid of Virginia Woolf?* in which real-life marrieds
Elizabeth Taylor and Richard Burton bludgeon each other with words and mind games for

Mike Nichols lines up a shot of Dustin Hoffman in the pool, one of many alienating techniques in
The Graduate (1967), the movie Nichols nearly made his debut on. Instead, he started the previous
year with *Who's Afraid of Virginia Woolf?*

129 minutes. It was one of Bette Davis's great disappointments that she didn't get the lead, and when Taylor says, "What a *dump*," she is doing a Davis impression.

Adapted from the Edward Albee play, *Who's Afraid of Virginia Woolf?* broke new territory for adult language and behavior on film. Burton and Taylor, whose own married life was said to be just as stormy, play academic couple George and Martha—the movie was filmed at Smith College—whose nightly war of words and humiliation sucks in and eviscerates their houseguests of the evening, Sandy Dennis and George Segal. (Dennis and Taylor both won Oscars.)

Albee was sour on the adaptation, citing the addition of two non-Albee lines, which he described as: "Let's go to the roadhouse!" and "Let's go back from the roadhouse!" "That's called 'opening up' the play for movies," he sneered.

The erudite Nichols, who with his sharp, refined nose and regal yet relaxed bearing would look at home in a velvet smoking jacket, says he never looks back at his movies. "It's a little bit like looking at yourself in the mirror. I just say, yeah, well, that's right, that's what we did. I have no reaction." But he graciously consented to meditate briefly on his first film. "I would say, if you force me to look, that *Who's Afraid of Virginia Woolf?* is a love story, and I knew it then and the more distance we have in looking back the clearer it is now. That the first, second, and third things you see about it is how rough they are on each other, but after that you realize they're deeply in love. That it's about their love. That without their love there's no story at all," says Nichols.

"I think that was slightly more evident in the picture than in the play, not because of anything I did, but because you took the audience away. With an audience, it's a prizefight, competing for the audience's laughs. Take away the audience and they're alone, just like George and Martha are in fact alone. And when that happens to them, because a movie is different from a play, we saw that they loved each other, that this was a way of finding a new way to love each other. I think to some extent my pictures have always been about that."

The lovers in Nichols pictures are not the type to embrace in slow-motion amid a field of daisies. If his films are about love, they are also about how hard it is to find it and keep it in a world where values are so thin. There's Jack Nicholson at the end of the wryly bleak *Carnal Knowledge* (1971), so screwed up by his screwing of women that he can't have sex unless a prostitute puts him through an elaborate ego-bolstering routine; pregnant Meryl Streep as the last person in Washington, D.C., to learn that her husband (Nicholson) is having an affair with an ambassador's long-necked wife in *Heartburn* (1986); Melanie Griffith achieving the ultimate Electra-complex fantasy by replacing her boss (Sigourney Weaver) in the boardroom and the bedroom in *Working Girl* (1988); Streep again as a recovering addict under the supervision of the showbiz mom (Shirley MacLaine) who drove her to drugs in the first place in *Postcards From the Edge* (1990); Harrison Ford awake from his coma and returning to the bed of a wife (Annette Bening) he doesn't even remember in *Regarding Henry* (1991).

The love between George and Martha in *Who's Afraid of Virginia Woolf?* is only apparent after a lengthy and horrifying descent into the vortex of their marriage; Nichols has an innate infrared detector for the complexities of relationships. And it is his ability to set these relationships within a social and moral context that enables his pictures to transcend their characters to work as trenchant, often bitterly funny social satire. *The Graduate* articulated a new generation's alienation with extreme wit, not only in Nichols's handling of the actors, but in the camera work that shot Dustin Hoffman in his isolation from within the disorienting murk of a fish tank or a swimming pool, from under the stockinged leg of Anne Bancroft in the foreground, from beyond a pane of glass that separates his anguished Christ-like image from the altar where Katherine Ross is marrying a rival.

Nichols movies really *are* postcards from the edge, *with* an edge. With his comedian's timing and keen eye for human foible, a Nichols love story is sophisticated and bittersweet. "I only have one thing I can compare things to, and that's life," says Nichols, who escaped from Nazi Germany at an early age with his parents. "If you don't have reality as a referent, I don't know what you turn to. I'm interested in human behavior."

Nichols's early works—*Who's Afraid of Virginia Woolf? The Graduate, Catch-22*, and *Carnal Knowledge*—were more ambitious projects, speaking for entire ranges of human entanglements and stretched against broad, often crazy social canvases. He has made good films since then, like *Silkwood*, starring Meryl Streep as the real-life whistle-blower on a nuclear parts plant. But his later films seem narrower in scope.

"Lately, because maybe I don't have the energy that I used to have, I'm more drawn to story, to forward motion and plot, because it's such a relief to be able to rest on the plot. For somebody who's always been juggling in order to invent a story when my concern is behavior, it's a great pleasure to have a plot like *Working Girl* or *Regarding Henry*," says Nichols. "I identify very strongly with New Yorkers who get the Häagen-Dazs out of the fridge and get back on the bed to watch television and call their friends to say, 'Are you watching Channel 13?' Because I think that's life for a lot of people, and it would be for me if I hadn't been lucky in my personal life and my work life. That's what I would be doing, without any question. Suspended animation is my basic state."

Who's Afraid of Virginia Woolf? 1966
Bach to Bach, 1967 (actor)
The Graduate, 1967
Catch-22, 1970
Carnal Knowledge, 1971 (also producer)
The Day of the Dolphin, 1973
The Fortune, 1975
Gilda Live, 1980
Silkwood, 1983 (also producer)

Heartburn, 1986 (also producer)
The Longshot, 1986 (executive producer)
Biloxi Blues, 1988
Working Girl, 1988
Postcards from the Edge, 1990 (also producer)
Regarding Henry, 1991 (also producer)
Remains of the Day, 1993 (exec. producer)
Wolf, 1993

SAM RAIMI

Director
First Film: *The Evil Dead* (1980)
Video Availability: HBO Home Video

Bag of horror tricks

*P*recocious horror filmmaker Sam Raimi debuted at the Cannes Film Festival in 1983, where *The Evil Dead* sprouted fans the way a tree branch that rapes a girl in the movie sprouts ever-more-thorny tendrils. It became a cult hit, spawned a similarly low-budget sequel, and made Raimi a wunderkind among gore fans.

The Evil Dead borrows heavily from horror-movie lore ("I study horror movies for their construction," says Raimi) to create a campy, scary scenario in a woodland cabin. Two teen couples are terrorized and hacked up when they accidentally reawaken long-dead evil spirits, represented more often than not by a low-to-the-ground point-of-view camera zooming determinedly through the underbrush and up to the cabin windows.

Raimi's comic-book influences are very clear in *The Evil Dead* and show up again with a bigger budget in *Darkman*, his breakthrough mainstream hit. In *Evil Dead* and its even campier sequel, severed hands play a big role, and in *Darkman*, Liam Neeson not only loses his looks in an acid flash fire, he loses his hand too and needs to graft a new one with special cloning technology; the creator's hand attacking himself.

Raimi delights in making the mundane scary. Normal household implements take on the kind of menace they do to a baby in a crib—insinuating clocks, wild porch swings, mysterious cellar doors, changeable mirrors.

Raimi jokes that he could have gone into furniture or been "the bra king of Michigan," since his father owns a furniture store and his mother runs Lulu's Braworld, "the largest bra shop in the world." Instead, his dad gave him an 8-mm camera when he was a kid, and he experimented right up into college, where he organized film groups and developed a tight core of filmmaking friends who still work with him. His older brother, Ivan, cowrote *Darkman* with him, and he gleefully put his younger brother, Ted, in a sweltering rubber suit for *Evil Dead II*, then buried him under a mound of dirt. "It was 120 degrees outside, and he was twenty degrees warmer in the suit, so we had to keep airing him out," says Raimi.

His early game plan? "Action-comedy was my first love, but no matter how badly you make horror movies, they always find a market, so that's the safest way to lure investors."

Directing is a hands-on job, and Sam Raimi sports waders for some of the swampland shooting of *The Evil Dead* (1980). For *The Evil Dead 2*, he spread the discomfort around by putting his brother Ted in a sweltering monster suit.

Still, he used care and ingenuity to make his first movie. "Putting in just a bunch of scary things doesn't work," he says. "What is scary is identifying with a character or situation, then putting him in danger, then building suspense, then punctuating it with a scare. Give them what they want, but not what they expect."

The boyishly handsome Raimi drew on everything from *Night of the Living Dead* to *The Beast With Five Fingers* to the Three Stooges to make the witch's brew that is *The Evil Dead*. "You could say it's an homage, or you could say I ripped them off," says Raimi evenhandedly. "I just know that *The Wizard of Oz* scared the *grunt* out of me. *Hey, get away from those apples!*"

For the language contained in the Book of the Dead, which figures in both *Evil Dead* movies, Raimi used "bits of Latin, Hebrew, pig Latin, kind of mushed together into fake words, like an ancient tongue. That stuff scares me."

Other things that scare him: "The abstract terror of pictures like *The Tenant* frightens me, when a character thinks everyone is trying to drive him insane, or abstractions of nightmarish imagery. Also the real subtle things, such as when you realize a character you've been following is very nasty and thinks very unpure and evil thoughts."

His aim with *The Evil Dead* was "to scare 'em and entertain 'em the best I can, by pulling every trick out of my bag."

The Evil Dead, 1980 (also screenwriter)
Crimewave, 1985 (also screenwriter)
Spies Like Us, 1985 (actor)
Evil Dead II: Dead by Dawn, 1987 (also screenwriter)
Thou Shalt Not Kill...Except, 1987 (actor)
Maniac Cop, 1988 (actor)
Easy Wheels, 1989 (exec. producer)
Intruder, 1989 (actor)

Darkman, 1990 (also screenplay)
Night Crew, 1991 (actor)
Miller's Crossing, 1990 (actor)
Innocent Blood, 1992 (actor)
Lunatics, a Love Story, 1992 (coproducer)
Army of Darkness, 1993
The Nutty Nut, 1993 (cowriter)
Tamakawa, 1993 (actor)

GEORGE ROMERO

Director
First Film: *Night of the Living Dead* (1968)
Video Availability: Various (public domain)

Zombies, consumerism, and the bottom line

*T*he scene is familiar. It is a bunch of men and women, walking slowly, arms outstretched, grasping for something. Are they zombies arisen from the dead, scavenging for human flesh?

No, they are the shareholders who helped George Romero fund his first movie, and now they want their due.

Night of the Living Dead never made any appreciable money for the original shareholders. Romero lost control of the movie and it went into public domain. Not until the 1990 remake did the investors recoup.

Who knew at the time that *Night of the Living Dead* would become a cult favorite, a horror movie whose simplicity, gore, and startling imagery would inspire years of deconstructionist theory and scores of imitators? In 1968 Romero had simply wanted to break into filmmaking, and the conventional wisdom was that horror was the easiest entrée. Although he has made several movies since and has not lacked for work, his first movie remains his best—certainly his most famous.

Shot in black and white on an extremely low budget in Romero's native Pittsburgh, the movie is about zombielike corpses that rise from their graves to eat human flesh. A band of bickering survivors hole up in a farmhouse, nailing wooden slats across the windows and arguing over leadership and strategy. The scene of the zombies stumbling inexorably toward

The zombies come out to play and eat human body parts in George Romero's seminal *Night of the Living Dead* (1968), the movie for which Romero remains revered.

the farmhouse, arms outstretched for a little something as if they were immigrants, beggars, or outsiders, is a classic.

Night of the Living Dead expanded the parameters of acceptable gore on-screen, with zombies gnawing on stringy raw meat on the lawn. But it made bigger statements too, about society's us-versus-them mentality, about consumerism (a theme Romero would later explore in more detail), and about racism—particularly since the black hero who manages to survive the horrors of the night is shot in broad daylight by trigger-happy lawmen who have come to the rescue.

Soon, people were reading into the movie far more than Romero ever planned. The movie not only spawned sequels and a financially motivated remake by Romero himself, but endless doctoral theses too.

"Speaking from my own standpoint, a lot of things in the first film were sort of unconscious and came out of just whatever our attitudes were at the time, whereas the remake was sort of a lot more conscious," says the voluble Romero. "The first time, when we cast Wayne Jones, he just happened to be a black man. We chose him because he was the best actor from among our group of friends, who were the only people we could sucker into being in the movie, because they weren't being paid. Whatever extent we were socially conscious about it, we didn't change the script because he was black."

And the use of black and white, so symbolic in many of the critiques of the film, was simply a budgetary decision: It was cheaper than color stock. In fact, Romero talks more about the bottom line than he does the meaning of his movies.

"The original *Night of the Living Dead* is why I'm here, why I have a career," he says. "I have a fond spot in my heart for it despite the rough road we have been over, despite rip-offs and everything else. How can I feel anything but grateful? It brought me a tremendous amount of attention, and it's really why I'm alive. Now I'd like nothing better than to sit back and smile and see three or four more sequels be made and all of us collect a few bucks. I don't want it to sound like it's all altruistic, we're trying to make a couple of dollars!"

He and twenty-seven other people put up about $125,000 for the original, and eventually made back about a million. "No one gets rich when there are twenty-eight people sharing," he says. "And there's been some expenses for lawyers, things like that. There has never been a lot of money spread around. But at least the people involved in the first film probably made more just in the initiation of the remake than they made over the entire twenty years from the last film, as a group. They are entitled to a profit percentage."

Night of the Living Dead, 1968
There's Always Vanilla, 1971
Hungry Wives, 1972 (also screenplay)
The Crazies, 1973
Martin, 1978
Dawn of the Dead, 1978 (also actor, screenplay)
Knightriders, 1981 (also screenplay)
Creepshow, 1982
Day of the Dead, 1985 (also screenplay)
Flight of the Spruce Goose, 1986 (also screenplay)
Creepshow 2, 1987 (screenplay)
Lightning Over Braddock: A Rustbowl Fantasy, 1988 (actor)

Monkey Shines: An Experiment in Fear, 1988 (also screenplay)
Two Evil Eyes, "The Facts in the Case of Mr. Valdemar," 1990 (also screenplay)
Tales from the Darkside, the Movie, 1990 (screenplay, "The Cat from Hell")
Night of the Living Dead, 1990 (exec. producer; screenplay)
The Silence of the Lambs, 1991 (actor)
The Dark Half, 1991 (unreleased)

MARTIN SCORSESE

Director
First Film: *Who's That Knocking at My Door?* (1967)
Video Availability: Warner Home Video

Italianamerican

Who's That Knocking at My Door? begins with Martin Scorsese's own mother, Catherine, baking a nice Italian dinner for the family. From the beginning, Scorsese's work would be grounded in his Catholic, Italian-American, Little Italy upbringing, and in fact Mama Scorsese has appeared in bit parts in several of his films as a cogent reminder of the childhood that shaped the director's sensibilities.

Scorsese is famous for his asthmatic childhood. Confined to his bed much of the time, he watched hours and hours of movies on television. The result is a comprehensive knowledge of film and an innate grasp of film language.

The NYU film school graduate made several shorts—including the cheerfully bloody *The Big Shave*—before the feature-length *Who's That Knocking at My Door?* It played the Chicago Film Festival and two years later was released theatrically after Scorsese threw in a nude scene, full of arty jump cuts. It marked the beginning of his lifelong collaboration with former film schoolmate Thelma Schoonmaker, whose editing is part and parcel of the Scorsese style. "When you work with someone as long as I've worked with Marty," said Schoonmaker at the 1992 Berlin Film Festival, where *Cape Fear* was booed because of its violence, "it's as if you're one person. You hardly have to talk; we know what the other is thinking."

In *Who's That Knocking at My Door?* Harvey Keitel—in his own first film appearance—plays J.R., part of the gang of Little Italy youths who hang out in what in a few years will be Scorsese's *Mean Streets*. J.R. falls in love with a cool, cultured girl (Zina Bethune) but cannot reconcile within himself the mother-whore dichotomy he was raised on in Catholic School. When he learns his fiancée is not a virgin—through no fault of her own—he pushes her away, labels her a whore, and ends up haunted by his religious and romantic conflicts.

Sin and redemption have always had a home in Scorsese films, reaching an apparent apex when Willem Dafoe played an all-too-human Jesus in *The Last Temptation of Christ*, only to be topped by Robert De Niro's divine-avenger figure in *Cape Fear*. The camera in *Who's That Knocking?* ferrets out the religious paraphernalia in J.R.'s life—the holy candle, the

286

statues of Mary and Jesus. Shots of J.R. at confession are jarringly juxtaposed against scenes of a rape.

The camera in *Who's That Knocking?* moves as quickly as Scorsese speaks—which is to say, very, very fast, as if there's not a moment to lose. Stylistically, the movie sets the tone for the naturalistic, repetitive, overlapping street language that dominates Scorsese soundtracks. To see where he got that from, one need only look at *Italianamerican*, an hour-long documentary in which Scorsese filmed his mother and father talking at cross-purposes over the kitchen table.

The director's boyhood love of film is also a big fixture of *Who's That Knocking?* J.R. woos the girl initially by discussing John Wayne movies with her; there is an extended sequence where they sit waiting for the Staten Island ferry, discussing *The Searchers* to absurd lengths. Later, before an attempted gang rape, J.R. and his pals sit around watching and discussing old Charlie Chan movies.

Keitel came to the movie via an ad in the trades and took the job for no pay. "I was a young actor at the time, looking for work," says Keitel, who later got a career boost when he starred with Robert De Niro, another Scorsese favorite, in *Mean Streets*. "I had a job working as a court stenographer, so we shot the film all through that winter on weekends. I recall vividly watching the scene inside the church when that song *Who's That Knocking at My Door?* is played, and watching that scene being cut, and being aware at that moment that something extraordinary was taking place in film."

Martin Scorsese made several distinctive shorts before *Who's That Knocking at My Door?* (1967), a movie that introduced Harvey Keitel and presaged the director's urban, Italian-American kind of cinema.

Scorsese films *are* extraordinary, but even though critics count *Taxi Driver* and *Raging Bull* among their favorites of all time, the box office has not always been so kind. Scorsese movies are as tough as the language in them; *GoodFellas* was essentially a comedy, but its violence was too much for broad audiences. His 1991 remake of the classic *Cape Fear* turned out to be a mainstream success, but even there, Scorsese couldn't resist adding biblical proportions to the revenge thriller. "I didn't mean to put that stuff in, it was already there is Wesley Strick's script, but I guess it tied into my obsessive behavior with those themes," says Scorsese. "It's like, if someone puts it in, I can't resist filming it. In *Boxcar Bertha* it was the same thing; everyone who saw the film thought that the crucifixion of David Carradine at the end was put in by me, but it was there in the original script. I was just sort of drawn to it."

Part of what makes Scorsese films so upsetting are his attempts to capture "a feeling of almost eavesdropping on someone's private world, and feeling that anxiety of hearing too much and feeling embarrassed by it. It's a very delicate area. I think the only one who I can remember being affected by with this technique over the years, a great teacher of mine, was [John] Cassavetes."

Scorsese tries not to use the word *art* in conjunction with his movies, because "I don't want to scare people away who would read certain articles and might want to see the film but thought they might be seeing an art film. It's the 'A' word. So I usually say, no, it's a film of entertainment."

Scorsese occasionally appears in cameos in other directors' movies. Here he plays the driven painter Van Gogh in a segment of Akira Kurosawa's *Dreams*.

What's a Nice Girl Like You Doing in a Place Like This? (short), 1963
It's Not Just You, Murray (short), 1964
The Big Shave (short), 1967
Who's That Knocking at My Door? 1967 (also screenplay)
Bezeten—het gat in de muur, 1969 (screenplay)
Street Scenes 1970, 1970 (production supervisor)
Woodstock, 1970 (asst. director, editor)
Medicine Ball Caravan, 1971 (assoc. producer)
Boxcar Bertha, 1972
Elvis on Tour, 1972 (coeditor)
Mean Streets, 1973 (also screenplay)
Alice Doesn't Live Here Anymore, 1974
Italianamerican (short), 1974 (also actor)
Cannonball, 1976 (actor)
Taxi Driver, 1976 (also actor)
American Boy, 1977 (also actor)
New York, New York, 1977
The Last Waltz, 1978 (also actor)
Roger Corman: Hollywood's Wild Angel, 1978 (actor)
Raging Bull, 1980 (also actor)
The King of Comedy, 1983 (also actor)
Pavlova, 1983 (actor)
After Hours, 1985
Round Midnight, 1986 (actor)
The Color of Money, 1986
Not Just Any Flower (short), 1987 (assistance)
The Last Temptation of Christ, 1988
New York Stories, "Life Lessons," 1989
Akira Kurosawa's Dreams, 1990 (actor)
Goodfellas, 1990 (also screenplay)
The Grifters, 1990 (producer)
Hollywood Magicians, 1990 (actor)
Cape Fear, 1991
Guilty by Suspicion, 1991 (actor)
Music for the Movies: Bernard Herrmann (docu), 1992 (actor)
Mad Dog and Glory, 1993 (producer)
The Age of Innocence, 1993
Naked in New York, 1993 (exec. producer)

BARRY SONNENFELD

Director, cinematographer
First Film (as director): *The Addams Family* (1991)
Video Availability: Paramount Home Video

"All the great directors faint...."

Working as cinematographer for the weird Coen brothers, Barry Sonnenfeld had to film such things as the Mysterious Flying Hat for *Miller's Crossing* or use the "baby-cam" to record the infant's-eye-view scuttlings of quints for *Raising Arizona*. In Rob Reiner's *Misery*, Sonnenfeld used the camera to emphasize the enormity of writer James Caan's imprisonment by fan Kathy Bates. Sonnenfeld was therefore well prepared to take the helm of the morbidly funny *Addams Family* for his directing debut.

One of the first things the first-time director did was to faint, an act that didn't inspire much confidence from cast and crew. "All the great directors faint at some point in their careers," protests Sonnenfeld.

First-time director Barry Sonnenfeld (left) and producer Scott Rudin show Christina Ricci and Jimmy Workman the world of the viewfinder on the set of *The Addams Family* (1991).

The transition from cameraman to director was not that difficult, according to Sonnenfeld, especially because *The Addams Family* is a very visual movie, full of sight gags and atmosphere. He sums up the job of director as "having to make hundreds of decisions a day that ultimately don't matter, but add up to mattering a lot. Yes, let's have six of those book covers, and no, we won't see their backs, and no it should be green and not red—you answer millions of questions like these every day. And the answers are very important to everyone asking them. Each question carries equal weight—should he park the car here? Or there? Oftentimes it doesn't matter what you say as long as you give an answer."

Sonnenfeld says that on a movie set, everyone feels the film revolves only around him or her. "Actors always feel the film is about their character, as they should. When you watch dailies, the assistant cameraman thinks the entire movie is about focus, and the soundman thinks it's about that noise. A director's job is to keep the balance and answer all the questions with authority. I've been lucky in that I've been immature and wacky enough as a person and director that everyone wants to help me."

Sonnenfeld may never leave his cinematographer's roots behind. When he talks about his directorial debut, he singles out visuals, like the point-of-view shot of a juggled knife "going right into Christopher Lloyd's tonsils." But he thinks the bigger issue in *The Addams Family*—about a clan of ghouls whose values are at odds with the wholesome world around them, based on the Charles Addams cartoons that originally appeared in the *New Yorker*— "is about how nonconformity is good." And that's the outlook he intends to keep as he continues to direct.

In Our Water, 1982 (camera)
Blood Simple, 1984 (camera)
Violated, 1984 (add. camera)
Compromising Positions, 1985 (camera)
Wisdom, 1986 (add. camera)
Raising Arizona, 1987 (camera)
Three O'Clock High, 1987 (camera)
Throw Momma From the Train, 1987 (camera)
Big, 1988 (camera)
When Harry Met Sally..., 1989 (camera)
Miller's Crossing, 1990 (camera)
Misery, 1990 (camera; 2nd unit director)
The Addams Family, 1991

STEVEN SPIELBERG

Director, producer
First Film: *Duel* (1972)
Video Availability: MCA Home Video

The supernatural in everyday life

A childlike appreciation of the uncanny is a staple of Steven Spielberg's cash-cow career. Only occasionally does he show a slightly darker side, as he did in his first full-length film, *Duel*, made in 1972 for television. Unlike other made-for-TV movies, *Duel* was so good that it had a European theatrical release, followed a few years later by a U.S. release. (He also made a two-hour science fiction film, *Firelight*, when he was sixteen, which played one night in a theater.)

The future maker of films involving close encounters and extraterrestrials had a more insidious object of wonder at the wheel of *Duel*—a mysterious and apparently driverless diesel truck with an evil mind of its own. The bad vehicle stalks a hapless motorist (Dennis Weaver) down the nation's highways, trying to run him off the road. The entire movie consists of this malevolent chase.

Steven Spielberg's movies often celebrate the enchantment and adventure of boyhood. His first movie, *Duel* (1972), is about a deadly truck.

Spielberg's skill was in creating and sustaining suspense and adventure on a slim story that could have been a throwaway segment on "Night Gallery," the Rod Serling sci-fi TV show whose episodes Spielberg occasionally directed at the start of his career. He clearly had a sense of pace and momentum that would next come in handy in *Jaws* (1975), in which the truck of *Duel* is replaced by a killer shark, the highway by a beach resort.

Often in his movies, supernatural forces upset the balance of suburban life, and it takes a child to set things right. In his benign work, like *E.T.*, the boy Elliot so empathizes with the alien that he experiences E.T.'s drunkenness telepathically. In the maligned *Poltergeist*, which Spielberg wrote and produced but didn't direct, it's the little girl who announces, "They're *heeeere*," while the parents are oblivious.

Poltergeist (1982), a horror movie about an unwitting suburban family whose home rests on a graveyard of restless spirits—something like Dorothy's house slamming down onto the Wicked Witch of the West—is another indication of Spielberg's occasionally darker intent, which is perhaps why he didn't direct it himself. A director so identified with the fun and fantasies of childhood treads a thin line with the public—the child labor and torture of *Indiana Jones and the Temple of Doom* came under attack and in fact precipitated a new movie rating, the PG-13, so that Spielberg wouldn't lose his core audience.

By the time of *Hook*, his 1991 yuppie update of the Peter Pan story, Spielberg's age was showing. This time, the story is told through the eyes of a grown man (Robin Williams) whose career success has made him lose sight of childhood pleasures, like flying through the air or throwing food. This chink in Spielberg's armor was a costly one; *Hook* was a critical and box-office disappointment, falling far short of its goals.

His biggest hits remain those that tell of unearthly wonders from a child's point of view, like *E.T.*, or at least from the child-within's point of view, like the *Indiana Jones* series. When Spielberg tried to break out of the familiar formula, he was criticized for sanitizing Alice Walker's novel to make *The Color Purple* (see WHOOPI GOLDBERG). Within the formula, however, he has had unparalleled success, with several of his films on the top-ten list of history's box-office hits.

He has also single-handedly given the special-effects industry a boost, what with aliens landing and temples of doom exploding. *Duel* is the least complicated film Spielberg would ever make, and it still plays powerfully.

Duel, 1972
Ace Eli and Rodger of the Skies, 1973 (story)
The Sugarland Express, 1974
Jaws, 1975
Close Encounters of the Third Kind, 1977 (also
    screenplay)
I Wanna Hold Your Hand, 1978 (exec. producer)
1941, 1979
The Blues Brothers, 1980 (actor)
Used Cars, 1980 (exec. producer)
Continental Divide, 1981 (exec. producer)

Raiders of the Lost Ark, 1981
Chambre 666, 1982 (actor)
E.T.: The Extra-Terrestrial, 1982 (also producer)
Poltergeist, 1982 (producer, screenplay)
Twilight Zone—the Movie, 1983
Gremlins, 1984 (exec. producer)
Indiana Jones and the Temple of Doom, 1984
Back to the Future, 1985 (exec. producer)
The Color Purple, 1985 (also producer)
The Goonies, 1985 (exec. producer)
Young Sherlock Holmes, 1985 (exec. producer)
An American Tail, 1986 (exec. producer)
The Money Pit, 1986 (exec. producer)
Batteries Not Included, 1987 (exec. producer)
Empire of the Sun, 1987 (also producer)
Innerspace, 1987 (exec. producer)
The Land Before Time, 1988 (exec. producer)
Who Framed Roger Rabbit? 1988 (exec. producer)
Always, 1989 (also producer)
Back to the Future II, 1989 (exec. producer)
Dad, 1989 (exec. producer)
Indiana Jones and the Last Crusade, 1989
Tummy Trouble (short), 1989 (exec. producer)
Arachnophobia, 1990 (exec. producer)
Back to the Future III, 1990 (exec. producer)
Gremlins 2: The New Batch, 1990 (exec. producer)
Joe Versus the Volcano, 1990 (exec. producer)
Listen Up, 1990 (actor)
Rollercoaster Rabbit (short), 1990 (exec. producer)
Hook, 1991
Cape Fear, 1991 (coproducer)
An American Tail: Fievel Goes West, 1991 (exec. producer)
The Warner Bros. Story (docu), 1991 (co-host)
We're Back, 1993 (producer)
Jurassic Park, 1993

294

OLIVER STONE

Director, writer, producer
First Film (as director): *Seizure* (1974)
Available: Prism Entertainment

The artist's nightmare

Screenwriting alone could not contain Oliver Stone's creative impulses back in 1974. So after cowriting a script with Edward Mann, he decided to direct. In *Seizure*, his alter ego, a novelist played by Jonathan Frid (of "Dark Shadows" TV fame), experiences what for Stone is not just a fantasy but "the ultimate nightmare" for artists—that the creations of their febrile minds will come to life.

Well, guess who's coming to dinner over at the home of this novelist? None but three of his nastiest literary inventions: the Queen of Evil, a huge black executioner, and Herve Villechaize as a nasty dwarf named the Spider. These houseguests will force Frid and his wife and friends, including Mary Woronov and Troy Donohue, to flirt with death all night

Oliver Stone teaches Michael Caine to use the prosthetic hand that will do him in in *The Hand*, the movie commonly thought to be Stone's first, but made a full seven years after the low-budget *Seizure* (1974).

long. The first to die is the family dog, who is found hung by the neck from his leash.

And so it goes in *Seizure*, Stone's little-seen directorial debut, a low-budget horror flick made in Quebec. "It wasn't great," says Stone dryly. "I felt back then the same way I do now, that I always wanted to direct. The horror genre was easier to break in with."

Stone took time out from a party in his honor in Dallas during the filming of *JFK* to talk about his first film, even though he was glassy-eyed with fatigue.

As awful as *Seizure* is, it still shows a certain style that can charitably be called seminal Stone. Its archetypes of evil would show up later in more subtle form: Tom Berenger as the amoral lieutenant of *Platoon* (1986); Michael Douglas as the unscrupulous trader of *Wall Street* (1987).

If *Seizure* does not immediately bring to mind the grand scheme of *JFK* (1991), which is about a moment in politics and time that changed the way America thinks about itself, still it is only a Stone's throw from *The Hand* (1981), his second directing job (he wrote it too) and the one that most people think is his first. Just as in *Seizure*, the artist's creations are so powerful they can carry out the master's hidden agenda or even turn on him. Michael Caine is a newspaper cartoonist whose career and marriage to Andrea Marcovicci are cut short by a car accident that lops off his hand. But the digits crawl back to kill off some of Caine's detractors.

In both early movies, symbols of the creative spirit—the figments of a writer's imaginations, the hand that makes the drawings—act out the artist's subconscious desires, particularly fantasies of revenge and megalomania. "I'm scared of something in me," says Frid, who plays Edmund the novelist in *Seizure*.

"It's the classic novelist's nightmare," explains Stone, "only the nightmare is happening in real life. Is the writer creating the monster within him? There is a confusion about whether he is a victim or doing the victimizing."

Beginning in *Seizure*, the psychology of Stone's protagonists is rooted in the early omnipotent fantasies of childhood, when children experience alternate rushes of megalomania and guilt because they believe their bad thoughts can really reach out and harm others.

Stone can relate another theme he was trying out in *Seizure* to one he later explored in *The Doors* (1991), and that is something he describes as "people's relationship to death." Jim Morrison, the lead singer for the short-lived but long-remembered sixties group the Doors, obsessed over drugs, death, and poetry until his overdose at age twenty-seven. His songs were full of allusions to transcendence and death.

Stone loves characters who, like himself, push the limits. He retains a certain amount of awe for his *Seizure* novelist, who is so enamored of his own imagination he would almost rather see his family killed than stop making fiction. The photojournalists of *Salvador* (1986) travel willingly into the jaws of death to get their stories. *Midnight Express* (1978) was written after Stone had been busted for drugs shortly after his return from duty in Vietnam.

He has admitted that the set of *Scarface* (1983) was rife with drug use which paralleled that of the characters in Stone's screenplay.

Oliver Stone is a man of extremes, and it shows in his work. Issues of morality, of good and evil, of hitting rock bottom and being born anew, crop up frequently. Edmund's existential nightmare threatens to regenerate itself every twenty-four hours for all eternity.

At least Edmund has only to deal with his own conscience. In later movies, Stone would split his screen metaphorically to accommodate opposing father figures who claw at the conscience of the protagonist and mirror his moral dilemma. Charlie Sheen as an ambitious young trader in *Wall Street* is torn between the homespun values of his blue-collar dad (played by his real dad, Martin Sheen) and the exhilarating buy-'em'-and-screw-'em megalomania of Michael Douglas. In *Platoon*, which won four Oscars, Charlie Sheen again must choose his moral center from the examples set by two warring lieutenants—angelic Willem Dafoe, who smokes pot with his men and dances to Motown, or scar-faced Tom Berenger, who eavesdrops on his men and kills his own kind.

A typical Stone image is the Christ-like martyr who dies for our sins, beginning in *Seizure* with the faithful family dog hanging from a tree. Later, there would be Dafoe's famous pose on the posters for *Platoon*, kneeling with his arms outstretched in final agony, or Val Kilmer as Jim Morrison blissfully breaking on through to the other side of consciousness at the end of *The Doors*.

Stone's canvases are writ large. His movies tend to excess, beginning with *Seizure*, in which there is not one but three forces of evil. There is not just cocaine in *Scarface*, for which he wrote the screenplay, there is wretched excess of coke. There is not just a change of heart for Tom Cruise's disillusioned Vietnam veteran in the double-Oscar winner *Born on the Fourth of July*; he goes on a holy crusade that lasts 144 minutes. "I'm *in the face* all the time," Stone admits in response to the frequent cry that his filmmaking lacks subtlety.

The war outside (Vietnam, El Salvador) and the war inside (fantasy, drug addiction, ethics) rage across screens that have been painted by Stone. Even an early screenplay like *Midnight Express* (1978) had Brad Davis not only jailed in Turkey on marijuana charges, but virtually thrown into hell.

Female characters have never been Stone's strong suit, and those in *Seizure* are no exception. The Queen of Evil (Martine Beswick) is everything a man could ever want and dread at the same time, "the majestic embodiment of all our desires and thoughts—the alluring eternal female of our soul...She is a mother and equally so the dark lady of the world." Edmund's own wife (Christina Pickels) is a bitch. "You're a worm, Edmund! A lump of mud! You want so much to live, and you don't know how!" And Mary Woronov as a houseguest wears a bikini to wrestle Edmund to the death.

Another important aspect of Stone's filmmaking, from a behind-the-scenes standpoint that probably has as much to do with his own personality as with the harsh realities of Hollywood, is that his films offer seemingly impossible challenges. He is not just a filmmaker, but a standard-bearer; the more difficult the path, the more spectacular the result. He is sparked by adversity.

Seizure was an early lesson in the perils of filmmaking. "I had to smuggle the work print out of Canada and try to sell it here because we ran out of money," says Stone. "We bootlegged it to the U.S." It finally opened to sparse attendance in New York on Forty-second Street, in a row of theaters more accustomed to kung-fu double features. Even Stone admits: "You have to stretch to like it."

Street Scenes 1970, 1970 (camera, sequence director)
Seizure, 1974 (also screenplay)
Midnight Express, 1978 (screenplay)
The Hand, 1981 (also actor, screenplay)
Conan the Barbarian, 1982 (screenplay)
Scarface, 1983 (screenplay)
Year of the Dragon, 1985 (screenplay)
8 Million Ways to Die, 1986 (screenplay)
Platoon, 1986 (also screenplay)
Salvador, 1986 (also producer, screenplay)
Wall Street, 1987 (also actor, screenplay)
Talk Radio, 1988 (also screenplay)
Blue Steel, 1989 (producer)
Born on the Fourth of July, 1989 (also actor, producer, screenplay)
Reversal of Fortune, 1990 (producer)
The Doors, 1991 (also screenplay)
JFK, 1991 (also screenplay)
South Central, 1992 (exec. producer)
Zebrahead, 1992 (exec. producer)
The Last Party, 1993 (actor)
Heaven and Earth, 1993
The Joy Luck Club, 1993 (exec. producer)

FIRST FILM SNAPSHOTS

An Album of Famous Beginnings

LAUREN BACALL

Copyright © Warner Brothers

Lauren Bacall gives future husband Humphrey Bogart that special up from beneath look, the one she later explained was because she was so nervous in her first film she had to keep her head down to control the shaking. She was nineteen when she made *To Have and Have Not* (1944; Warner Home Video) after being discovered by Slim Hawks, the wife of director Howard Hawks. Slim marched the former Betty Bacall around the canyons in Beverly Hills, making her scream until her voice dropped to the husky tones Slim thought were correct for a role loosely based on herself. To this day, Bacall has a smoky voice.

JACK NICHOLSON

Jack Nicholson means business as he awkwardly pulls a gun on one of his storeroom hostages in *The Cry Baby Killer* (1958; d. Jus Addiss; not available on video). The juvenile delinquent turns crybaby when he thinks he's killed the two guys who beat him up; Nicholson was probably ready to cry too, because he thought this movie was going to be his ticket to the big time. The Roger Corman-produced cheapie turned out to be a ticket to another ten years of treading water in B-movies, until 1969, when he played the drunken lawyer out for a joyride with freewheeling bikers Peter Fonda and Dennis Hopper in *Easy Rider*.

MARLON BRANDO

Former GI Marlon Brando angrily works his upper body after his lower is paralyzed by a war injury in his famous film debut in *The Men* (1950; d. Fred Zinnemann; Republic Home Video). Amazingly, the stage-trained Method actor who would be considered one of the greatest of all time had screentested in Hollywood more than two years earlier and never got any work from it.

DUSTIN HOFFMAN

Photofest

Dustin Hoffman is being led by the nose as an inept G-man on a mission to Italy to recover money stolen by Cesar Romero in *Madigan's Millions* (1968). Although *The Graduate* is touted as his first film, he actually made *Madigan's Millions* before that—it was released a year later—and was even earlier seen in a cameo in *The Tiger Makes Out* (1967; d. Arther Hiller; not available on video). Hoffman got $5,000 to go to Rome for *Madigan's Millions*, an awful Spanish-Italian flick originally called *Un Dollaro per Sette Vigliacchi*. He graduated to $17,000 on *The Graduate*, Mike Nichols' paean to a new generation's alienation.

SUSAN SARANDON

Susan Sarandon finds the hippie life tough going when her father accidentally murders her druggie boyfriend in her impressive debut in *Joe* (1970; d. John Avildsen; Vestron). This intelligent, accomplished actress has a cult following from her appearance in the 1975 "midnight" movie *The Rocky Horror Picture Show*, and recently came out on top, along with Geena Davis, as a female road warrior in *Thelma and Louise* (1991) and a take-no-prisoners mother of an ailing child in *Lorenzo's Oil* (1992).

Photofest

RICHARD GERE

Richard Gere is the best pickup a girl ever had in *Looking for Mr. Goodbar* (1977), with Diane Keaton as the lonely single looking for excitement on a one-night-only basis. Gere does a set of studly push—ups in his jockstrap and leather jacket, and is so memorable that this is famously thought to be his film debut. Actually, it was the debut for Tom Berenger, who played Keaton's *other* pickup. Gere first showed up in *Report to the Commissioner* (1975; d. Milton Katselas; MGM/UA Home Video) as a streetwise hood brought in for questioning in a cop's death.

KEVIN KLINE

Kevin Kline makes a swashbuckling debut as the manic-depressive lover of Meryl Streep, a guilt-torn Polish survivor of the Nazi death camps, in *Sophie's Choice* (1982; d. Alan J. Pakula; CBS/Fox Home Video). He was already a presence on the stage, with two Tonys under his scabbard sash—for *On the Twentieth Century* and *The Pirates of Penzance*—when he signed on for the affecting but somewhat lugubrious adaptation of the William Styron novel. The movie also stars Peter MacNicol as the young Styron alter ego who watches the doomed love affair progress. Kline almost made his debut in the steamy *Body Heat*, a role that went to William Hurt, but he didn't give his rival the cold shoulder when they made *The Big Chill* together in 1983. In 1992, Kline returned to swashbuckling to play Douglas Fairbanks in *Chaplin*.

DOLLY PARTON

Courtesy *New York Post*

When Dolly Parton says no, she doesn't mean yes, and boss Dabney Coleman soon finds out she means business in *9 to 5* (1980; d. Colin Higgins; CBS/Fox Home Video). Parton teamed up with Jane Fonda and Lily Tomlin in this silly, enjoyable comedy as three secretaries out for revenge on their piggish boss. Parton brings her own special charm to the role; in fact, she doesn't like playing characters other than herself. "When I find a part that's greater than my image, than I'll consider it," she says. "I'm not really an actress, and I don't have that burnin' desire. Music is my first love." Directors who plan to "direct" Dolly had better be forewarned: "I'm a southern girl. I have a big mouth and a big heart. I'm real honest with people. If they ask me somethin', I tell 'em, and sometimes if they don't ask me and I need to tell 'em I'll tell 'em anyway."

CYBILL SHEPHERD

Cybill Shepard drives Timothy Bottoms wild with desire in *The Last Picture Show* (1971; Columbia/Tri-Star). The former Miss Teenage Memphis was chosen when the director, Peter Bogdanovich, spotted her posing on the cover of *Glamour* magazine. He gave her the sexy part of Jacy Farrow, the town flirt in rural Anarene, a town that's practically too dead to notice. Jacy's petulant complaint—"Nuthin' turns out like it's supposed to"—is the theme of this bleak but richly textured black-and-white movie. Shepherd and Bogdanovich went on to live together for eight years, and through the eyes of his adoring camera she has never looked quite as lovely, luscious, and dangerous. Nor has she looked as awful as when he photographed her and most of the original cast in the sequel, *Texasville*, nineteen years later. That's probably because nuthin' turns out like it's supposed to.

Copyright © Columbia Pictures

303

INDEX

ABOUT THE AUTHOR

Jami Bernard is the film critic for the *New York Daily News* and formerly of the *New York Post* and past chairwoman of the New York Film Critics Circle. Her work has appeared through the L.A.Times Syndicate and in dozens of publications, including the *Washington Post, Allure, Seventeen, Self, Video Magazine, Billboard*, and *Spin*. Bernard has been a guest on numerous television shows, including "The Joan Rivers Show," "Entertainment Tonight," "A Current Affair," and "Now It Can Be Told," as well as on radio in North America and Europe. Her work takes her round the world to international film festivals, where many of the celebrity interviews for this book took place.